Convertible Bonds . . . Selling Short . . .
Dow Theory . . . Straddle . . .
Down Tick . . . Yield Spread . . .
Puts and Calls . . . Ex-Dividend . . .
Preferred Stock . . . Unit Trust

These are just a few of the thousands of terms described with jargon-free clarity in this comprehensive dictionary of investment terminology. Arranged for easy reference, defining key terms and concepts that every investor needs to know, it is the one book that covers the entire spectrum of investment language. Whether you are just learning the ins and outs of trading or are a sophisticated investor, whether you're heavily into the stock market or dabbling in real estate, coins or collectibles, *THE A TO Z OF INVESTING* is one of the best investments you'll ever make (tax deductible)!

CHRISTINE AMMER is coauthor, with her husband, Dean S. Ammer, of the highly regarded *Dictionary of Business and Economics*.

THE
A to Z
OF
INVESTING

CHRISTINE AMMER

A MENTOR BOOK

NEW AMERICAN LIBRARY

NEW YORK AND SCARBOROUGH, ONTARIO

NAL BOOKS ARE AVAILABLE AT QUANTITY DISCOUNTS WHEN USED
TO PROMOTE PRODUCTS OR SERVICES. FOR INFORMATION PLEASE
WRITE TO PREMIUM MARKETING DIVISION, NEW AMERICAN LIBRARY,
1633 BROADWAY, NEW YORK, NEW YORK 10019.

Copyright © 1986 by Christine Ammer

Library of Congress Catalog Card Number: 86-62311

 MENTOR TRADEMARK REG. U.S. PAT. OFF. AND FOREIGN COUNTRIES
REGISTERED TRADEMARK—MARCA REGISTRADA
HECHO EN CHICAGO, U.S.A.

SIGNET, SIGNET CLASSIC, MENTOR, ONYX, PLUME, MERIDIAN
and NAL BOOKS are published *in the United States*
by NAL PENGUIN INC,, 1633 Broadway, New York, New York 10019,
in Canada by The New American Library of Canada Limited,
81 Mack Avenue, Scarborough, Ontario M1L 1M8

First Printing, December, 1986

2   3   4   5   6   7   8   9

PRINTED IN THE UNITED STATES OF AMERICA

HOW TO USE
THIS BOOK

This book is an encyclopedic dictionary, defining and explaining the thousand or so most used terms in the language of investment. It does not just tell you what a term means but also, where necessary, explains it. It includes the terminology of stocks and bonds, options and warrants, commodity and financial futures, mutual funds, pension accounts, gold and silver, mineral and oil leases, interest-bearing bank accounts, life insurance, real estate, collectibles and coins—in short, every kind of investment. It includes those accounting terms especially needed for understanding a company's annual report, balance sheet, and other compendia of facts and figures used to assess investments and explains how those data can be used. It also includes information for the growing number of investors who wish to use a personal computer for their financial record-keeping, planning, and strategy.

The terms in this dictionary, whether they consist of one word or several words, are listed in strict alphabetical order, letter by letter, up to the comma in case of inversion. When a numeral is part of a term, as in *10-K form*, the term is alphabetized as though the number were spelled out (*Ten-K*). Identical terms with different meanings are defined under a single heading with a series of numbered definitions. Terms mentioned in one entry and further explained in another, where the reader is advised to seek them out, are printed in small (and, where appropriate, regular) capital letters, such as COUPON STRIPPING or TREASURY BILL.

Although this book is intended to be helpful to readers who wish to understand and compare different kinds of investment, it does *not* purport to give investment advice. Each investor's financial situation and particular goals are unique, and no book can or should tell individuals what to do. Investors must make their own decisions, but the better informed they are, the wiser their decisions can be. With this end in mind, Appendix B lists important sources of financial information.

Appendix A lists the stock and commodity exchanges where their decisions may be carried out and Appendix C the most important stock indexes and averages.

A

accelerated depreciation A method of calculating depreciation on a fixed asset so as to charge more to the early years of its service life than to the later years. Its chief advantage is that it helps a company defer taxes, because depreciation is tax-deductible. The principal methods used are the DECLINING BALANCE METHOD and the SUM-OF-DIGITS METHOD.

acceptance, bankers' See BANKERS' ACCEPTANCE.

account, brokerage A regular relationship between a securities broker and a customer or client, who receives certain services in exchange for payment of a commission. The broker's principal service is to act as agent for the client in purchasing securities and/or commodities. Other services may include holding or reinvesting the proceeds of the client's investments, supplying credit for margin purchases, and furnishing credit cards, special checking accounts, tax-record services, or even complete management of assets.

account executive See REGISTERED REPRESENTATIVE.

accounts payable The amount owed by a business for its purchases of raw material, supplies, equipment, services, and so on.

accounts receivable The amount owed to a business, mainly by its customers, most of whom can be expected to pay such debts within a given period.

accredited investor According to Regulation D of the Securities and Exchange Commission (SEC), an individual who has a net worth of at least $1 million or an annual income of at least $200,000, or who invests at least $150,000 in the enterprise in question, an amount not representing more than one-fifth of his or her net worth. An accredited investor does not count as one of the maximum number of persons who may invest in an issue for it to be considered a PRIVATE PLACEMENT and therefore able to waive SEC registration.

accrual method Also, *accrual basis*. An accounting method whereby transactions are recognized when they occur rather than when they are settled (that is, paid for). Thus a sale to a customer is counted as income even though the customer need not pay for the purchase for ninety days. See also CASH BASIS.

accrued Describing an item of income or expense that has occurred but has not yet been paid. In accounting, *accrued income* has been earned but not actually received during a given accounting period, and an *accrued liability* has been incurred but not yet paid. An example of the former is rent, and of the latter taxes. With fixed-income securities, *accrued interest* is the interest earned on a bond or note since the last regular coupon payment. When a bond is sold, the accrued interest must be paid by the buyer to the seller, the exact amount being based on the number of days since the last interest payment. This kind of sale is also called *full* or *and interest*. See also FLAT.

accumulation Term used by technical analysts for a stock price that fluctuates within a relatively narrow range for a time and then moves much higher, indicating that there is rising demand for it. See also DISTRIBUTION, def. 2.

acid test Another name for QUICK-ASSET RATIO.

active market Also, *broad market, heavy market*. A high volume of trading in a particular security, commodity, or the market as a whole. See also BREADTH, MARKET; THIN MARKET.

adjustable-rate See ADJUSTABLE-RATE MORTGAGE; FLOATING-RATE.

adjustable-rate mortgage   Abbreviated *ARM*. Also, *adjustable mortgage loan (AML)*, *renegotiated-rate mortgage (RRM)*, *variable-rate mortgage (VRM)*. A long-term mortgage, typically running thirty years, on which the interest rate may be adjusted over short periods according to current economic conditions. There may or may not be limits on the size and frequency of changes in the interest rate. A common limit on interest is a change of plus or minus 0.5 percent between two consecutive periods and a maximum of 5 percent over the life of the loan. With some mortgages negative amortization may be allowed, permitting monthly interest payments to stay low during periods of temporary high interest rates but increasing the principal (term) of the mortgage. The interest rate is adjusted semiannually, annually, or at some other interval. Adjustable-rate mortgages often carry a lower interest rate than traditional fixed-rate mortgages because the lender undertakes less risk that the rate will be far out of line with future market rates, but they also carry more uncertainty for the borrower. See also FLOATING-RATE.

adjusted basis   In tax terminology, the cost of acquiring property after making appropriate allowances for increases such as capital expenditures and decreases such as depreciation. The amount received after resale of the property minus the adjusted basis shows whether there has been any capital gain or loss on the transaction. In the case of a stock or bond, the amount it is sold for is adjusted to allow for broker's commission, stock splits since the initial purchase, etc.

adjusted gross income   The basis on which an individual's taxable income is computed, found by deducting nontaxable income (such as interest on municipal bonds, etc.) and expenses (such as business expenses, charitable contributions, or allowable child care) from gross income.

adjustment bond   See INCOME BOND.

ADR   Abbreviation for (1) AMERICAN DEPOSITARY RE-
CEIPT; (2) automatic dividend reinvestment (see under
DIVIDEND).

advance/decline line   The number of stocks whose
prices rose relative to the number of those whose
prices fell during a given time period, usually presented as a cumulative figure or a moving average.
Analysts widely believe that this figure shows the
general direction of the market; if advances exceed
declines, the market is rising, and if declines exceed
advances, it is falling. Several formulas are commonly used. The simplest one subtracts the number
of stocks with price declines each week (or each day)
from the number with price advances, and the results
are plotted on a graph, yielding a straight line that is
level (no change), slants up (rising market), or slants
down (declining market). Another formula divides
the difference between advances and declines by the
total number of stock issues changing in price. Still
another divides the number of advancing issues by
the number of declining issues on a given day; if the
result is higher than 1 the market is advancing, while
below 1 it is declining. This last calculation is also
called the *advance/decline ratio* or the *overbought/
oversold index*. Technical analysts often combine figures on market volume (how many stocks are involved) with advance/decline calculations, to obtain
more information on market BREADTH.

advance refunding   See under REFUNDING.

after-tax yield   The rate of return on a bond or other
long-term investment after deducting an estimate of
tax payments. This calculation may be fairly complicated but is important in comparing alternative investments when income tax is a significant factor.

agencies   See FEDERAL AGENCY ISSUE.

all or none   Abbreviated *AON*. In the securities trade, a buy or sell order for which no partial trade is to be executed; that is, the total number of shares called for must be bought or sold. There is no time limit on the transaction, however, and the order can remain open until the customer indicates it should be closed.

allotment The amount of securities of a new issue that is apportioned to each of the underwriters.

allowance In accounting, a sum set aside for bad debts, depreciation, taxes, or some other liability, either anticipated or unexpected. It is also called reserve (see RESERVE, def. 2). See also SINKING FUND.

alpha The volatility of a stock price independent of advances or declines in the general market, instead resulting from conditions unique to the issuing corporation. A stock with an alpha of 1.15, for example, will presumably advance in price by 15 percent a year even if the price of an average stock (as based on a large price index, such as Standard & Poor's 500) remains the same. The alpha is influenced by such factors as the rate of the company's earnings increase per share. A stock selling below a price implied by its alpha is considered undervalued and therefore a good buy, whereas one that is outperforming its alpha is considered overvalued and a candidate for selling. Of course, stocks also are affected by general market conditions, which are accounted for by their BETA coefficient.

alternative minimum tax A tax imposed by the Internal Revenue Service to prevent large numbers of the well-to-do from escaping taxation entirely through the use of tax-sheltered investments and other enterprises. Consequently, a person who enjoys the benefit of substantial tax preferences may incur a higher tax under the alternative minimum tax, which is computed quite differently from other income-tax calculations.

AMBAC See under MUNICIPAL BOND.

American Depositary Receipt Abbreviated *ADR*. Also, *American Depositary Shares,* abbreviated *ADS*. A negotiable receipt issued by an American bank for shares of stock in a foreign corporation. The underlying stock certificates are deposited in a bank—usually a foreign affiliate of the American bank—and the ADRs are traded in American markets in their stead. In many cases ADRs are the only means for Americans to own such shares, because Japan and many other countries do not allow stock certificates to leave the country. Even without this restriction, ADRs are useful because they eliminate some of the differences between American and foreign stocks, thereby facilitating trading. Thus, with ADRs the bank converts dividends from the original foreign currency into dollars and also adjusts the lot sizes and price scales of foreign stocks to conform to domestic ones, such as issuing one ADR for every ten or twenty shares when appropriate. Further, foreign corporations often issue unregistered (bearer) shares, which are inconvenient to trade in the United States. Also, when a foreign company does not register an issue with the Securities and Exchange Commission (SEC), as is often the case, American citizens may not subscribe to RIGHTS offers or may find it difficult to sell rights. When such an issue is transformed into ADRs, the bank can sell such rights directly in the foreign market, to which it has much readier access than most individual stockholders do.

There are two kinds of ADR, sponsored and unsponsored. With a sponsored ADR, a foreign company asks an American bank to issue the ADRs in the U.S. and the company participates more actively, standing behind dividend payments and sending an annual report, and sometimes interim reports, to shareholders. With an unsponsored account, an American broker approaches a U.S. bank and convinces it that there is a sufficient market for a given security to merit issuing an ADR for it. The foreign firm must provide the bank with a letter saying it does not object and must agree to furnish the SEC with any information made public in its own home country. The cost of distributing dividends is subtracted from the dividends by the bank, and annual reports are usually sent only on request, often at the stockholder's expense. Commissions on ADRs are the same as for regular stock purchases, and a growing number of ADRs are quoted in the financial pages daily. See also FOREIGN INVESTMENT.

American Stock Exchange Also, *AMEX*. See APPENDIX A.

amortization

 1. An accounting method whereby the cost of an asset is spread out over its life. It may be applied to any fixed asset whose life is limited but, unlike a piece of equipment, does not wear out with use, as well as to intangible assets such as patents, good will, and the like.

 2. The liquidation of a long-term debt, such as a bond or mortgage, by means of regular installment payments that reduce both principal and interest.

analyst In the investment trade, an individual who specializes in studying a particular security or group of securities, industry, or, more often, the market as a whole. Analysts are employed by brokerage houses, banks, mutual funds, insurance companies, and other large investors; they also may be self-employed. See also FUNDAMENTAL ANALYSIS; TECHNICAL ANALYSIS.

annual report A yearly financial report that all publicly owned U.S. corporations are required to make to their shareholders. It generally includes the president's letter to stockholders, summarizing the financial highlights of the previous year; an income statement or earnings report that summarizes the year's sales and other income, costs, net profit or loss, and comparative information for the previous year; a consolidated balance sheet itemizing assets, liabilities, and shareholders' equity; announcement of the stockholders' annual meeting and summaries of the major activities and future plans of the company; and an auditor's statement showing that the company's books have been investigated by an independent outside auditor. Investors can glean considerable information from a company's annual report and should read all of it carefully, including the footnotes, which frequently explain the company's position in more specific terms. See also 10-K FORM.

annuity A form of insurance in which the insured, called the *annuitant,* pays a predetermined sum, either all at once or in installments, to a life insurance company, for which at a predetermined time he or she receives a sum of money for a specific period or for life. If the time of annuitization is in the future—at retirement, for example—the interest in the annuity compounds tax-deferred; such a plan is also called a *deferred annuity.* In contrast, an *immediate annuity* begins to pay income at once, and tax on it is not deferred. Annuities may be part of a company pension plan or purchased by individuals. One usually can cash in all or part of an annuity any time by notifying the insurer, but there generally is a surrender fee for early liquidation. Since the policy's cash value increases daily, one receives accrued interest with the return of the principal, assuming that the annuity has been held for a reasonable time. Annuities are available for as little as $2,500. In addition, most companies invoke charges for expenses in the premiums; these include a sales fee (unless it is a no-load plan), annual fee, and other costs. Prospective policyholders should check not only on fees but the charges and tax penalties for early withdrawal. See also JOINT AND SURVIVORSHIP ANNUITY; VARIABLE ANNUITY.

appraisal Estimating the value of a property for the purposes of tax assessment, resale, insurance, and so on.

appreciation An increase in the value of property, such as the market value of a stock. For real estate it often is expressed as a percentage increase per year.

arbitrage Matching purchases and sales of the same security, currency, commodity, or other product in two different markets in order to take advantage of a slight price difference. For example, if cotton sells for 72 cents a pound in London and 72½ cents in Amsterdam, the commodity arbitrager would try to buy in London and sell in Amsterdam. In securities trading, arbitrage may consist of buying and selling short the same security to profit from a price difference, or of buying RIGHTS to a stock and selling that stock. The same technique may be applied to the stocks of companies that are about to merge or be taken over. Called *merger arbitrage, risk arbitrage,* or *acquisition arbitrage,* it usually involves acquiring the shares of the target company (the one to be taken over), which tend to sell at a discount from the offering price until the takeover has been completed, and then selling them at the higher price of the new stock. Both the selection of firms that are candidates for takeover and the timing of stock purchases are extremely tricky, and merger arbitrage is generally considered far too risky an undertaking for most individual investors. See also RISK ARBITRAGE.

ARM Abbreviation for ADJUSTABLE-RATE MORTGAGE.

arrears A sum of money that is due but not paid at the specified time, for example, a charge-account bill, mortgage payment, or stock dividend. The person or firm responsible for paying the sum is then said to be "in arrears."

ask Also, *asked, offer.* In the securities and commodities trade, the lowest price a seller will accept; in the over-the-counter market it is the price at which a broker can sell stocks. See also BID.

assessed valuation The dollar value assigned to real property by a municipality for the purpose of tax assessment. It is important to investors in municipal bonds that are backed by property taxes, as well as to property owners who must pay these taxes. It is often expressed in *mills*, one mill being equal to 1/10 cent; thus, if a locality's tax rate is 30 mills and a property is assessed at $1 million, the tax is $30,000.

asset In accounting, any property, physical or intangible, that has a monetary value. Tangible assets include plant, machinery, cash, prepaid expenses, etc. Intangible assets include patents, good will, trademarks or copyrights, etc. A current asset can readily be turned into cash (for example, marketable stocks and bonds); a fixed asset, such as land, plant, machinery, or the like, cannot.

asset management account Also, *cash management account.* A money-management program offered by some full-service brokers, banks, and mutual funds that links brokerage services with a checking account, money-market fund, or other investment. Thus any cash in an account is automatically invested rather than being allowed to lie idle. A brokerage account of this kind usually requires a minimum first investment of about $20,000 in securities and/or cash (although some require as little as $5,000); it is most suitable for investors who value their broker's investment advice and tend to trade frequently. The accounts offered by mutual funds tend to center on a money-market fund and offer the services of a dis-

count broker, a credit card, and a variety of computerized transaction services. They generally require a
much lower minimum investment. Bank asset management accounts normally involve some kind of
checking account, either conventional or interest-
bearing, with automatic investment of "extra" cash
into a money-market fund. Usually discount brokerage service is also provided, and unlike the other two
types of account, the bank account offers federal
insurance for the funds in the checking account. One
can write checks and charge purchases to the account
and also borrow against securities, as in a regular
margin account. From the broker's and bank's standpoint, such accounts induce customers to trade and
borrow more, increasing their earnings from commissions and interest.

asset play   Term for a stock that is undervalued relative to the company's assets (not its earnings) and is
therefore attractive to investors.

asset turnover   The proportion of sales per dollar of
assets during a year, calculated by dividing net sales
(shown on the income statement) by average assets
(shown on the balance sheet). This figure helps show
whether funds are productively invested. If an expansion in facilities does not produce more sales, there
may be a weakness in marketing strategy, although
sometimes it takes time for demand to grow up to
capacity.

assignment   The transfer of rights to a contract to a
different party, including the transfer of stock ownership from one party to another. Most registered stocks
provide a form on the reverse side of the stock
certificate whereby the owner may "assign" ownership. See also STOCK POWER.

articles of incorporation   See under CHARTER.

at the market   Another term for MARKET ORDER.

at the money Also, *on the money*. Describing an OPTION or WARRANT whose strike price is equal to the current market price of the underlying investment and therefore has no INTRINSIC VALUE. See also IN THE MONEY; OUT OF THE MONEY.

audit An inspection of financial records and accounting procedures by an expert, called an *auditor*, who examines them for accuracy, completeness, and conformity to generally accepted accounting procedures.

authorized issue The total number of shares of stock a corporation may sell under its charter, or the total number of bonds that may be sold under a given indenture. A company is not obliged to sell all the stock it is entitled to sell, but if it wants to sell more than the maximum allowed it may generally do so only with the approval of a majority of its stockholders.

average A statistical calculation that represents the central value of a series of numbers. In common usage it most often refers to the arithmetic mean; for example, in the series 7, 8, 9, the mean is $7 + 8 + 9 \div 3 = 8$. In the securities trade the term is used for both averages and indexes of stock prices, such as the Dow Jones Industrial Average and Standard & Poor's Index. See also STOCK INDEX/AVERAGE.

average up (down) Buying securities in a rising (falling) market so as to lower the average price paid for a company's shares. To average up, an investor may buy 100 shares at $15, $16, $17, and $18, thus averaging up 400 shares at $16.50. Or similarly, the investor may decide to buy a total of 1,000 shares, first buying 200 at $30, another 200 at $28, and so on, until 1,000 have been acquired, thus lowering (averaging down) the average purchase price.

away from the market A LIMIT ORDER for which the ask price is higher or the bid price lower than the current market, so that it cannot be executed at once. On stock exchanges it is held by the SPECIALIST for later execution unless it is marked FILL OR KILL; see also BOARD BROKER.

B

b An abbreviation used in stock tables next to the dividend figure to indicate that it signifies an annual cash dividend plus a stock dividend.

baby bond Also, *small piece*. A bond with a face value less than $1,000, usually $100 or $500. Although they may attract small investors, such bonds are generally harder to sell than ordinary bonds and hence are less liquid.

bag In investing in U.S. silver coins, the basic unit of trading, which consists of 10,000 dimes or 4,000 quarters or 2,000 half-dollars. Thus each bag has a $1,000 face value.

balanced fund A MUTUAL FUND that has a dual goal of growth and high income in the form of dividends or interest. It generally divides its investments among common and preferred stocks and bonds.

balance sheet A financial statement that shows a company's assets, liabilities, and capital (stockholders') equity at a given time, usually the last day of its fiscal year. The account form of balance sheet shows assets on the left and liabilities and equity on the right, with the totals equal ("in balance," hence the name balance sheet). The report form of balance sheet presents the same information arranged in vertical columns. Basically the data show what the company owns, what it owes, and the ownership interest of its proprietor(s) or stockholders. Balance sheets vary in the amount of detailed data they provide. A *consolidated balance sheet*, the kind normally included in corporate annual reports, combines the assets and liabilities of a parent company and its subsidiaries as though they were a single organization.

A balance sheet reveals a great deal about a firm's financial condition, such as how deeply it is in debt, how well it can meet its short-term financial commitments, and what assets underlie its stock. For example, one can calculate the firm's debt relative to total capitalization (which will indicate to what extent its profits will be eroded by interest payments). Total capitalization is computed by subtracting intangible assets and current liabilities from total assets; debt should be less than two-thirds of capitalization. Another important figure is net working capital, the difference between total current assets and total current liabilities, which is how much it can spend to expand. Another way to assess this is to calculate the current ratio (current assets divided by current liabilities); a ratio of 2:1 is considered ideal. Some authorities believe the quick-asset ratio (quick assets, meaning current assets minus inventories, divided by current liabilities) is even more revealing. Still another calculation is net asset value per common share, which is total equity divided by the number of shares outstanding. Ideally this figure should have been rising over the past few years. Also, if the current market price of the stock is less than the net asset value, the stock may be undervalued.

balloon mortgage A short-term mortgage, typically for three to five years, in which periodic interest and principal payments only partly pay the debt. At the end of the specified period the entire balance of the loan falls due, and the lender may either renew the mortgage or call for full payment.

balloon payment A large final payment that is made to close out a long-term obligation, such as a mortgage, following a series of smaller payments.

bankers' acceptance Also, *banker's acceptance, bank*

acceptance, all abbreviated *BA*. A negotiable TIME DRAFT extensively used in international trade and also as a safe, short-term investment in the money market. The typical BA matures in ninety days and is so called because a bank accepts responsibility for it—that is, guarantees payment at maturity. The yield is the difference between the amount the manufacturer (exporter) receives for its goods and the full face value of the acceptance that is paid to the bank by the buyer (importer). Because BAs usually involve quite large denominations, such as $100,000, they rarely are bought by individual investors but are frequently traded among banks and large institutions, including money-market funds.

bankruptcy   The inability of an individual or business to pay its obligations and the consequent administration of some or all of its affairs by a trustee or receiver. In the case of a corporation, the bankruptcy proceeding most often is a Chapter 11 proceeding (referring to the section of the Federal bankruptcy law involved), which requires that the company's business be operated under supervision and court regulation until it is liquidated or until its debts or capital structure (or both) can be reorganized.

bank statement   A monthly (or other periodic) statement that shows all the transactions of a bank account during the month concerned, that is, deposits, withdrawals, interest earned, etc.

base

1. A standard of measure used in constructing an index. For example, in constructing price indexes, a *base period* is usually selected—a year or an average of years, a month, or some other time period. Thus the U.S. consumer price index is constructed by comparing prices in a current month with prices in the *base year* 1967. Similarly, for comparing security prices a *base market value*, the average market price

of a group of securities at a given time, may be selected. The New York Stock Exchange Index had an original base of 50.00 as of December 31, 1965.

2. In technical analysis, a stock is said to be *building a base* when its price remains largely unchanged for some time but is presumed to be getting ready for a major advance or decline.

basis

1. The price difference between a designated futures contract and the cash price of the same commodity.

2. With financial futures, the difference between the contract price and the cash price of the underlying securities or currencies.

3. With bonds, the yield to maturity at a given price. Nearly all municipal securities are quoted on a yield-to-maturity basis rather than the percentage-of-par basis used for corporate or U.S. government bonds. Thus a 5 percent coupon municipal bond with 15 years to maturity might be quoted 5.40 percent bid, 5.30 percent offered. To find out what this quotation means in dollars, one must look in a *basis book*, which gives dollar prices if the yield is known.

basis point A unit of measure used for the interest rates of notes and bonds. One basis point equals one-hundredth of one percentage point (so 100 basis points = 1 percent).

bear An investor who thinks a stock price or the market or the economy in general will decline and behaves accordingly, selling stocks short and/or buying put options in order to profit from the decline. By extension, a *bear market* is one that reflects this sentiment and therefore is declining. A *bear raid* is an organized attempt to manipulate a stock price by selling short a large number of shares, and, after the price declines enough, repurchasing the stock at the lower price. Securities and Exchange Commission regulations make this practice illegal. For *bear spread* see under SPREAD, def. 3.

bearer bond A bond not registered in the owner's name and therefore payable to the bearer and negotiable. Coupon bonds generally are bearer bonds. See also REGISTERED BOND.

beneficiary The recipient of an inheritance, or of the proceeds of a life insurance policy, annuity, trust, or the like.

best-efforts selling See under UNDERWRITING, def. 1.

beta Also, *beta coefficient*. A Greek letter, written , used to represent the volatility of a stock's price compared to the rest of the market. Some stocks move up fast in rising markets and drop just as fast in weak markets; other stocks also move up and down with the rest of the market but change less than the average stock. The former are said to have a high beta and the latter a low beta. Riskier stocks usually— but not always—have a high beta, whereas fairly safe stocks tend to have a low beta.

Several investment services calculate the beta for each listed stock, comparing the fluctuation of the stock's price with the movement of an overall average such as the Standard & Poor's 500 Index. A stock that moves in precise correspondence with the market (as represented by such an index) has a beta of 1.0. A volatile stock with a beta of 2.0, such as that of a savings and loan association, is expected to advance and decline twice as much as the market; if the market average moves from 1000 to 1400, this stock can be expected to move from 10 to 18 in response to market change alone. In the same market a stock with a beta of 0.6, such as a public utility, will move up or down only 60 percent as much as the general market. The beta is considered useful mainly for investors who own at least fifteen stocks in eight or more industries, because it enables them to calculate the market risk of a whole portfolio in terms of its volatility. The more different securities there are in the portfolio, the more accurate is the predictability of the beta over a period of time. Each stock is influenced by many factors, expected and unexpected, favorable and unfavorable. These factors tend to offset one another in a portfolio consisting of a dozen or more stocks, so that the beta for the portfolio as a whole becomes a more reliable forecasting tool. To calculate the beta of a portfolio, one multiplies each stock's beta by the number of shares held and their current market value. The sum of these figures is then divided by the total value of the portfolio, yielding its beta.

bid In the securities and commodities trade, the highest price a buyer offers for a particular security or commodity at a given time. Along with the ASK price, bid prices appear in price quotation tables for the over-the-counter market in stocks and for mutual funds. See also QUOTATION.

bid price See REDEMPTION PRICE, def. 1.

Big Board Nickname for the New York Stock Exchange.

bill Abbreviation for BILL OF EXCHANGE; DUE BILL; TREASURY BILL.

bill of exchange Also, *draft*. A written order by one party upon a second party to pay, either on demand or at some future date (see TIME DRAFT), a specific sum to a third party. If the second party is a bank, the order is called a *bank draft*. If the bank agrees to make the payment, it is said to accept the order, which then may be called a BANKERS' ACCEPTANCE. Bills of exchange are an extremely common form of payment in both domestic and foreign trade. They are negotiable instruments and are frequently traded in the money market.

blanket mortgage A mortgage on more than one parcel of property.

blind brokering Acting as an intermediary between

the buyer and seller of a very large order of Treasury securities where the buyer or seller does not know the identity of the other. For example, if a large investment banker or other dealer wants to accumulate $1 billion worth of Treasury bonds for its various customers (including pension funds and the like), it does not want other dealers to know, lest the price rise unduly. It therefore pays to go through an intermediary who will keep the transaction private (and, of course, charge a commission for the service). In the mid-1980's about half of all Treasury transactions were handled in this way.

block A large quantity of stock—10,000 shares or more—or a large dollar-value of bonds—$200,000 worth or more.

blue chip The common stock of a well-known corporation with a high reputation for the quality of its products and its ability to earn profits and expand. Blue-chip stocks tend to be high-priced, in exchange for representing lower-than-average risk.

Blue List, The Also, *Blue Book.* A trade publication issued daily that lists the names and quantities of municipal bonds being offered by dealers to other dealers, including the coupon price and yield of each. Some Federal agency issues and corporate bonds are also included. Its full name is *The Blue List of Current Municipal Offerings,* and "blue" refers to the fact that it is printed in blue ink on blue paper.

blue sky laws General name for state laws concerning the sale of new securities, principally new stocks and mutual fund shares. Most stages require the issuer to register the offering and provide detailed financial information about the issuing firm and the securities.

board broker On the Chicago Board Options Exchange, an employee who keeps track of option orders that are AWAY FROM THE MARKET and therefore cannot be executed. Some board brokers act as agents and execute such orders when it becomes possible, in which case they notify the exchange member who originally entered the order. On the Pacific and Philadelphia stock exchanges the same function is fulfilled by an employee called an *order book official*.

board of directors The individuals who are elected by the stockholders of a corporation to make broad policy decisions, appoint the company's chief operating officers, and declare dividends. The top management executives usually also serve on the board. The board meets several times a year, and members are paid for their work. Under Securities and Exchange Commission rules each is considered an INSIDER.

board room

1. Room in a brokerage office where customers can watch the consolidated tape displayed on a screen.

2. Room in the corporate main office where the board of directors meets.

boiler room An office from which individuals use high-pressure tactics to sell dubious securities over the telephone to prospective investors, whose names appear on ''sucker lists.'' While not necessarily illegal, the practice is unethical according to the rules of fair practice stated by the National Association of Securities Dealers. See also BUCKET SHOP.

bond A long-term obligation (debt) of a corporation or government. Bonds are issued by the United States government (TREASURY BOND, U.S. SAVINGS BOND); by federal agencies (FEDERAL AGENCY ISSUE), by foreign governments or corporations in the United States (YANKEE BOND); by state and local governments and their agencies (MUNICIPAL BOND); and by private corporations. The last-named are technically called ''corporate bonds,'' but the word ''bond'' alone generally means a corporate bond. A bond is basically a promise to pay a specific amount of interest at intervals over a given period of time, and to repay the principal, stated on the bond itself and called its face or par

value, on the date of maturity (expiration). The interest on most bonds is paid twice a year in fixed
payments, either made automatically (REGISTERED
BOND) or when the bondholder sends in a coupon
(COUPON BOND). The interest rate, called coupon rate
(for any kind of bond), is usually a fixed percentage
of the bond's face value, which for the majority of
American bonds is $1,000. The period of time from
bond purchase to maturity, called term to maturity,
varies from one year to forty or more; most bonds
run for twenty to thirty years.

There are exceptions even to these basic character-
istics. Bonds are sold at prices equal to their face
value (par), less than par (at discount), or more than
par (at a premium). Some deep-discount bonds, sold
at considerably less than par, are non-interest-bearing,
that is, interest is not paid out regularly but accrues
and is paid together with the principal at maturity.
Some bonds allow the issuer to retire them before
maturity (CALLABLE BOND), and others require the
principal to be repaid over a long period rather than
at maturity (installment bond). With some bonds, the
coupon rate, rather than being a fixed amount, is tied
to the interest on three-month Treasury bills or some
other variable (FLOATING-RATE BOND).

Bonds are considered a safer investment than stocks
because bondholders' claims on assets take precedence over stockholders' claims if the issuer goes
bankrupt. Many corporate bonds are secured, either
by a mortgage (MORTGAGE BOND) or a pledge of
collateral (COLLATERAL TRUST BOND). Even then, their
safety ultimately depends on the financial quality of
the issuer, which can be checked by consulting its
rating (see BOND-RATING AGENCY). Municipal bonds
are considered safer still, and Treasury securities
backed by the U.S. government the safest of all.

Bonds are traditionally regarded as a long-term

investment that yields a fixed income. The investor's return from a bond is called its yield, and the measure most commonly used to calculate it is YIELD TO MATURITY; a quicker but less complete assessment is CURRENT YIELD. Because bonds are a favorable investment when interest rates in general are declining (since they continue to pay the fixed interest rate determined at the time of purchase) and unfavorable when interest rates are rising (for the same reason), bond issuers have devised numerous devices to attract investors who are reluctant to tie up their money at fixed interest over several decades. For example, a CONVERTIBLE DEBENTURE allows the holder to exchange the bond for stock or some other security. Some bonds carry an attached WARRANT to buy additional bonds at a given coupon rate, or a put option allowing early redemption at a specific rate (PUTABLE BOND).

Prices of corporate bonds listed on the New York Stock Exchange and American Stock Exchange are quoted in the financial pages of large newspapers. (Many are not so listed, but these are recorded in *Standard & Poor's Register* and in *Moody's Bond Record,* available in large brokerage offices and also in many public libraries). The price is expressed in 100's (that is, a percentage of par), so one must add a 0 to each figure, and fractions are of $10. For example, a price of 74¼ means $742.50. The listings show the corporation issuing the bond, its coupon rate (annual interest rate), maturity date, current yield, the volume of trading (the dollar amount traded the previous day in bond denominations of $1,000), and the previous day's high, low, and closing prices and net price change. Municipal bonds are quoted on a yield-to-maturity basis (see BASIS, def. 3).

The minimum bond purchase usually is $1,000 or $5,000, and the standard trading unit is a round lot of 100 bonds, or $100,000 (however, see BABY BOND).

Bonds can be bought through most brokers, bond dealers, and from the issuing corporation (the latter usually in amounts too large for most individual investors). Brokers and dealers do not charge a commission on new issues but do collect a handling fee for buying a previously issued bond or selling one before maturity. Such fees are set at their own discretion and range from $2.50 to $30 for a $1,000 bond. One can also acquire an interest in bonds by buying shares in a bond mutual fund.

bond anticipation note   Abbreviated *BAN*. A short-term debt instrument issued by a state or local government to tide it over until the actual issue of a forthcoming bond, whose proceeds will be used to pay off the note. Like municipal bonds, BANs may be exempt from federal income tax, but depending on the purpose of the actual bond, they may be judged preferential items subject to the alternative minimum tax.

Bond Buyer's Index   An index published daily by *The Daily Bond Buyer*, a financial publication specializing in the municipal bond market; investors use the index to compare the yield of municipal bonds. There actually are two indexes, one made up of twenty long-term bonds rated A or better and the other made up of eleven bonds rated AA (see also BOND-RATING AGENCY).

bond-rating agency   A private company that assesses the quality of bonds issued in terms of the issuer's ability to meet interest payments and repay the principal. The two best-known rating agencies are Standard & Poor's Corporation and Moody's Investor Service, which both rate bonds and other fixed-income securities. Moody's expresses its ratings for corporate bonds as (from best to worst): Aaa, Aa1, Aa2, Aa3, A1, A2, A3, A, Baa, Ba, Caa, Ca, and C. Standard & Poor's are: AAA, AA+, AA, AA−, A+, A, A−, BBB, BB+, BB, BB−, B+, B, B−, CCC, etc., to C; a D rating indicates default, and the + and the − signs on the ratings from AA to B show relative standing within the major rating category. Although the two agencies frequently agree on the quality of bonds, they sometimes do not, so that Moody's may rate a bond as Aaa while Standard & Poor's rates it AA+ or lower; such a bond is said to have a *split rating*. Split ratings are the rule for convertible debentures, which Moody's nearly always rates one grade lower than nonconvertible bonds. Both Moody's and Standard & Poor's employ a similar rating system for municipal bonds; see also WHITE'S RATING.

bond ratio The proportion of a company's bonds to its total capitalization. If bonds represent one-third or more of total capitalization, the company is regarded as highly (perhaps excessively) leveraged, except in the case of utilities, which tend to have more long-term debt. Also see DEBT-TO-EQUITY RATIO; LEVERAGED, def. 1.

bond swap See SWAP.

bond yield See AFTER-TAX YIELD; CURRENT YIELD; YIELD TO MATURITY.

bonus stock Shares of common stock offered as a bonus to the purchasers of preferred stock or bonds, or to the underwriter of an issue.

book-entry securities Also, *book shares, certificateless bonds, uncertificated shares.* Securities that are not represented by certificates of ownership. Instead, ownership is simply recorded in customers' accounts. This system is used mainly for mutual fund shares, some municipal bonds, and some foreign stocks. It reduces both paperwork and the risk of losing valuable certificates.

book value

1. In accounting, the value of an asset recorded on the balance sheet, which may be quite different from its current market value. This figure is reduced each year as depreciation is deducted from it.

2. In corporate finance, the value of a company, computed by deducting liabilities from assets; in effect, the same as net assets.

book value per share   The theoretical value of a share of common stock if a company were liquidated. It is found by subtracting from a firm's total assets its liabilities, both current and long-term, and its outstanding preferred stock at par value, and dividing this figure by the number of outstanding shares of common stock. For a manufacturing company, book value is far less important than earnings and prospects, although the trend over a period of years can be significant. The book value of common stock of financial firms such as banks and insurance companies is more significant, since their assets, unlike manufacturers' plant and equipment, can readily be turned into cash.

Boston Stock Exchange   See Appendix A.

bot   In the securities and commodities trade, widely used abbreviation for "bought."

boutique   Name borrowed from a specialty retail establishment to describe a small, exclusive brokerage firm that specializes in a limited number of securities or services.

breadth, market   The percentage of stock issues being traded on a particular day, or during a given time period. If the majority of stocks listed on an exchange are traded, an upward or downward price trend has more validity than if only a small percentage are traded. The analysis of market breadth simply involves counting the number of stocks going up or down in price or establishing new price highs or lows. One commonly used measure of market breadth is the ADVANCE/DECLINE LINE.

break   Sudden drop in a security price or the market in general.

breakout   Also, *upside breakout, volume breakout.* A

sudden upward spurt in a security price, usually accompanied by a similar large increase in trading volume, after a period of steady or declining prices and volume. The sudden spurt often, but not always, is the beginning of a steady climb upward, signaling the penetration of a RESISTANCE LEVEL. A *downside breakout*, in contrast, is the same phenomenon in the opposite direction.

breakpoint The dollar-value level of a purchase of mutual fund shares at the precise point where the percentage of sales charge decreases. Sales charge schedules, which must be stated in the fund's prospectus, usually include five or six breakpoints.

broad market See ACTIVE MARKET.

broad tape A service that provides current financial information and news to its subscribers by projecting it on a screen. It is so called because it provides much more comprehensive information than the TAPE projected on stock exchange floors and in fact is not allowed to be used there lest it give floor traders an unfair advantage. It is shown mainly in brokerage offices. Some confine use of the term ''broad tape'' to the Dow Jones news service, but others apply it to all such services, which are provided by the Associated Press, Reuters, and other agencies.

broken lot Another name for ODD LOT.

broker An individual or firm that acts as agent for customers in the purchase and sale of securities or commodities, in return for a commission (called a *brokerage fee*). Stockbrokers specialize in stocks, commodity brokers in commodities, and broker-dealers buy for their own accounts as well as for customers. Some brokers are licensed stock exchange members or belong to an exchange member firm; others do not. All brokers who are registered with the Securities and Exchange Commission (SEC) are members of the Securities Investor Protection Corporation

(SIPC), which protects their customers' accounts; firms that deal entirely in mutual fund shares or annuities or other investment instruments generally are not SIPC members. In order to act as an agent, a stockbroker must be a *licensed registered representative*, which requires passing one of the examinations devised and administered by the National Association of Securities Dealers (NASD). There are four such exams, covering sales of general securities (stocks and bonds), mutual funds, municipal bonds, and tax shelters respectively. Licensing is done by the state. (See also UNIFORM SECURITIES AGENT STATE LAW EXAMINATION.) Senior members of brokerage firms may also become Chartered Financial Analysts (CFA), which involves passing a series of difficult examinations administered by an association based in Virginia. Some become Certified Financial Planners (CFP) after taking a prescribed university course of study covering pension planning, estates, taxes, etc. Some brokers also are registered Investment Advisors, indicating they are qualified to manage investment portfolios after meeting all the requirements imposed by and registering with the SEC. See also DISCOUNT BROKER; FULL-SERVICE BROKER; INVESTMENT ADVISER; REGISTERED REPRESENTATIVE.

Despite regulation, not all brokers are honest. Investors who suspect they are being cheated are advised to complain either to the New York Stock Exchange or one of the fourteen regional offices of the NASD. If they feel it is warranted, officials will reprimand or fine the broker. To get one's money back, one usually must ask for arbitration; in most cases investors cannot sue a broker if they have signed an arbitration-only agreement or started arbitration proceedings. One can also take one's complaint to a regional office of the SEC.

broker's loan Cash borrowed by a broker from a bank to buy securities, carry a customer's margin account, or underwrite a new issue, for which the securities in question serve as collateral. It is nearly always a call loan, meaning it can be terminated within twenty-four hours should the market value of the securities decline substantially.

bucket shop A brokerage operation that accepts customer's orders but does not execute them at once, instead waiting until it is advantageous to the broker. The practice, also called *bucketing*, is illegal.

bulge A rapid rise in the price of a security or commodity, or the market as a whole.

bull An investor who believes a stock price or the market or the economy in general will advance, and behaves accordingly, buying stocks and/or call options in order to profit from rising prices. By extension, a *bull market* is one that reflects this sentiment and is characterized by rising prices and, often, high trading volume. For *bull spread,* see under SPREAD, def. 3.

bullion Bars, or ingots, of refined gold, silver, or another precious metal. Gold ingots must be at least .995 fine to qualify for trading. See also GOLD.

bullion coin A gold or silver coin that is purchased as an investment. It normally sells at a price slightly above the value of the metal in the coin. See also under COIN COLLECTING.

business cycle A more or less continuous pattern of alternate expansion and contraction in the entire economy. During the period of expansion, industrial production increases, and with it, employment, prices, wages, interest rates, and profits all rise. After the cycle reaches a high point, it gradually begins to contract, with production shrinking and employment, prices, wages, interest rates, and profits all declining. After a low point is reached the economy begins to recover and business activity again increases. Although the general pattern holds true, the duration of each phase, the precise high and low points, and the overall duration of the cycle vary. Moreover, economists frequently disagree about exactly what stage of the business cycle the current economy is in.

buyers' panic Also, *buying climax*. A market in which many investors suddenly want to buy stocks because of a widespread belief that prices will rise (see also BULL). As a result prices do rise sharply and quickly, and trading volume is exceptionally high. A buyers' panic frequently marks the end of a BEAR market and the beginning of a new bull market.

buying power Also, *purchasing power*. In the securities trade, the total amount of securities that may be bought on margin without generating a MARGIN CALL.

buyout The purchase of a company by its employees. See also LEVERAGED BUYOUT.

buy stop order A STOP ORDER to buy.

C

calendar List of securities about to be offered for sale, for example, municipal bond calendar, or convertible debenture calendar.

calendar spread See under SPREAD, def. 3.

call Also, *call option.* An option contract for the right to buy a certain stock, or commodity, or futures contract at a certain price within a certain time period. See OPTION.

callable The privilege of early redemption of a bond or preferred stock. See CALLABLE BOND.

callable bond Also, *call privilege, call provision, redeemable bond.* A bond that the issuer may retire before its maturity date. Usually the issuer then pays the bondholder a premium (above the face value of the bond). The existence of this privilege and the amount of the premium (if any) must be stated on the bond INDENTURE. Generally it is preferable to buy bonds that are protected against early redemption for a specific period, such as ten years from the issue date. Also, one must take into account that the redemption price quoted for calling in a bond effectively limits its market price. The majority of American corporate bonds are callable, but Treasury bonds and notes often are noncallable. Many preferred stocks carry a similar call provision. See also SINKING FUND.

call loan A loan for which the creditor can demand repayment at any time, though in practice a brief period of notice may be required. Broker's loans are nearly always call loans.

capital asset An asset that a company holds long-term and does not sell during the normal course of business. Such assets include fixed assets, such as land, buildings, and machinery, as well as long-term investments.

capital asset pricing model Abbreviated *CAPM*. A complicated mathematical calculation that describes the relationship between the premium paid for extra returns on capital and extra risk. It is based on the theory that a high-risk stock, for example, must pay a higher return in order to attract investors.

capital expenditure Also, *capital expense*. The price paid for a CAPITAL ASSET. For tax purposes a capital expenditure usually cannot be deducted from a firm's gross income, but it is depreciable according to a schedule based on the asset's life. An investor may be interested in a company's *capital spending per share*, that is, the outlays for plant and equipment for the year divided by the number of shares of stock outstanding.

capital gain (loss) The profit (or loss) from the sale of disposition of property, based on an increase (or decrease) in the property's market value. The tax rate on capital gains varies depending on whether the owner is an individual or business and on the amount of income. Consequently, investors can benefit by planning sales of securities in order to adjust annual income and minimize taxes. In the case of a mutual fund, the capital gains may be distributed to shareholders, but frequently investors prefer to have them automatically invested in additional shares of the fund. In selling one's home, the capital gain is equal to the sale price (minus commissions and any other sale-related expenses) minus the purchase price (adjusted for home improvements and similar items). For an owner-occupied house, the tax on this income can be postponed if the seller buys another house of equal or greater value during the period stipulated by current income-tax law.

capital growth   An increase in the market value of the securities held by a mutual fund, which is reflected in the NET ASSET VALUE of the fund's shares. Capital growth is a specific aim of many mutual funds and is so stated in their prospectuses.

capitalization   The sum total of all securities issued by a corporation, including common and preferred stock, bonds, debentures, and both paid-in and earned surplus. Security analysts frequently look at a company's *capitalization ratios*, that is, the percentage of total investment capital represented by each type (long-term debt, preferred stock, and common stock). A company's capitalization depends on the industry, its financial position, and policy. Relatively stable industries like utilities usually have a higher proportion of debt than manufacturing companies. (See also DEBT-TO-EQUITY RATIO.) The higher the ratio of common stock equity, the less are the prior claims on the company ahead of the common stockholders.

capital market   The market for buying and selling long-term debt instruments (bonds, mortgages, etc.) and equity securities (stocks), as opposed to the *money market* and its trading of short-term funds.

capital spending per share   See under CAPITAL EXPENDITURE.

capital stock   The sum total of all the securities representing ownership (equity) of a corporation, including both common and preferred stock. The term is often used to mean only common stock because the rights of preferred stockholders usually are more limited.

capital structure   The common stock, preferred stock, and bonds that make up a corporation's CAPITALIZATION. If the bulk of securities issued is common stock, the capital structure is termed conservative; if bonds represent a considerable proportion (one-third or more), the capital structure is said to be LEVERAGED (def. 1).

capital surplus The difference between the balance sheet value of a stock and its nominal, or par, value. It is usually identical to PAID-IN SURPLUS.

carat A measure of the percentage of gold in an alloy, with 24 carats representing 100 percent, 12 carats 50 percent, and so on.

carryback (carryover) The transfer of one year's tax deductions, losses, or credits backward (or forward) to another tax year. U.S. tax law allows individuals to carry over a certain amount of net capital loss in this way.

carrying cost Also, *carrying charge(s)*. The storage, insurance, interest, and other costs incurred by owning a physical property (such as commodities or real estate) over a period of time.

cash account Also, *special cash account*. A normal brokerage account in which the customer trades securities with his or her own money, as opposed to a margin account, where trading is partly financed by credit.

cash basis A method of accounting on the basis of when transactions are paid for, rather than when they are incurred. See also ACCRUAL BASIS.

cash flow The payments received during a given accounting period, which represent a company's ability to service debt, reinvest in new assets, and pay dividends. Securities analysts use the term to mean reported earnings plus depreciation, that is, the amount a company has earned to replace or expand plant and equipment, provide working capital, and pay dividends. *Cash flow per share*—the net profit plus noncash charges (depreciation, depletion, and amortization) minus preferred stock dividends, divided by the number of common stock shares outstanding—is considered by some analysts to be a better indicator of a company's financial standing than earnings generated by the company's operations, a figure that can be made to look higher by changing the method of depreciation accounting.

cash management account   See ASSET MANAGEMENT ACCOUNT.

cash market   See SPOT MARKET.

cash surrender value   See under LIFE INSURANCE.

CD   Abbreviation for CERTIFICATE OF DEPOSIT.

certificate of deposit   Abbreviated *CD*. A certificate for a bank deposit that earns a specific interest rate for a given time period, ranging from seven days to several years. At the end of that time the bank pays both principal and interest. A CD may be either negotiable or nonnegotiable, that is, transferable or not to another person. Negotiable CDs, especially those with maturities of 14 to 180 days, are widely traded in the money market. CDs are issued by commercial banks and savings institutions and sometimes sold by brokerage firms. All are insured up to $100,000 by the federal government and consequently are a low-risk investment. They yield more than an ordinary savings account. However, yield information is not always clear, the annual yield quoted sometimes assuming that investors will reinvest principal and interest. This is misleading not only because one may prefer a different investment but because yields are based on current rates, which are likely to have changed by maturity. Therefore investors are advised to ask for the yield through maturity. Further, for bank-issued CDs there usually is a substantial penalty for early withdrawal. On very short-term CDs, maturing in thirty-one days or less, there is a government-required minimum deposit. A number of special kinds of CD have been developed. Among them is the *small savers' certificate* (SSC), a thirty-month bank certificate of deposit whose interest rate is tied to that of thirty-month Treasury securities. See also EURO-CD; YANKEE CD; ZERO-COUPON ISSUE.

certificate of incorporation　See under CHARTER.

Chapter 11　See under BANKRUPTCY.

charter　A document issued by a government authority that grants certain rights and privileges and imposes certain restrictions on a bank or a corporation. A corporation charter consists of *articles of incorporation*, which state the corporation's name, purpose, amount and type of stock it is to issue, location of main office, and names of officers and directors, and, when this document is approved, a *certificate of incorporation* issued by the state.

chartist　An investment analyst who uses charts to plot the price movements of securities. (See also TECHNICAL ANALYSIS.) The most popular kinds of chart so used are the bar chart, which analyzes price changes at certain time intervals (for example, daily, weekly, monthly), usually also taking volume into account, and the POINT AND FIGURE CHART. Because price patterns frequently assume certain forms, bar chartists have named some of the familiar patterns for the geometric figures (triangles, rectangles) or other shapes (flags, pennants, saucers) they resemble. A common one is *head and shoulders*, so named because it resembles the outlined head and shoulders of a person. Prices move up first to form the left "shoulder," drop, rise even higher to form the "head," and drop more sharply to form the right "shoulder." This pattern signals a declining price trend. In contrast, a *reverse head and shoulders* pattern, with the head at the bottom of the chart (or viewed upside down), signals a rising price trend.

check-writing privilege　A service offered by money-market and bond funds that allows holders to write checks against their holdings, which continue to earn interest until the checks have cleared. Such privileges usually are confined to checks of some minimum amount, such as $500, and often only a limited number of checks may be written per month.

Chicago Board of Trade   See Appendix A.

Chicago Board Options Exchange   See Appendix A.

Chicago Mercantile Exchange   See Appendix A.

churning   Also, *twisting*. Excessive trading in a brokerage customer's account, an illegal practice that increases the broker's commissions but rarely improves the customer's portfolio. Investors who suspect their brokers of churning are advised to save the confirmation slips that show when their orders were executed, and look at the trend in total commissions paid and the trend in their net equity. If the commissions are rising and equity is not, or even if equity is rising as well, there may be churning. Confirmation slips often are the only record of commissions paid on stock trading, since this information does not always appear on monthly reports from brokers.

Cincinnati Stock Exchange   The first completely automated American stock exchange, operating by means of the National Securities Trading System (NSTS), which enables brokers to deal entirely through a computer and eliminates the need for a trading floor. Agency orders and market makers' bids and offers are entered and disseminated nationally; the computer matches bids and offers, based on price and time priorities, and automatically executes the transactions. Once a transaction is executed it is displayed immediately to the buyer and seller on their computer terminals, as well as being reported to the CONSOLIDATED TAPE. The computer also keeps track of limit orders by means of a composite LIMIT ORDER book.

class   In options trading, options of the same kind (all puts, or all calls) on the same underlying security. Thus all calls on Red Hot stock would be considered

one class of option, and all Red Hot puts another. See also CLASSIFIED STOCK.

classified stock Also, *Class A, Class B stock.* A common stock that is divided into two or more classes, each of which has different rights and privileges. For example, Class A might have voting rights and Class B not, or Class A might be given some dividend advantage over Class B.

Clifford trust A tax-saving device that calls for the return of its capital to the grantor (donor) after ten years or more and the payment of its income to a beneficiary during that period. The beneficiary of such a temporary trust is usually either a minor child or an elderly parent in a low tax bracket; the donor is usually in a high tax bracket and would be helping the beneficiary financially under any circumstances. However, tax law holds that the trust income may not be used to buy what the donor is already legally obligated for, such as food and shelter for one's own child, and since March 1, 1986, most of these tax benefits have been eliminated or greatly curtailed.

close

1. On a stock exchange, the last thirty minutes of trading.

2. Also, *closing price.* The price at which a security last changed hands the previous day. This is usually the price listed in the following day's financial pages.

3. In commodity markets, the last few minutes of trading. See also SETTLEMENT PRICE.

close a position Eliminate the risk of loss in an investment, either by selling it outright or by offsetting the risk by taking an opposite position in the futures or options market.

closed corporation Also, *close corporation, private corporation.* A corporation in which most or all of the stock is owned by a few individuals, often family members or top management, and none is available for sale to the public.

closed-end investment company Also, *closed-end investment trust, publicly traded investment fund.* An INVESTMENT COMPANY that has a relatively fixed number of shares that are purchased through brokers or dealers on a stock exchange. Unlike a MUTUAL FUND, therefore, the shares are not redeemable but are traded in the open market, as stocks are. See also DUAL FUND.

closing costs The expenses incurred in the transfer of real estate from one owner to another. They include lawyers' and surveyors' fees, title searches, insurance, and fees to file deeds and mortgages.

Coffee, Sugar and Cocoa Exchange See Appendix A.

coin collecting Collecting gold coins, silver dollars, and rare coin issues (so-called *numismatic* coins) for investment purposes, that is, in the hope that their value will increase appreciably during the period they are held. Minting of gold coins in the United States ceased in 1933, and in 1954 the U.S. Treasury declared that all coins minted before 1933 would be presumed to be rare, deriving most of their value from their scarcity. In addition, *bullion* or *intrinsic* coins, which are not especially scarce, sell at only a nominal premium (5 to 10 percent) above their bullion content, and are primarily bought by investors in gold or silver (rather than in coins). Among the numismatic coins traded are both circulated and uncirculated coins; the former show some signs of wear, which affect their value. Coins that have never circulated also may show signs of wear called "bag marks," nicks and abrasions resulting from storage and moving. Because condition affects value, a grading system has been developed, ranging from 1 (poor condition) to 70 (perfect). There also are special gradings for uncirculated coins and *proof* coins (coins specially struck and never meant for circulation). As a rule, only coins that rate a score of 60 or higher for uncirculated coins qualify as investment-grade coins. In addition, the American Numismatic Association uses a standard series of terms that precisely describe a coin's surface. Among American coins, not only silver and gold coins, such as silver dollars and gold pieces, but also pennies, nickels, dimes, quarters, and half-dollars may have collector's value. For example, a copper-nickel cent piece minted in 1859 was worth about $2,500 in the mid-1980's.

Recently minted gold and silver coins (bullion coins) derive their value from their content, so their price is closely related to the price of the metal they contain. Among the gold coins traded are the Austrian 100-Corona and Hungarian 100-Corona, each containing 0.9802 troy ounce of gold; U.S. Gold Double Eagle (0.97 troy ounce); Mexican 50-Peso (1.0256 troy ounces); British Gold Sovereign (.2354 troy ounce); and Russian Chervonetz (.2488 troy ounce), along with the South African Krugerrand, Canadian Maple Leaf, Mexican Onza, Isle of Man Angel, and China Panda, each of which weighs exactly 1.0 troy ounce. Some of these also are available in fractional coins of one-half, one-quarter, or one-tenth of an ounce. Despite the fact that some of these coins have the same weight in troy ounces, they do not contain identical quantities of gold. The Canadian Maple Leaf is .999 fine while the Krugerrand and Angel both are .9167 fine; the Maple Leaf is pure gold and wears more readily, while the other two contain gold alloyed and hardened with copper, making them more durable but less desirable for jewelry purposes. All such coins should be handled carefully to avoid nicks and scratches. (See also under SILVER.)

Unlike stocks and bonds, the coin market is largely

unregulated. Therefore investors are advised to deal only with a reputable concern such as a bank, foreign-exchange dealer, member of a stock exchange, or coin dealer who has been in business for some time and preferably is a member of a recognized professional organization such as the American Numismatic Association, International Association of Professional Numismatists, or Professional Numismatists Guild. An unscrupulous dealer might not only sell counterfeit (fake) coins but pass off restrikes (coins minted from dies of earlier years) as originals, so experts suggest that investors ask for a guarantee of authenticity from the dealer. Bullion coins are not a particularly liquid investment. When reselling them one rarely gets back the premium paid upon purchasing them. Also, there is a sales tax on bullion coins in most U.S. states and Canadian provinces, adding to the transaction's cost. In 1985 American public feeling against the South African government led to a ban on the importation of Krugerrands into the United States.

collateral Security for a loan in the form of assets with monetary value. The creditor holds either the asset itself or title to it until the loan is repaid.

collateralized mortgage obligation Abbreviated *CMO*. A mortgage-backed security (see under SECONDARY MORTGAGE MARKET) that separates mortgage pools by maturities into short-, intermediate-, and long-term certificates. With Ginnie Maes and similar securities, interest and a portion of principal are repaid at regular intervals, but they differ according to how long it will take for principal to be repaid in full, ranging from five (short-term) to twenty (long-term) years.

collateral trust bond Also, *collateral trust certificate*. A bond that is backed by collateral deposited with a trustee, usually a bank. The collateral generally consists of securities, most often stocks and bonds of firms controlled by the bond-issuing corporation.

collectibles A blanket term for objects with scarcity value that are purchased as investments in the hope that their price will appreciate considerably during the period they are kept. Included are paintings and other works of art, Oriental rugs, antiques, gems, postage stamps, numismatic coins, baseball cards, comic books, marbles, and dozens of other items. There are numerous risks and problems with such investments, and most experts advise that only those who have a genuine interest in and considerable knowledge of a particular area should undertake them. Works of art are not interchangeable; each is unique, making them a very illiquid investment. Dealers are not regulated and unless one is knowledgeable it is easy to be sold a fake. In addition, the items must be stored and protected against theft and damage, thus incurring some costs. See also COIN COLLECTING; GEM INVESTMENT.

collection period The average time it takes for a company to be paid after selling its goods or services; it is calculated by dividing accounts receivable by average daily sales. Thus if a firm has $2 million in accounts receivable and average daily sales are $100,000, the collection period is twenty days.

combination In options trading, purchasing a call and a put on the same underlying security with different strike prices but the same duration (expiration date). See also STRADDLE, def. 1; STRAP; STRIP.

combined ratio In analyzing insurance company stocks, a measure of their profitability. The combined ratio is the sum of a company's loss ratio and its expense ratio, with the break-even point at one-to-one, or 100 percent. Thus a combined ratio of less than 100 percent represents an underwriting profit, and a combined ratio higher than 100 percent means an under-writing loss.

Comex (COMEX)   Abbreviation for Commodities Exchange, Inc. See Appendix A.

commercial paper   Also, *prime commercial paper*. A short-term corporate loan, backed only by the credit rating of the firm, which is usually excellent (hence "prime"). Maturing in less than nine months (most often in 30 to 120 days), commercial paper generally is sold at a discount by the corporation to a dealer, which in turn sells it to brokers or banks. Occasionally, however, a firm sells such notes directly to purchasers. Most commercial paper has a face value of $100,000 or more. It is freely traded in the money market and so is readily available to individual investors through a money-market fund. Interest rates, which are usually lower than those on conventional bank loans, are published monthly in the *Federal Reserve Bulletin* and weekly by the Federal Reserve Bank of New York. The rates are quoted on a discount basis, the yield being the difference between the discounted purchase price and the face amount. Commercial paper quality is, like that of bonds, rated by several investors' organizations. They are Moody's (P-1, P-2, P-3), Standard & Poor's (A-1, A-2, A-3, B, C, D) and Fitch Investor's Service (F-1, F-2, F-3, F-4); in each case the "1" means highest quality.

commission house   Also, *futures commission merchant.* A firm that buys and sells futures contracts for the accounts of its customers, who include both commercial and speculative traders. In effect, a commodity broker.

Commodity Exchange, Inc.   See Appendix A.

commodity fund   See COMMODITY POOL.

commodity futures exchange   An organized market for trading commodity futures, comparable to the stock exchange for trading stocks. Unlike the stock market, however, the commodity exchange serves not only those who take delivery of the goods for which they contract but also a much larger number of traders who never intend to take delivery of the underlying commodity. Of this latter group, many are hedgers who wish to protect themselves against unfavorable price fluctuations in the spot (actual) market (see HEDGING), and some are speculators who trade in futures purely to make a profit. In order to prevent excessive speculation and illegal market manipulation, the U.S. Commodity Futures Trading Commission (CFTC) regulates all American commodity exchanges and approves their rules and regulations concerning futures and options trading, which cover practically every aspect of trading, including limits on the amount of futures bought or sold by an individual, as well as price limits.

The exchanges, which numbered about a dozen in the mid-1980's (see Appendix A), are nonprofit membership organizations similar to the organized stock exchanges. The members include floor brokers and traders, who trade for their customers' and their own accounts (see also FLOOR TRADER, def. 2); trade houses, which are in the spot market (for the actual commodities) and engage primarily in hedging; and commission houses or futures commission merchants, which act as brokers for customers trading either commodities or futures contracts. Trading takes place by open outcry and hand signals in specific areas, called pits or rings, each designated for a particular commodity traded on an exchange. As the prices change they are recorded through a computerized communications system that enables prices (high, low, and last three changes) to be displayed on a large electronic screen near each ring. Summaries of price changes are sent daily to the media and are available in the financial pages of major newspapers.

Originating in 1848, when the Chicago Board of Trade was established, commodity futures exchanges expanded enormously from the mid-1970's on, when trading was no longer confined to agricultural commodities such as sugar, grains, and soybeans, but broadened to include lumber, heating oil, precious metals and, fastest-growing of all, FINANCIAL FUTURES. Because the futures market is fairly risky and quite specialized, several forms of professional management for investors have developed. *Commodity pools*, usually in the form of a limited partnership, operate much as a mutual fund does, enabling individuals to participate with a smaller investment than is possible in an individually managed account. *Commodity trading advisers*, individuals who specialize in studying futures markets, will for a fee advise clients on futures trading. Both kinds of management are regulated by the CFTC, as well as by the National Futures Association, an industry self-regulatory body. With a trading adviser, however, the investor must still deal with a commodity broker to execute the actual trading. The growth in futures trading has also led to criticisms of the traditional system of open outcry and hand signals and suggestions that it be replaced by a computerized system, but in the mid-1980's only the fairly small Bermuda-based International Futures Exchange had instituted such a system.

commodity pool   Also, *commodity fund*. A kind of mutual fund or, usually, a limited partnership whose shareholders are speculators in the commodities market, most often in futures contracts, and which is managed by an expert in commodity trading. See also under COMMODITY FUTURES EXCHANGE.

common stock   A security that represents a share of ownership in a corporation, entitling the holder to receive dividends and voting rights in the running of the business. Of the various securities issued by a corporation, common stock carries the highest risk and the greatest possibility for appreciation. See also CAPITAL STOCK; PREFERRED STOCK.

competitive trader   See FLOOR TRADER, def. 1.

computer, use of for investors   See DATA BASE; INSTINET; INVESTMENT ADVISER; PORTFOLIO MANAGEMENT PROGRAM; PROGRAM TRADING; REGRESSION ANALYSIS; SCREENING; SPREADSHEET; TECHNICAL ANALYSIS.

condominium   Abbreviated *condo*. Absolute ownership of a unit of real estate within a larger property and a share of the common property (for example, lobbies, grounds, and elevators), which is usually maintained by a management company paid a fee by each owner. Each individual owner is taxed separately and may sublet or sell his or her unit at will. See also COOPERATIVE.

confirmation   Form sent by a broker to a customer following the execution of an order, with details as to price, commission, in what market, date of execution, and how much the customer owes or is owed. It also indicates if the broker acted as a dealer in the transaction.

conflict of interest   A situation in which an individual makes a decision in a business or professional capacity that can be of personal benefit. In the securities trade, trading on the basis of INSIDER information and advising brokerage customers to buy stocks in which the broker has an interest as either owner or underwriter are two examples of conflict of interest.

conglomerate   A corporation that consists of numerous companies engaged in a variety of businesses and industries. Unlike a HOLDING COMPANY, it is created through a series of mergers with and purchases of other companies. The chief advantages of a conglomerate are centralized financial management and a broader market for securities; the main disadvantage is that its very size and diversity make it difficult to run efficiently.

consolidated balance sheet   See under BALANCE SHEET.

consolidated tape   Stock market TAPE that reports transactions in securities listed on the New York (Network A) and American (Network B) stock exchanges in all the markets where they occur, that is, including also the regional exchanges where they are traded. The quotations are broadcast first to the exchanges themselves and then, after a fifteen-minute delay, to ticker machines, display boards, and cable-access television across the United States and internationally. These ticker quotations are not the same as the securities quotations available at a QUOTE TERMINAL.

constant dollar plan   See under FORMULA INVESTING.

contra broker   Broker on the opposite side of a transaction, that is, representing the buyer on a sell order, or the seller on a buy order.

contractual plan   Also, *periodic payment plan*. A MUTUAL FUND in which the investor acquires shares by periodically paying a fixed dollar amount over a long period, such as $50 a month for fifteen years. Frequently such a plan involves a considerable FRONT-END LOAD.

controller   Also, *comptroller*. The principal accountant of a firm, who is responsible for all its accounts and financial reports, tax returns, and internal auditing, and for carrying out the budget.

conversion premium   The difference between CONVERSION VALUE and MARKET VALUE of a bond, expressed as a percentage. If the conversion value of a $1,000 bond is $800 (since the 25 shares it may be converted into now sell for $32 each), the conversion premium is 25 percent ($1,000 − $800 = $200 = 25% of $800). This figure represents the judgment of investors with respect to the worth of the bond.

conversion price   The effective price paid for common stock obtained by converting either convertible preferred stock or convertible debentures. For example, if a $1,000 bond is convertible into 20 shares of stock, the conversion price is $50 ($1,000 ÷ 20).

conversion ratio Also, *conversion rate*. The number of shares of common stock that may be obtained by converting a convertible bond or share of convertible preferred stock.

conversion value Current value of total shares of common stock into which a convertible security may be converted. For example, the conversion value of a $1,000 bond with a conversion ratio of 25 shares is $800 when the common stock is trading at $32 per share (25 × 32 = 800).

convertible debenture Also, *convertible bond*. A debenture (unsecured bond) that may be exchanged by its owner for common stock or some other security, usually a fixed number of shares of the bond issuer's common stock. The terms of conversion are generally spelled out precisely as to price and time. Convertible debentures can be freely traded, and they pay a fixed amount of interest, just as ordinary bonds do. However, their coupon rate tends to be lower than that of equivalent ordinary bonds because of the potential gain arising out of convertibility (and at the same time tends to be higher than the dividend rate on the underlying common stock). The prices of convertibles reflect both bond prices and the price of the underlying stock. Investors in convertibles hope that the underlying stock's price will advance and the debenture's price will rise correspondingly. Unlike buying the underlying stock itself, however, buying the convertible affords a partial protection against a stock price decline, since the convertible should continue to pay regular interest regardless of the stock price. Estimating the price one should pay for a convertible can be complicated. One needs to compare the yield on the underlying stock (divide annual dividend by recent stock price) with the convertible coupon, as well as the CONVERSION PREMIUM (the difference between the convertible's price and its market value upon conversion). In addition, one should consider whether or not there is call protection, since companies often call convertibles to reduce their debt (holders then either accept the call price, usually a shade higher than par, or convert the bond into common stock). Although convertible bonds usually have the possibility of greater price appreciation than comparable nonconvertible issues, they can decline in price, either because the price of the underlying stock drops or because interest rates rise, or both. One can offset some of these risks by investing in a mutual fund that invests in convertible bonds. See also CONVERTIBLE PREFERRED STOCK.

convertible hedge   A form of HEDGING with a convertible security, most often involving the purchase of a convertible bond and the simultaneous short sale of the stock into which the bond is convertible. If the stock goes up, there should be a profit in the bond and a loss in the stock. If the stock goes down, there should be a profit in the stock and a loss in the bond. Obviously, the profit in either case must exceed the accompanying loss and the commission and other trading expense for the hedging to succeed. Such hedging does reduce the risk of loss, however. Another advantage is the ability to sell the stock short without margin (down payment) because the corresponding convertible security serves as collateral. (See SELLING SHORT for further explanation of this process.)

convertible preferred stock   Preferred stock that may be exchanged by its owner for common stock, usually but not always the common stock of the same company. The terms for such an exchange are spelled out carefully as to price and time. Convertible preferred stocks can be traded freely on exchanges and over-the-counter, just as ordinary preferred stocks are, and in other respects are very similar to a CONVERTIBLE DEBENTURE.

cooperative Abbreviated *coop*, *co-op*. An organization that is owned by its members. In real estate it is usually a corporation that acquires ownership of land and/or building(s), for which the funds are raised by selling shares to persons who will reside in or otherwise use them. Buying a given number of shares gives a tenant a proprietary lease, granting the right of possession of a portion of the property for a given period of time; in addition the tenant must pay maintenance, which consists of a prorated share of the funds needed to cover operating expenses, mortgage, and taxes. In most cases shareholders may not assign their shares or sublet their portion without the approval of the corporation. See also CONDOMINIUM.

cornering the market Acquiring control over the supply of a commodity or stock, so that persons who have sold it short (see SELLING SHORT) and want to cover their sales (buy the underlying stock or commodity) must now pay an excessive price for it. Although it seems blatantly unfair, cornering the market is perfectly legal (although many of the measures used to do so, such as forming a pool, are illegal).

corporate bond Also, *bond*. A BOND issued by a corporation, as opposed to a government or government agency.

corporate pension plan See PENSION PLAN.

corporate restructuring Changing the organization of a corporation, which usually but not always involves some RECAPITALIZATION. Restructuring is undertaken to make a company more profitable, more attractive to investors, more highly leveraged, more protected against unwanted takeover, or for any number of other purposes. For example, a company may sell an unprofitable subsidiary at a loss and take a large tax write-off. This sale also reduces depreciation charges against the former subsidiary's assets and enables the company to use the proceeds of the sale to buy its own stock. The number of shares of outstanding stock is thereby reduced, increasing earnings per share and causing the stock price to rise, as well as bolstering the position of the present management and giving it more protection against a possible unfriendly takeover.

corporation Abbreviated *Corp.*, *Inc.* (for *incorporated*). A form of business organization that consists of a group of owners, called stockholders, who are legally considered a single entity (''one person''). A corporation may own property, incur debts, and sue or be sued. Its owners have *limited liability,* that is, they are liable for the firm's debts only to the extent of their investment. If the firm goes bankrupt, a stockholder who owns 100 of its shares bought at $15 a share can lose only $1,500. Ownership in a corporation is readily transferable; anyone can buy or sell shares in it at any time. Further, the corporation continues to exist even if all of its stockholders die. It can raise more money by issuing more stock or by borrowing (issuing bonds or in some other way). Legally, the firm is controlled by its stockholders through exercising their voting rights. In practice, most publicly owned modern corporations have thousands of stockholders who have little interest in the running of the company provided that it earns profits, (in which they share through dividends and the increased value of their stock), and consequently nearly all corporations are run by professional managers. In the United States corporations are subject to various government controls, which vary from state to state.

correction A temporary change of direction in the

movement of the price of a security or commodity, usually downward. For example, a stock price may be moving generally up, but despite broadly increased demand for the stock some investors will want to cash in on their profit and sell it. If enough do so, the price may temporarily drop as a result of such PROFIT TAKING and then resume its upward course. See also TECHNICAL RALLY.

correspondent A bank, brokerage firm, or other financial agency that acts as agent for another on a regular basis. Brokerage firms frequently have correspondents on exchanges to which they do not belong, or on exchanges in other countries.

coupon bond A bond with interest certificates (coupons) attached to it. The holder "clips" (detaches) the coupons as they become due and presents them for payment of interest. A coupon bond is usually a BEARER BOND and therefore is negotiable. See also REGISTERED COUPON BOND.

coupon rate The annual interest paid on a bond, stated as a percentage of its par (face) value. The term comes from the practice of submitting a coupon whenever an interest payment is due (see COUPON BOND), but applies to registered bonds as well.

coupon stripping Separating the individual coupon (interest) payments of a bond from the par value due at maturity, thereby creating two kinds of security that can be sold separately: a ZERO-COUPON ISSUE and the coupons. Brokerage houses have created pools by buying the underlying bonds, most often U.S. Treasury issues, and selling certificates that represent ownership of coupon and/or principal payments on securities in the pool. Known by such acronyms as TIGR (for Treasury Investment Growth Receipt), CATS (Certificates of Accrual of Treasury Securities), and LYON (Liquid Yield Option Note), these certificates can be purchased from the various brokerage houses that offer them, and some are traded on the New York Stock Exchange. Like zero-coupon bonds, they offer no actual income (in the form of interest payments) until maturity, but individual investors must pay income tax on the interest that accrues even though it is not paid out. Thus, they are most suitable for pension funds, IRAs, and other tax-sheltered accounts.

covenant See PROTECTIVE COVENANT; RATE COVENANT.

cover In SELLING SHORT, the purchase of an equal number of securities to be delivered against the short position (or the deposit of an equivalent amount of cash).

coverage The ability of a corporation to pay interest (fixed charges) on its bonds and dividends on preferred stock out of its earnings. To calculate *interest coverage*, divide the operating profit shown on the income statement, or the balance available before income taxes and interest charges, by the annual interest charges (fixed charges). Ordinarily a manufacturing company should cover interest at least five times, although for highly leveraged companies like public utilities a three-times average coverage is considered satisfactory. To calculate the *combined* or *overall coverage*, which includes interest and preferred-stock dividends (the latter being paid after taxes), divide the annual interest and debt costs plus preferred dividends into the adjusted operating profit (before interest but after taxes). For a manufacturer a combined coverage of four is usually regarded as satisfactory, whereas for a public utility three times again is considered adequate. Although these proportions represent a measure of the safety of a company's bonds and preferred stock, too high a ratio (excessive safety) may show that the firm is not highly leveraged enough.

covered forward sale See under FORWARD CONTRACT.

covered option See under OPTION.

credit
1. In general, the purchase of goods or services or cash in exchange for a promise of future payment. The widespread use of credit by individuals and businesses has given rise to the *credit rating* industry, that is, agencies that investigate the trustworthiness of individuals and firms in meeting their financial obligations.
2. In accounting, an entry on the liability side of the balance sheet, indicating a deduction from assets.
3. In a brokerage or other customer's account, an increase in the customer's equity.

cross order   Also, *crossed trade, crossed sale.* An order to a broker to buy and sell the same security. If it comes from a single customer, it constitutes a WASH SALE subject to special tax treatment. If it comes from two or more customers, the broker is obliged to process the order through the exchange, lest a customer otherwise be deprived of getting a better price.

cum dividend   Literally, "with dividend," meaning that the buyer of a stock will receive the next dividend, which has been declared but not yet paid. Since five business days is the normal interval allowed for REGULAR WAY DELIVERY of a stock, stocks usually are sold cum dividend up to five days preceding the RECORD DATE and EX-DIVIDEND thereafter.

cumulative dividend   A preferred-stock dividend that, if not paid out because the company cannot or will not pay it, will accumulate and be paid, along with current dividends, before any dividend is paid to holders of common stock. Almost all preferred stock carries a provision for cumulative dividend.

cumulative voting   A system of voting for the directors of a corporation that allows holders of common stock to multiply the number of their shares by the number of positions being voted on and cast the total number of votes they are entitled to for a single person, or to split them as they wish. This system is much less common, however, than STATUTORY VOTING.

Curb Exchange   Original name of the American Stock Exchange; see Appendix A.

currency futures   See under FINANCIAL FUTURES.

current assets   Property that can reasonably be expected to be converted into cash, sold, or consumed during normal business operations in twelve months or less. Current assets include cash, U.S. government bonds and other highly marketable securities, accounts receivable, and inventories.

current coupon bond   A bond whose coupon (interest) rate is close to current market rates.

current liabilities   Debts that will fall due within twelve months. Among them are accounts payable, wages, taxes, installments on long-term debt, and notes payable.

current position   An analysis of a firm's WORKING CAPITAL.

current ratio   The proportion of a firm's current assets to its current liabilities, representing a measure of its liquidity. For most companies, experts say, the current ratio should be at least 2:1, although for utilities and businesses with small inventories it can safely be somewhat lower. See also QUICK-ASSET RATIO.

current yield   The amount of interest paid per year on an investment, divided by its current market price. The current yield for bonds is indicated in the corporate bond listings published in the financial pages. Thus a bond that pays 8½ percent interest and sells for 76½ ($765.00) has a current yield of 11.1 percent, which usually is rounded off to 11 percent. While this figure can be important to the investor who is spending the coupon payments, it does not describe the return from those bonds whose market prices are far above or below their redeemable par value, which is calculated in YIELD TO MATURITY. For stocks, current yield is computed by dividing the stock price by the dividend payout. A stock selling for $20 a share and paying a $2 yearly dividend is yielding 10 percent. This figure alone, however, can be misleading, because a rising current yield can mean either a rising dividend or a falling stock price.

cushion bond Another name for PREMIUM BOND.

cushion theory The idea that a large volume of short sales in a security will drive its price up, because these sales will have to be covered by actual purchases of stock. The name comes from the fact that SELLING SHORT serves as a "cushion" for consequent buy orders. Technical analysts regard a ratio of 2:1 (twice as many short sales as normal transactions in the stock) as large enough to signal a price advance. The SHORT INTEREST THEORY is a similar notion applied to the market as a whole.

custodial account

1. An account under which a bank stores property owned by a customer.

2. An account held by a parent for a minor child. The Social Security number on the account is the child's, so no income tax is paid by the parent on dividends, interest, or capital gains. Rather, these returns are listed on the child's own tax return. However, beginning in 1986 such income shifting to children under 14 has earned no tax benefits.

customer's man See REGISTERED REPRESENTATIVE.

cv In bond and stock tables, abbreviation for convertible.

cyclical stock A stock that tends to mirror the ups and downs of the business cycle, rising in price when the economy expands and falling when the economy shrinks. Examples include the stock of companies in capital goods industries such as steel, machine tools, and heavy equipment.

d In stock price quotations, usually appearing in the "low" column, an indication that the price represents a new 52-week low.

database Computer term for an electronically transmitted library of information. Individuals may use a personal computer equipped with a modem (enabling communication over telephone lines) and a communications program (software) to obtain investment information from a database. Such information is sold by an on-line information service, which stores data from numerous databases in its own computers and retransmits it. This service usually requires users to pay an initial fee, which often includes some free on-line time to give new users a chance to become familiar with it. Thereafter charges depend directly on the time the service is used—so much per minute. In the mid-1980's investment information was available from more than forty information services. Investors could use a database to obtain price quotations for stocks, bonds, commodities, and options to update their portfolios; historical pricing information on the markets and on individual securities and commodities in order to perform technical analysis; fundamental information about different companies; news about specific firms and the economy in general; research information; current reports of insider trading; earnings forecasts; surveys of money markets and foreign exchange trends; and more. Each information service provides information about compatible software. Although only a communications program is needed to obtain data to read on the home screen, most investors want to use the data they obtain, entering figures into their SPREADSHEET or automatically updating their portfolios or drawing graphs to show the patterns of individual securities or industries or the entire market. These applications all require software of their own. See also PORTFOLIO MANAGEMENT PROGRAM.

day order   An order to buy or sell securities on specific terms that must be executed by the end of the trading day or it automatically expires. All orders are registered as day orders unless the investor specifies they are good for a longer period (for example, a week, a month, until canceled, etc.).

dealer   An individual or firm that buys and sells securities and commodities for its own account. Both brokers and specialists may act as dealers, selling to other customers from their own inventory, besides acting as agents who enter into transactions on behalf of their customers.

debenture   A BOND that is backed only by the general credit of the issuer and is not secured by collateral such as a mortgage or lien on real property. The majority of corporate bonds issued are debentures. See also CONVERTIBLE DEBENTURE; SUBORDINATE DEBENTURE.

debt   Cash, goods, or services owed by one person or organization to another. It is one of the two principal forms of investment, the other being EQUITY (ownership). Securities that represent debt (so-called *debt instruments*) include the bill, note, debenture, bond, commercial paper, certificate of deposit, banker's acceptance, and bill of exchange. Another important form of debt for investors is the MORTGAGE.

debt-to-equity ratio   The proportion of a company's debt, both long-term and short-term, to its equity capital, which includes common and preferred stock, earned and unearned surplus, and surplus reserves.

Businesses with fairly predictable earnings, such as utilities, can safely carry a higher debt-to-equity ratio than can companies with fluctuating earnings, such as auto and steel producers.

declining balance method An accounting method that charges more depreciation in a fixed asset's early years and less later. It is so called because the annual charge is based on a fixed percentage of the asset's value after the depreciation for the previous years has been deducted. See also DOUBLE DECLINING BALANCE METHOD.

deep discount bond A bond that is selling at much below its par (face) value, usually 80 percent of par or less, most often because interest rates were much lower when the bond was originally issued.

default

1. In general, failure to pay the interest or principal on a loan when it is due. The term is used for bonds, deeds of trust, mortgages, and many other forms of obligation.

2. In commodities futures trading, the inability of a firm or individual to meet margin requirements, that is, the down payment required by the exchange for a futures contract.

defeasance A term borrowed from the law, where it means "a rendering null and void," whereby an old, low-interest debt security is converted into either a new, higher-interest obligation or a stock, thereby reducing debt on the balance sheet and improving earnings. For example, a corporation might buy high-yielding Treasury securities to repay principal and interest on an old bond issue paying much lower interest but not maturing for another fifteen years. The old bond issue, which is now defeased debt, can be removed from the balance sheet, and the difference between its face value and that of the Treasury notes can be added to quarterly earnings. Or the corporation might tell a broker to buy the outstanding portion of the old bond issue, which the broker might then exchange for a new issue of the company's stock with the same market value.

defensive position   Also, *defensive investment*. Selling higher-risk growth stocks in favor of income-producing bonds and/or income stocks that respond less to the ups and downs of the business cycle, in anticipation of an economic downturn.

deferred annuity   See under ANNUITY.

deferred income   Also, *deferred revenue*. Income that has been received but not yet earned, as, for example, rent paid in advance. On the balance sheet it is listed as a liability.

defined-benefit plan   See under PENSION PLAN.

defined-contribution plan   See under PENSION PLAN.

delayed opening   Postponing the beginning of trading in a particular listed security because exchange officials believe there is a gross imbalance of buy and sell orders, usually due to some event such as an announced takeover. A company itself also may ask for a delayed opening if it is about to announce a major change of some kind.

delisting   Removing a listed stock from an organized exchange because it no longer meets exchange requirements.

demand deposit   Money that may be withdrawn without advance notice from a bank account, usually by writing a check.

depletion   An accounting allowance for the shrinkage or exhaustion of an asset, nearly always a natural resource such as an oil or gas well. When tax laws allow for depletion, it is stated in the form of a credit against taxes due.

Depository Trust Company   Abbreviated *DTC*. A central place of safekeeping for securities through which members exchange the certificates for sales among one another. Most such exchanges are now effected by means of computerized bookkeeping entries rather than the actual handing over of paper certificates. A member of the Federal Reserve, the DTC is owned by the industry, mainly the New York Stock Exchange and Wall Street brokerage firms.

depreciation An amount charged against earnings to allow for the aging of plant and equipment owned by a firm, or any other decline in the value of physical assets. Normally depreciation is allocated over the life of the asset, so much during each accounting period. There are numerous ways of calculating depreciation, but they fall into two basic categories: charging off the same amount each year for each item, or deducting higher amounts in the early years and decreasing amounts in later years. (The principal accounting methods used are DECLINING BALANCE METHOD, STRAIGHT-LINE DEPRECIATION, and SUM-OF-DIGITS METHOD.) Since depreciation is deductible from taxable income, the method of accounting is an important part of tax planning. Moreover, the government can change the tax treatment of depreciation as part of its fiscal policy, making it easy to write off assets and thus encouraging investment, or shortening or lengthening the period of time over which an asset may be depreciated. On the balance sheet, there may be a series of credits on the asset side, showing the reduced value of a fixed asset. Called a *depreciation reserve*, it is not actually a fund set aside but simply shows the change in value of the company's assets. On the income statement a footnote usually discusses the company's depreciation policy. U.S. tax law also allows individuals to deduct depreciation from taxable income, provided that the items so treated are used in business or held for the production of income, have a useful life for a determined period that exceeds one year, and wear out or become obsolete. Depending on how they are used, an automobile, personal computer, and home office space all might qualify.

devaluation   An officially declared decrease in the value of one country's currency in relation to other currencies and/or gold. Devaluation is generally carried out when there is a serious balance of payments deficit, that is, when a country's imports greatly exceed its exports and it needs more foreign exchange to pay for imported goods. With devaluation, its goods become cheaper for foreigners and imports become costlier.

digits deleted   An incomplete price on a stock exchange TAPE, meaning the tape has been delayed and therefore some digits have been dropped. Thus, for example, a price sequence of 13, 13¼, 13⅞ appears as 3, 3¼, 3⅞.

dilution   An increase in the number of shares of common stock issued by a corporation without a comparable increase in its assets. This would occur if all of a corporation's convertible securities were converted and all its warrants and options exercised. Most convertible securities are protected against dilution by an *antidilution clause*, whereby the conversion price is reduced in case of dilution.

diminishing balance method   Another name for DE-CLINING BALANCE METHOD.

directors   See BOARD OF DIRECTORS.

direct placement   Another name for PRIVATE PLACE-MENT.

discount

  1. The amount by which an asset is priced under its face value, book value, or the value of a comparable asset. Thus, the term is used for the amount by which a bond sells below its face value, a stock below its book value, or a coin below the value of its metallic content. See also PREMIUM.

  2. In commodity futures trading, the amount by which a futures contract price is below the spot price

(current market price for the actual commodity). See also BASIS. Also, the price difference between futures contracts of different delivery months. For example, "October at a discount to August" means the October futures price is lower than that for August.

3. In finance and banking, the interest on a loan that is charged in advance and deducted from the amount lent.

discount bond A bond selling at a price below its par (face) value. The difference between these two figures, or discount, affects the return on the investment (see YIELD TO MATURITY). The term applies both to bonds that originally sold at par and are currently selling for less (usually because interest rates have risen) and to bonds that are sold at a discount from the time of issue (original-issue discount bonds). The latter often have a very low coupon rate or are non-interest-bearing, that is, interest is not paid out regularly but accrues to the time of maturity and is paid then together with the principal. See also DEEP DISCOUNT BOND; DISCOUNT YIELD; PREMIUM BOND.

discount broker A brokerage house whose services consist mainly of executing customers' orders to buy and sell securities or commodities, and that charges lower ("discounted") commissions than a full-service broker. Discount brokers are used mainly by investors who do not seek a broker's advice but make their own investment decisions. Fees vary, sometimes being based on the dollar amount of transactions and sometimes on the number of shares traded. There also may be volume discounts and/or negotiable rates for very active traders.

discounted cash flow Also, *present-value method*. A method of calculating the return on a capital investment in terms of a compound interest rate discounted over the life of the asset. If, for example, funds can be invested today to yield 10 percent per year, a payment of $100 to be made in one year has a present value of $90.90. Such calculations are based on the time value of money, that is, its value depends partly on when money is received.

discount rate Also, *rediscount rate*. The interest rate charged by Federal Reserve banks on loans to member banks. An increase in the discount rate discourages banks from making loans in excess of their reserves, since it becomes too costly for them to borrow from the Federal Reserve, which in turn slows down business growth. Conversely, a lowered discount rate encourages borrowing and stimulates business expansion.

discount yield The annual yield on a security that is sold at a discount from its face value. For example, to calculate the yield on a $10,000 Treasury bill bought for $9,250 with 270 days until maturity, divide the discount ($10,000 − $9,250 = $750) by the face value ($10,000) and multiply the result (750 ÷ 10,000 = 0.075) by the approximate number of days in the year (360) divided by the number of days to maturity (360 ÷ 270 = 1.33): 1.33 × 0.075 = 0.10 or 10 percent.

discretionary account A brokerage account in which the customer gives the broker some control over the purchase and sale of securities, commodities, etc. on the customer's behalf, without the customer having to approve each order placed.

disintermediation The removal of deposits from banks, savings and loan associations, and other savings institutions to higher-yielding investments such as Treasury bills. Formerly a severe problem, disintermediation became less marked in the 1980's when deregulation allowed savings institutions to pay whatever interest rates they chose to.

distribution

 1. Also, *offering, public offering*. The sale to the

public of a large amount of stock, either an entire issue (see PRIMARY DISTRIBUTION; SECONDARY DISTRIBUTION) or a large block. In order to avoid flooding the market and depressing its price, the stock may be sold over a period of time.

2. Term used by technical analysts to describe a stock price that fluctuates within a relatively narrow range for a time and then moves much lower, indicating that there is declining demand for it. See also ACCUMULATION.

diversification Spreading one's investments among different types of security, different companies, different industries, and/or different geographical locations, in order to protect against unforeseeable risks. Most authorities agree that a portfolio of twenty or more carefully selected stocks is adequately diversified. For small investors who cannot afford such diversification, spreading assets among several well-chosen mutual funds and a relatively risk-free government security can achieve the same goal.

diversified investment company A MUTUAL FUND with three-fourths of its assets so allocated that it has no more than 5 percent of its total assets invested in any one company, and that it holds no more than 10 percent of the outstanding voting stock in any other company.

divestiture Disposing of a major asset, such as a block of stock or a company subsidiary, through sale, liquidation, or SPINOFF. Reasons for divestiture include a court order enforcing an antitrust decision, lack of profitability in a subsidiary, a need for cash, etc.

dividend The portion of a corporation's earnings that it distributes among its stockholders, in proportion to the number and kind of shares they own. The decision to pay dividends is made by the board of directors, and they usually are paid quarterly, in the form of cash, stock (called *stock dividend*), or, rarely, some other property. Preferred stock dividends usually are fixed over a period of time, whereas common stock dividends are more dependent on the company's earnings and current cash position. Some companies offer their stockholders *automatic dividend reinvestment* (*ADR*), whereby the dividends automatically buy more shares of common stock; this saves brokerage fees and postpones payment of income tax on dividends, which otherwise must be paid the year they are received (see also DIVIDEND EXCLUSION). The investor's rate of return on a stock is usually calculated in terms of its *dividend yield* (*return*), the annual dividend per share divided by the market price per share. Investors whose main aim is current income are advised to compare a company's dividend yield and the prospects for future dividend increased against the more reliable but fixed return from bonds, preferred stocks, or savings bank deposits. Analysts also consider a company's *dividend payout ratio*, the percentage of earnings on common stock that is actually paid out in dividends, which varies according to the stability of earnings, the need for new capital, and general policies. Some companies prefer to reinvest earnings for expansion without relying on borrowing, and such growth companies usually pay less in dividends than older companies in stable industries, such as utilities. See also CUM DIVIDEND; EX-DIVIDEND; PASSED DIVIDEND.

dividend exclusion The exclusion of a fixed amount of annual dividend income from federal income tax. In the mid-1980's $100 could be deducted by individuals, $200 by married couples filing joint returns; and 85 percent by U.S. corporations on dividends paid to them by other U.S. corporations, but the 1986 tax law eliminated these provisions.

dollar bond

    1. Another name for YANKEE BOND.

    2. A municipal TERM bond, which has a single

coupon and maturity for an entire issue that is quoted on a percentage-of-par basis, as corporate bonds generally are, instead of the yield basis customary for municipal bond quotations.

dollar cost averaging Also, *dollar averaging*. A system of spending a fixed amount of money to buy securities at regular intervals, for example, $150 a month. Consequently one buys more when prices are low and less when they are high. See also FORMULA INVESTING.

Donoghue's Money Fund Average An average constructed of the yields of all major money-market mutual funds, which is published weekly for seven-day and thirty-day yields and appears in the financial pages of some newspapers. See also LIPPER MUTUAL FUND INDUSTRY AVERAGE.

don't know Another term for QUESTIONED TRADE.

double declining balance method A method of calculating depreciation whereby the annual depreciation charge is twice the percentage set by the STRAIGHT-LINE METHOD applied to the undepreciated balance at the beginning of each year.

double entry The conventional bookkeeping system in which every transaction is entered twice, as a credit in one account and a debit in another. From it, a BALANCE SHEET and INCOME STATEMENT can be generated almost automatically.

double spread Same as STRADDLE, def. 1.

Dow Jones average See under STOCK INDEX/AVERAGE.

down tick Also, *minus tick*. In the securities trade, any stock price that is lower than that of the immediately preceding transaction, designated by a minus sign just before the price shown on the screen. See also ZERO-MINUS TICK.

Dow theory A type of market analysis based on tracking the performance of the Dow Jones industrial and transportation averages (see under STOCK INDEX/

AVERAGE). If one rises significantly and the other also advances, the market is moving upward. When both decline below a predetermined level, the market is moving down.

draft   A written order directing the payment of a sum of money from the drawer's account to a designated person or firm called the payee. One form of draft is the BILL OF EXCHANGE.

dual fund   Also, *dual-purpose investment fund*. A special kind of CLOSED-END INVESTMENT COMPANY that issues two classes of share: income shares and capital shares. Holders of income shares receive all interest and dividends earned on the fund's portfolio, as well as a specific price for their shares, which the fund promises to pay them at a specified future date. On that date the holders of capital shares receive whatever assets are remaining over and above the amount paid out to the income shareholders. At that time the fund may liquidate completely, dividing its assets among the capital shareholders, or it may continue in business as an ordinary MUTUAL FUND. Income shareholders of a dual fund are basically lenders; they lend the fund the purchase price of their shares, receive interest periodically over a period of time, and then are paid back. Capital shareholders use it as a long-term investment; they receive nothing for a period of years, but if stock prices rise considerably during that time, their shares increase in value considerably more than the prices of individual stocks invested in by the fund.

dual listing   A security that is listed on more than one STOCK EXCHANGE. Listing on both the New York and American stock exchanges is not permitted, but many securities are listed on one of these plus one of the regional exchanges.

due bill   A written acknowledgment of indebtedness, similar to an IOU. The term is often used for security transactions in which the seller's broker gives title to the buyer's broker for a certain number of shares or a dollar amount representing a dividend payment because the securities themselves cannot be delivered in time.

dummy   An individual or firm that serves in another's place, for reasons of expediency or secrecy. For example, a board of dummy directors may be appointed by a new corporation until there is time for the stockholders to elect the real board. Similarly, title to property (real estate or securities, for example) may be held by a dummy owner because the real owner does not wish to be named.

dumping   Selling large blocks of stock at whatever price the market will pay.

E

earned income Income that is derived from work performed, products sold, and so forth, as opposed to income from investments. Different tax rates may apply to earned and unearned income.

earned surplus See RETAINED EARNINGS.

earnings per share A company's net income, after taxes and payments of preferred stock dividends, divided by the number of common stock shares outstanding. This figure is called *primary earnings per share* if it is based on average shares outstanding or *fully diluted earnings per share* if it is based on actual year-end or average shares outstanding plus all shares reserved for the conversion of convertible senior securities and the exercise of all stock warrants, rights and options. All publicly owned U.S. corporations are required by law to report their earnings each quarter, and they are periodically listed in the financial pages of large newspapers. In addition, the year-end figures appear in the company's annual report. See also PRICE-EARNINGS RATIO.

earnings report Another name for INCOME STATEMENT.

earnings yield A company's twelve-month earnings (the previous six months' actual earnings plus the coming six months' estimated earnings) divided by the current stock price. Analysts use this figure to compare the yield of stocks and bonds. It is the inverse of the PRICE-EARNINGS RATIO.

ECU bond A corporate bond denominated in European Currency Units (ECUs), which represents a market basket of European Economic Community (EEC, or Common Market) currencies. It differs from the

EUROBOND mainly in that it is not denominated in dollars. The ECU, which is a hypothetical rather than a real currency (no ECU bills or coins exist), is actually a weighted average of member countries' currencies, the specific weights reflecting the relative size and share of trade of each participating nation's economy. The interest rate on ECU bonds is usually lower than on dollar-denominated bonds, but they can be quite profitable when the U.S. dollar is falling in value against other currencies.

efficient market hypothesis The idea that in a free market with numerous buyers (investors) who prefer the highest possible profits with the least risk, no amount of information can affect the results. Consequently a stock market investor cannot over time achieve more than a fair return relative to the risks undertaken. See also RANDOM WALK.

efficient portfolio A selection of investments that earns the maximum returns relative to the risks undertaken. It can be determined statistically by calculating the EXPECTED RETURN of each security owned and its volatility with respect to the market (see BETA) and the other securities in the portfolio.

8-K Form A report that all publicly owned U.S. corporations must file with the Securities and Exchange Commission (SEC) concerning unscheduled material events or corporate changes considered of importance to shareholders or to the SEC; it must be filed within fifteen days of their occurrence. Such events include: changes in the control of the company; acquisition or divestiture of assets; bankruptcy or receivership; changes in the company's independent auditors; resignation of any directors owing to disagreement.

employee stock ownership plan Abbreviated *ESOP*. Also, *employee stock purchase plan*. The purchase by employees of stock in their own company, usually at less than the current market price, by means of payroll deductions. It is one means of effecting a buyout, that is, the employees eventually take over the company. It also may help keep a not very profitable business going, if the employees agree to accept lower wages in exchange for stock with voting rights, giving them more voice in company affairs. Most often such a plan operates as a tax shelter, the employee not taking possession of stock until retirement, and the corporation receiving tax benefits. However, changes in the tax law passed in 1986 curtailed the tax benefits of such plans.

endorsement   Signing a negotiable instrument such as a check or stock or bond certificate on the back, thereby transferring the amount of that instrument to someone else.

equipment trust certificate   A bond that is secured by the equipment used to conduct the issuer's business, which is nearly always a form of transportation (such as a railroad, airline, or trucking firm).

equity

   1. An investment that represents an ownership interest, principally the portion of a corporation's assets that is owned by the holders of its preferred and common stock, also called *stockholders' equity*. Stock rights, stock options, and stock warrants also represent a form of equity.

   2. In banking and real estate, the difference between the sum a property could be sold for and the claims held against it.

   3. In accounting, the excess of assets over liabilities, also called *net worth*.

escrow   The placement of assets with a third party to insure the performance of the terms of a contract or some other specified condition. Escrow is frequently used in real estate transactions in which deed and purchase money are held by a third party, as well as in some brokerage transactions, such as the deposit of a mutual fund's sales charge.

Eurobond A bond floated by a corporation or government outside the issuer's own country. Most Eurobonds are denominated in dollars, meaning both interest and principal are paid in dollars. (See also EURODOLLAR.) The center of the Eurobond market is London.

Euro-CD A EURODOLLAR certificate of deposit, that is, a negotiable CERTIFICATE OF DEPOSIT denominated in U.S. dollars that is issued outside the United States by either a branch of a U.S. bank or by a foreign bank. Euro-CDs in units with a $1 million face value are traded in the money market.

Eurocurrency A deposit in a bank located outside the country in which the currency of the account was issued, such as a U.S. dollar account in a Swiss bank, or a Swiss franc account in a British bank.

Eurodollar A U.S. dollar deposit in a bank located outside the United States, either in Europe (where the market was first located, hence the name) or anywhere else in the world. It may be owned by an individual, business, or government. In most places Eurodollar banking is free of such regulations as a required reserve against deposits, and in some places, such as the Bahamas, tax rates are very low. Huge amounts of Eurodollars are lent, borrowed, and traded each day in financial centers around the world. These transactions are for cash, with the funds exchanged electronically among the trading institutions. Thus few if any of these funds, which are estimated at a total of at least $2 trillion in the mid-1980's, literally change hands. Most Eurodollar funds are in fixed-rate time deposits (TDs), where maturities range from overnight to a few years. Negotiable receipts for such deposits, called Euro-CDs, are actively traded in the international money market, as are Eurodollar floating-rate CDs and Eurodollar floating-rate notes. The principal Eurodollar market is London, and Eurodollar borrowing rates, including those of Eurodollar futures and options, are based on the London interbank offer rate (LIBO, or LIBOR).

excess margin Equity in a margin account that is above the MAINTENANCE MARGIN required. It usually can be withdrawn or used to buy more securities. See also SPECIAL MEMORANDUM ACCOUNT.

exchange distribution The sale of a large block of stock in a direct exchange-floor transaction, with a broker accumulating enough buy orders to complete the trade, and the seller paying the broker's commission. Such a transaction is marked DIST (for ''distribution'') on the BROAD TAPE.

exchange privilege Also, *conversion privilege, switch privilege*. The right to exchange the shares of one mutual fund for the shares of another fund under the same sponsor, at little or no charge. However, capital gains realized from the first fund are subject to income tax.

ex-dividend Also, *ex-stock dividend*. Literally, ''without dividend,'' meaning that the buyer of a stock will not receive the dividend that has already been declared for the current quarter, but the seller will. A stock usually is sold ex-dividend from four days prior to the RECORD DATE, in order to allow enough time to complete a transaction and notify the corporation of change of ownership; a transfer earlier than that is CUM DIVIDEND. The ex-dividend factor is taken into account in the stock's price, which usually drops by the per-share amount of the declared dividend until the payment date (when dividend checks are mailed). In newspaper listings of stock prices it may be marked *x* or *xd*.

exercise Carry out the terms of an OPTION contract, that is, buy the underlying security of a call option or sell the underlying security of a put, at the strike price.

exercise price   Same as STRIKE PRICE. This term is more often used for warrants, and *strike price* for options.

expected return   Also, *expected rate of return, mean return*. In security analysis, the weighted arithmetic average of all possible return rates for each security in a portfolio, the weights consisting of the probability that each return will occur.

expense ratio   The proportion of an investment company's expenses to its assets. With mutual funds it represents operating expenses expressed as a percentage of the fund's total assets, a figure that helps investors compare the expenses incurred by different mutual funds; this figure appears in the fund's prospectus and annual report. A similar calculation can be made for real estate investment trusts (REITs), where it represents expenses other than interest expressed as a percentage of total assets.

expiration date   The last day on which one may exercise an OPTION. It falls on the third Friday of the month named in the option contract.

ex-rights   A stock that is sold without the RIGHTS to buy more of the same company's stock at a discount, which the previous owner of the stock was entitled to until a given date. After that date the rights may be traded separately.

extendable bond   A bond that allows the holder to postpone redemption (and payment of the face value) beyond the maturity date. This option is advantageous in times of declining interest rates, when the fixed coupon rate of the bond is higher than the current market.

extra dividend   An additional dividend that is declared by a corporation's directors after a particularly profitable year.

ex-warrants   A stock or bond that is sold without the
WARRANT attached to it, which remains the property
of the seller. In financial-page listings it may be
marked *xw*.

f Also, *F*. In bond tables, abbreviation for FLAT, that is, a bond trading without accrued interest.

face value The monetary value of a stock or bond, insurance policy, coin or paper money, printed or otherwise marked on its face. Face value and market value frequently differ. For stocks and bonds some writers prefer the term PAR VALUE; others use the two interchangeably.

fair market value The price on which a buyer and seller who are under no compulsion will probably agree. See also MARKET PRICE.

fair rate of return See under RATE BASE.

family of funds A group of mutual funds owned by the same investment company, each with a different objective (for example, one for growth stocks, another for money-market instruments, a third for municipal bonds, and so on). Usually shareholders may switch their holdings from one fund to another. See also MUTUAL FUND.

Fannie Mae Popular name for the *Federal National Mortgage Association* (abbreviated *FNMA*), a government-sponsored private corporation that buys mortgages from banks and other lenders and sells them to investors. Fannie Mae is owned by its stockholders and its shares are traded on the New York Stock Exchange. It is the single largest home-mortgage investor in the United States. It finances its purchases by issuing two kinds of security: long-term debentures and shorter-term notes, backed by Fannie Mae's ability to borrow from the federal government rather than by any real property; conventional pass-through securities called participation certificates (or PCs), which represent an interest in a pool of mortgages (see under SECONDARY MORTGAGE MARKET for explanation).

FDIC See FEDERAL DEPOSIT INSURANCE CORPORATION.

Federal agency issue Also, *agencies*. A bond or other debt security issued by a government agency or government-sponsored agency, such as the Tennessee Valley Authority (TVA), SMALL BUSINESS ADMINISTRATION (SBA), Export-Import Bank (ExIm), FEDERAL HOME LOAN BANK, Federal Home Loan Mortgage Corporation (FREDDIE MAC), Federal National Mortgage Association (FANNIE MAE), Government National Mortgage Association (GINNIE MAE), Student Loan Marketing Association (SALLIE MAE), and numerous others. Although considered a very safe investment, ranking just below U.S. government securities, federal agency issues are not necessarily backed by the full faith and credit of the United States, as Treasury issues are. However, the guarantee of the underlying agency, backed by Congress, is considered nearly as good. Also unlike Treasury issues, the interest on these obligations is not necessarily exempt from state and local income taxes. Federal agency issues are available only through intermediaries; the agencies do not sell them directly. For a new issue, the agency uses a selling group of brokers, dealers, and banks, announcing the offering in newspapers a few days beforehand. One can buy from any of these firms without paying a commission, though there usually is a small service charge. Agency issues are available in denominations as low as $1,000 and are, after their initial issue, actively traded in the over-the-counter market and on some stock exchanges (and can then be purchased through a broker or bank). Also, many mutual funds, including money-market funds, invest in Federal agency issues and sell an interest in their holdings to their shareholders. The obligations of several international agencies, which combine the debts of several different countries, are also treated as federal agency issues. The most important of them in the mid-1980's were World Bank bonds, Inter-American Development Bank bonds, and Asian Development Bank bonds; all required a $1,000 minimum purchase and were taxable on the local, state, and federal levels. Listings for Federal agency issues are found only in the largest financial papers, although occasionally some smaller papers list international bonds at the beginning of the New York Stock Exchange bond quotations.

Federal Deposit Insurance Corporation Abbreviated *FDIC*. An independent federal agency that insures bank deposits and periodically examines insured state-chartered banks that are not members of the Federal Reserve System. It insures deposits in member banks up to a statutory limit, and may make loans to or buy assets from insured banks to facilitate mergers or consolidation in order to protect depositors against the risk of bank failure.

Federal funds rate The rate of interest charged for an overnight loan from one bank to another of excess reserves, that is, cash and deposits in excess of the reserves it is required to have on hand. Because the rate of interest for such loans depends largely on conditions of supply and demand, it is regarded as a very sensitive barometer of monetary conditions at any given time.

Federal Home Loan Bank Abbreviated *FHLB*. A system of twelve regional banks that lend money to their membership, which consists largely of thrift institutions—savings and loan associations, mutual savings banks, and insurance firms—which in turn are the principal lenders of home mortgages. All federal mutual savings banks, federal savings and loan associations, and every state-chartered savings and loan association insured by the Federal Savings and Loan Insurance Corporation (FSLIC) is required by law to become a member of its regional Federal Home Loan Bank by buying some of its stock. In addition to funds so obtained, the Federal Home Loan Banks raise additional money for lending by issuing consolidated Federal Home Loan Bank notes and bonds. Though the FHLB is a federal agency, these notes and bonds are not guaranteed by the full faith and credit of the United States; in case of need, however, the Treasury is authorized to buy these debts up to a certain amount.

Federal Home Loan Mortgage Corporation See FREDDIE MAC.

Federal Housing Administration Abbreviated *FHA*. A government agency, part of the Department of Housing and Urban Development, that insures private lenders of housing funds, principally home mortgages, against default by borrowers. FHA insurance covers mortgages for single- and multifamily private residences, rental housing, cooperatives and condominiums, mobile homes, medical facilities (nursing homes, hospitals, group-practice facilities), and land bought for residential development, as well as loans for property improvement. On FHA-insured mortgages, the FHA sets the down payment required of home purchasers, which in the mid-1980's ranged from 3 to 5 percent, depending on the total price of the home. (Before 1934, when the FHA was established, mortgage lenders often required a down payment of 40 to 50 percent.) The interest rate for FHA-insured loans is negotiated between buyer and seller. FHA loans are subject to a maximum limit, which varies with the location of the home, and they may be assumed by subsequent buyers of the home.

To obtain FHA insurance the buyer must meet certain financial qualifications; for example, monthly housing payments may not exceed a certain percentage of the home buyer's net income.

Federal National Mortgage Association See FANNIE MAE.

Federal Open Market Committee Abbreviated *FOMC*. A committee of the FEDERAL RESERVE SYSTEM that buys and sells securities in order to offset cyclical economic swings, support the credit and money needed for long-term growth, and accommodate seasonal demands of businesses and consumers for money and credit. The securities traded are mostly U.S. government obligations (Treasury issues) but also include Federal agency obligations and bankers' acceptances. The committee also undertakes transactions in foreign currencies in order to help safeguard the value of the dollar in international exchange markets. The committee is made up of the members of the Federal Reserve Board of Governors and five additional representatives of the reserve banks, each of whom is elected annually. Its meetings are secret, lest premature news of its decisions on short-term monetary policy, which directly affect the level of interest rates, give unfair advantage to one or another group of traders.

Federal Reserve System Also, *The Fed* (nickname). The central bank of the United States, charged with administering and making policy for the nation's credit and monetary affairs and supervising and regulating its banking system. It consists of six parts, a President-appointed seven-member Board of Governors in Washington, D.C.; twelve Federal Reserve banks, their twenty-five branches, and other facilities located throughout the country; the FEDERAL OPEN MARKET COMMITTEE; the Federal Advisory Council; Consumer Advisory Council; and member commercial banks, which include all national banks and those state-chartered banks that elect to join the system. The Federal Reserve regulates the nation's money supply, sets reserve requirements for member banks, and acts as a clearinghouse of funds throughout the banking system.

Federal Savings and Loan Insurance Corporation Abbreviated *FSLIC*. An agency administered by the Federal Home Loan Bank Board that insures investors' savings accounts in various thrift institutions engaged in home financing (up to $100,000 in the mid-1980s). The institutions include all federal SAVINGS AND LOAN ASSOCIATIONS, and those state-chartered building and loan, savings and loan, and homestead associations and cooperative banks that qualify. FSLIC similarly insures individual retirement accounts (IRAs) and Keogh accounts.

FedWire An electronic network that links the Federal Reserve banks, their branches, and key Washington offices, enabling banks to transfer funds among one another very quickly and also to transfer Treasury securities by means of computerized bookkeeping entries.

FHA See FEDERAL HOUSING ADMINISTRATION.

fidelity bond A form of insurance against employee dishonesty (lack of "fidelity"), which brokerage firms are required by law to carry.

fiduciary An individual or organization that holds assets in trust for another, called the beneficiary, for example, a trustee, receiver in bankruptcy, or executor of a will.

FIFO Abbreviation for FIRST IN, FIRST OUT.

fill or kill Abbreviated *FOK*. An order to buy or sell a security, commodity, or futures contract, which a broker must carry out at once or, if the price or another condition cannot be met, must cancel immediately.

financial futures   Also, *interest-rate futures*. Futures contracts in foreign currencies and certain fixed-income securities, principally Treasury bills, notes, and bonds, government-guaranteed mortgages (Ginnie Maes), bank certificates of deposit, and Eurodollar time deposits. The organized financial futures market originated in 1972 on the Chicago Mercantile Exchange with futures in half a dozen foreign currencies, and that exchange still handles principally short-term money-market futures (T-bills, bank CDs, Eurodollars). The market grew enormously in the next decade. Exporters and importers use foreign-exchange futures to meet due bills and to protect themselves against exchange-rate fluctuations. The interest-rate futures can be used to speculate on the direction of the rates over any period of time, to hedge securities, bank deposits or loans, or to exploit the spreads between various kinds of rate. Hedgers include government securities dealers and traders, banks, thrift institutions, pension funds, insurance companies, and mortgage lenders whose assets are affected by changes in interest rates. For the average small investor, the financial futures market is both too high-priced and too risky. For the longer-term futures such as Treasury bonds, a contract represents the equivalent of $100,000 with a margin (down payment) of $2,000; for the money-market short-term futures like T-bills, the typical contract is for $1 million with a $1,000 margin. In the case of T-bonds, a change in interest rate of only .12 point can change the value of a Treasury bond contract by $1,500, and only .6 point can effect the same change for a T-bill contract. For the mechanics of futures trading see FUTURES CONTRACT. See also STOCK INDEX FUTURES.

financial instruments   General name for a variety of negotiable instruments, ranging from corporate and Treasury securities (stocks, bonds, debentures, bills, notes) to the short-term debt instruments traded in the MONEY MARKET.

financial leverage See under LEVERAGE.

financial statement A formal statement of an individual's or company's accounts at a particular time. For corporations the principal forms of financial statement are the BALANCE SHEET and INCOME STATEMENT.

finder's fee A kind of commission paid to a third party for bringing together a buyer and a seller.

fineness The purity of gold or silver as a percentage of total gross weight. Gold that is .995 fine means its weight is 99.5 percent pure gold; the remainder is another metal, often copper, with which it is alloyed.

firm quote A price quotation that is binding when accepted. See also NOMINAL QUOTE; SUBJECT QUOTE.

first in, first out Abbreviated *FIFO*. A method of inventory accounting in which the items acquired earliest are counted as those used during a given accounting period, and they are valued at the prices at which they were purchased rather than at current market prices. (See also LAST IN, FIRST OUT.) On the sale of securities, tax laws require that for determining taxable gains the cost is the price of the first lot purchased, unless the seller specifies which lot is being sold.

fiscal year Abbreviated *FY*. Any twelve-month period used by a corporation or other organization for its financial accounting. For example, the fiscal year of the United States government begins October 1 and ends September 30.

Fitch Short for Fitch Investor's Service, an agency that rates corporate bonds and commercial paper, supervises mutual funds, and publishes other data for investors, notably *Fitch Sheets*, a chronological listing of successive trade prices for listed securities.

fixed asset An asset required for the normal operations of a business and purchased for long-term use: for example, land, buildings, machinery.

fixed charge   Charges such as rent and interest, which must be paid by a business regardless of how well or how poorly it is doing. In calculating earnings, fixed charges are generally the first items deducted from income.

fixed-charge coverage   A comparison of income to funded debt. See under COVERAGE.

fixed-income security   A security that earns a fixed return, in the form of interest or dividends, over a specific period of time. The principal securities of this nature are bonds, notes, bills, preferred stocks, mortgage-backed securities or pools, and shares in some unit investment trusts (those with fixed portfolios not tied to any floating rate). There are separate entries for all these securities.

fixed investment trust   See NONDISCRETIONARY TRUST; also UNIT INVESTMENT TRUST, def. 1.

fixed liability   An obligation that must be met, regardless of how well or poorly a company is doing. It includes FUNDED DEBT and lease obligations.

flat   Describing a bond sale in which the buyer need not pay the seller ACCRUED interest. A flat sale generally occurs only when the bond issuer has defaulted on interest payments, or with an INCOME BOND.

flat market   In the securities market, little change in the price of a security, mainly because there is little trading in it. It differs from a situation in which a stock is heavily traded but changes little in price.

float

   1. Money that is seemingly created by the time lag between the writing of a check and its collection at the bank on which it is drawn.

   2. The number of outstanding shares of a corporation's stock owned by the public and not by insiders. A small float (fewer shares) is more volatile in price than a large one, since it is more easily influenced by large buy or sell orders; this situation is also described as a THIN MARKET.

floating an issue   See under ISSUE.

floating debt   The short-term debt of a company or other organization, such as bank loans, commercial paper, or Treasury bills and notes. See also FUNDED DEBT.

floating-rate   Also, *adjustable-rate*. Describing a bond or preferred stock in which the interest is adjusted periodically according to some predetermined formula. One kind of floating-rate issue adjusts the coupon rate of a bond to a given value every six months—to, for example, a percentage slightly higher than that of three-month Treasury bills. Because such securities share some of the advantages of shorter-term securities, their yields tend to be below those of fixed-rate bonds. See also ADJUSTABLE-RATE MORTGAGE.

floor broker   A stock exchange member, employed by a member firm, who executes orders on the floor of the exchange on behalf of the firm's clients (unlike the FLOOR TRADER, def. 1, who buys and sells for his or her own account).

floor trader

   1. Also, *competitive trader, market maker, registered (competitive) trader*. A stock exchange member who trades for his or her own account, pays no brokerage commission, and must follow the same rules of the exchange as the SPECIALIST (who may trade on behalf of others), including the rule that 75 percent of their trades be stabilizing (selling only on an UP TICK and buying only on a DOWN TICK).

   2. Also, *local*. In commodity trading, the equivalent of the specialist on the stock exchange. The floor trader is a licensed member of the exchange who buys and sells futures contracts for his or her own account, trying to take advantage of momentary price fluctuations to make a profit. Accounting for much of the activity on the commodity exchange floor, the floor trader continuously makes a market in a futures contract by bidding and offering for sale the same futures.

flower bond   Nickname for certain U.S. Treasury bonds that can be turned in at par (face) value before maturity for payment of federal estate taxes, provided they were owned by the deceased at the time of death.

flow of funds   The cash position of a business firm, other organization, or entire economy during a given period, viewed as a circular flow. In a business, cash is used to buy supplies and other merchandise, which are eventually sold and converted into accounts receivable, which in turn are collected and turned into cash, used to buy more supplies, and so on. See also CASH FLOW.

Forbes 500   An annual directory, published by *Forbes* magazine, of the five hundred largest American publicly owned corporations ranked in terms of sales, assets, profits, and market value of shares. See also FORTUNE 500.

forced conversion   Inducing the holder of a convertible security to exchange it for common stock, which has become a preferable alternative owing to the company's declaring a much higher dividend or because the convertible's current market price is well above its call price (so that without converting the holder would have to accept the lower call price).

foreign investment   Investment in foreign securities, currencies, or other assets, such as real estate. A major factor in such investment is the exchange rate of various foreign currencies in comparison to the U.S. dollar. Generally, when the dollar is strong, the dollar value of a foreign investment declines, and when the dollar weakens, the dollar value of a foreign investment increases. With currencies, in addition to direct investment by buying Japanese yen, British pounds, French francs, etc., investors can buy foreign currency options and futures. For example, in the mid-1980's the Philadelphia Stock Exchange dealt in options on six major currencies (the British pound, Japanese yen, West German mark, Swiss franc, French franc, and Canadian dollar), and futures on all these except the French franc were traded on the International Money Market at the Chicago Mercantile Exchange. With options, an investment of several hundred dollars may be sufficient to control contracts worth up to almost $40,000. (See also FINANCIAL FUTURES; FORWARD EXCHANGE; FUTURES CONTRACT; OPTION.)

A long-term form of foreign investment is the purchase of an ANNUITY. For example, Swiss insurance companies offer annuities that will pay a fixed amount yearly in Swiss francs for a given period or for life.

Americans can invest in foreign securities through direct purchases of foreign stocks and bonds. The latter tend to yield much less than U.S. bonds, so the investment is really in a favorable change in exchange rates. Although foreign-currency-denominated securities are not regulated by the Securities and Exchange Commission, they can be acquired through a number of American brokers, as well as through specialty brokers. They also can be purchased by buying AMERICAN DEPOSITARY RECEIPTS (ADRs) of foreign companies. These receipts, equivalent to shares of stock of an overseas company, are bought and sold on the basis of a dollar price and traded on stock exchanges or in the over-the-counter market. Some foreign countries, however, do not permit ADRs to be issued for their securities (Switzerland is one). Other countries may create a separate class of common stock especially for purchase by nonresidents. Often a class B stock, it generally has no voting rights and has a different par value, dividend, and market price from class A common stock. Most foreign countries do not have a capital gains tax, although an American stockholder still must pay capital gains tax on foreign stock holdings to the Internal Revenue Service. Most countries do, however, have a withholding tax on dividends and interest, but it is not applied consistently. Some securities will be subject to this tax, and others, seemingly quite similar, will not. Therefore each instance should be checked with the broker. In cases where securities must be purchased on a foreign market, the shares usually are held in the home country, and for this service the American investor is charged an annual safekeeping fee.

Another way to invest in foreign securities is through an international mutual fund, which gives the benefit of greater diversification than most individuals could readily achieve. Most mutual funds that invest abroad are open-end funds, but a few are closed-end funds, with a limited number of shares. There are three main kinds of mutual fund that invest in foreign securities: a *global fund*, which holds both American and foreign securities; an *international fund*, which buys only foreign securities; and a *regional fund*, which specializes in securities from a specific area or country. With a global fund the investor can select from a worldwide variety of stocks, bonds, and currency. The proportion of foreign and U.S. holdings is determined by the fund's management, not the investor. Investors who want to decide for themselves what percentage of their portfolio will be in foreign stocks may choose an international fund. Regional funds give investors the opportunity to focus their money where they expect the biggest gains, as, for example, in the highly developed Pacific nations (Japan, Australia, Hong Kong).

Form 8-K   See 8-K FORM (alphabetized as "Eight-K").

Form 10-K, 10-Q See under 10-K FORM (alphabetized as "Ten-K").

formula investing Buying securities and maintaining a portfolio in accordance with some predetermined course of action. The most common kind of formula involves one or another specified ratio among the securities in the portfolio. With the *constant ratio plan*, one maintains the same relative value of different securities, for example, a 2:1 ratio of growth stocks to fixed-income securities. The *constant dollar plan* is the same scheme but calculated in terms of dollar value rather than percentages. With either, the desired ratio is maintained by selling and buying accordingly. With a *variable ratio plan*, one adjusts the proportion of securities according to some market indicator like the Standard & Poor's 500 Index, or some other indicator such as the price/earnings ratio of stocks. See also DOLLAR COST AVERAGING; PERIODIC PAYMENT PLAN.

Fortune 500 Annual directory, published by *Fortune* magazine, of the five hundred largest American publicly owned industrial (manufacturing) companies, ranked by sales, assets, net income, stockholders' equity, number of employees, earnings per share, and total return to investors. The magazine also publishes a similar directory of the five hundred largest American service (nonmanufacturing) companies, which includes banks and other financial institutions, life insurance companies, transportation, and utilities. See also FORBES 500.

forward contract A contract calling for the delivery of a commodity for a certain price at a specific future date. It differs from a FUTURES CONTRACT in that it calls for actual delivery and is not traded on any regulated commodity futures exchange. Forward contracts are generally based on the buyer's expectation that a commodity's price will rise and that the negotiated price will be lower than the eventual market price. A *covered forward sale* is the sale of a commodity the seller actually owns for delivery and payment at a later date. See also FORWARD EXCHANGE.

forward exchange   Forward buying or selling of foreign currency, based on the anticipation of a less favorable exchange rate in the future. (See also FORWARD CONTRACT.) Forward exchange contracts are traded on an interbank market rather than on an organized exchange. They are, however, similar to currency futures contracts, which are traded on a number of organized COMMODITY FUTURES EXCHANGES. Long used for hedging by businesses with active international operations that involve the use of foreign currencies, forward exchange in the 1980's began in part to be replaced by the use of currency options (see OPTION) as a hedging tool.

401 (k) plan   See SALARY REDUCTION PLAN.

fourth market   The trading of large blocks of securities by mutual funds and other institutional investors among themselves, without the use of dealers or brokers. Such trading is nearly always done by means of a computerized system such as INSTINET.

fractional share   Part of a single share of stock. Such shares generally are created through a dividend reinvestment plan, in which one cash dividend may not be sufficient to buy a full share of stock. The shareholder then is credited with the appropriate portion of a share until enough dividends have accumulated to pay for a full share. See also SCRIP.

Freddie Mac   Popular name for the *Federal Home Loan Corporation* (abbreviated *FHLMC*), a government-sponsored private agency set up in 1970 to provide a secondary mortgage market for FHA-insured and VA-guaranteed mortgages. In a decade it became one of the largest buyers of conventional home mortgages, mainly from savings and loan associations. It finances its purchases by issuing mortgage participation certificates or Freddie Mac PCs in minimum denominations of $25,000, representing undivided interests in pools of conventional home mortgages. (See also SECONDARY MORTGAGE MARKET.) Both interest and principal payments are passed through from the lender to the PC holder, which may be a depository institution, investment company, or individual. In addition, Freddie Mac issues short- and long-term credit instruments and periodically issues COLLATERALIZED MORTGAGE OBLIGATIONS (CMOs).

front-end load   A sales charge, often quite large, for investing in a mutual fund, annuity, life insurance policy, limited partnership, or other enterprise, which is paid when one first invests in it (at the beginning, or "front end"). See also NO-LOAD.

full faith and credit   A phrase indicating that the complete power to raise funds by taxation and borrowing are pledged in the payment of both interest and principal for a government or a municipal debt instrument (such as a bond or note.) All federal government securities and any GENERAL OBLIGATION BOND issued by a state or local government are backed by this pledge.

full-service broker   A brokerage firm that provides a wide range of services to customers. The main difference from a discount broker is that the full-service broker generally maintains a research staff and offers considerable investment advice to customers. It may also offer an ASSET MANAGEMENT ACCOUNT, new stock issues, and various financial services ranging from checking accounts to tax-record services and credit cards.

fully diluted earnings per share   See under EARNINGS PER SHARE.

fundamental analysis   A system of analyzing investments that considers mainly the basic financial data about a company and derives from them such figures as net worth per share, current assets, debt-equity ratios, and the like in order to project future earnings and dividends. Unlike TECHNICAL ANALYSIS, it does not take into account investment opinions about the company or industry as reflected in purchases and sales of its securities. Critics of fundamental analysis point out that everyone has access to the same financial figures and their calculations are so rapidly reflected in a stock's prices that they are useless. In recent years, however, the process has been assisted by computer programs that greatly speed up fundamental analysis. Such programs enable one, for example, to know which companies have debt below 10 percent of their total capital, share prices at least 25 percent below book value, and price-earnings ratios of 7 or less. There are numerous such programs. In selecting one, experts advise checking to see the number and kind of securities and financial facts a program can handle, and how far back historical data go (at least five years is best). See also PORTFOLIO MANAGEMENT PROGRAM.

funded debt   The long-term liabilities of a company or other organization, consisting of bonds and other long-term obligations. See also FLOATING DEBT.

futures contract   Also, *future*. A contract calling for the delivery of a commodity or financial instrument at a specific future time for a specified price, which is determined by auction on a COMMODITY FUTURES EXCHANGE. All futures contracts are traded in the same way, the price being determined by open outcry and other conditions of sales established by the exchange where the particular commodity is traded. Buyers of futures contracts, who are referred to as *long*, enter them in the expectation that prices will rise; sellers of futures, referred to as *short*, enter because they think prices will fall. An important

function of futures contracts is protection against unfavorable price changes through HEDGING, that is,
taking an opposite position in futures from what one
takes in the actual, or spot, market. (See also SELLING
SHORT.) The initial investment in a futures contract is
the *margin*, a percentage of the contract's total value
that is set by the exchange. Though the margin is
small compared to the total contract, trading in futures is considerably riskier than trading in options,
because a futures contract involves a legally binding
agreement to take or make delivery of a commodity
on a certain date, whereas an option involves only a
right to perform. (See also OPTION.) The delivery date
may be anywhere from one month to more than two
years in the future. Each contract is standardized with
respect to size and delivery requirements. In practice
only a small percentage of futures contracts actually
are received or delivered; most contracts are liquidated through an exchange-associated clearing facility,
which supervises and assigns all deliveries. Thus
contracts for selling and buying the same commodity
offset one another. Among the more than fifty commodities and financial instruments involved in futures
trading on American exchanges in the mid-1980's
were various grains, live cattle and hogs, potatoes,
pork bellies, lumber, sugar, coffee, cocoa, oil and
gasoline, cotton, frozen orange juice, precious metals, aluminum, foreign currencies, Treasury bills and
bonds, certificates of deposit, Eurodollars, and at
least five different stock market indexes.

Futures prices are listed in the financial pages of
large newspapers and also are available through
databases serving home or office computers. The
listings generally include such data as the season's
high and low prices, the day's opening, high, low,
and close prices (the last is sometimes the SETTLE-
MENT PRICE), net change in price from the previous

day, and open interest (number of futures contracts
outstanding in that commodity). The first line normally gives the name of the commodity, the size of a
single contract (100 ounces for gold, 40,000 pounds
for cattle, etc.), and how prices are quoted (for example, dollars per troy ounce for gold, cents per
pound for cattle). The first column on the left displays the months for delivery. Trading is usually
limited to six months of a year up to two years in the
future, but it varies by commodity. Firms that sell
futures contracts on regulated exchanges are regulated
by the Commodity Futures Trading Commission and
must belong to the National Futures Association,
which requires them to provide a document disclos-
ing the risks of futures trading to prospective customers.

   Another way of investing in futures is through a
COMMODITY POOL. While such pools make it possible
to participate with a much smaller investment, their
success is heavily dependent on the skill of the fund's
manager, who must be able to react very quickly to
rapidly changing trends in a highly volatile market.
See also FINANCIAL FUTURES; FORWARD CONTRACT; FU-
TURES OPTION; INDEX FUTURES.

futures market   See COMMODITY FUTURES EXCHANGE;
   FUTURES CONTRACT.

futures option   An option on a FUTURES CONTRACT. As
   with other options, a call option conveys the right to
   buy and a put option the right to sell a futures
   contract at a specific price (the strike price) within a
   specific time period (before the expiration date). Such
   an option is traded in the same way as stock options
   are, but instead of exercising it for 100 shares of
   stock the investor exercises it for a futures contract,
   or, in some cases, cash. As with stock options, the
   buyer of a put or call need do no more than pay the
   premium (price) for the option in question and may
   allow it to expire. However, the seller (writer) of a

futures option is committed to deliver the future at the strike price if a buyer exercises the option, and therefore is required to deposit margin (see MARGIN, def. 2).

Option trading in futures contracts began in late 1982 with Treasury bond futures, and in the next few years became available for futures in gold, the West German mark, sugar, Eurodollars and several stock indexes. (See also OPTION; STOCK-INDEX FUTURE; INDEX OPTION; INTEREST RATE OPTION.) Depending on the underlying futures contract, the terms of futures options differ somewhat from those of stock options. For example, the trading unit in options on Eurodollar futures in the Chicago Mercantile Exchange is a single $1 million Eurodollar ninety-day time deposit for one of four contract months (March, June, September, December), with strike prices in terms of the International Money Market (IMM) Index in increments of .50 (for example, 89.50, 90.00, 90.50) and a premium quoted in terms of IMM Index points (where each .01 point, or basis point, equals $25; thus 0.35 represents a premium of $875). Eurodollar futures options on the Chicago Mercantile Exchange are exercised in terms of futures contracts; those traded on the Philadelphia Stock Exchange are settled in cash and cannot be exercised before the underlying contract expires.

gap See PRICE GAP.

gem investment Buying precious stones in the hope that their value will appreciate considerably during the time they are held. The most important gems for investment are diamonds, emeralds, rubies, sapphires, and pearls. The larger and more perfect (flawless) the stone, the more valuable it is. Unless there is some use for the gems other than their speculative value, they are not considered appropriate for the average investor. There is no ready market for them, as there is for stocks or gold. They are difficult to buy at other than retail prices, which include a large markup, they must be stored and protected against theft, and consequently they must appreciate enormously in price in order to earn a reasonable return.

general obligation bond A MUNICIPAL BOND that is backed by the full faith, credit, and taxing power of the municipality that issues it, which must raise sufficient funds through levying taxes to meet interest and principal payments. If the municipality's tax rate is limited by state law, the bond is called a *limited-tax bond*. See also REVENUE BOND; SPECIAL-TAX BOND.

general partner See under LIMITED PARTNERSHIP.

gilt-edged A security of unusually high quality. In the United States the term is used more for bonds than for stocks, for which BLUE CHIP is more common. In British usage it applies to bonds and is sometimes shortened to ''gilts.''

Ginnie Mae Popular name for *Government National Mortgage Association* (abbreviated *GNMA*), a U.S. government corporation within the Department of

Housing and Urban Development that guarantees timely payment of interest and principal on privately issued securities backed by pools of FHA-insured and VA-guaranteed mortgages. Ginnie Mae's guaranty is backed by the full faith and credit of the U.S. government. Although Ginnie Mae certificates in a new pool are worth at least $25,000 each when first issued, representing an undivided interest in the underlying mortgages, securities firms have formed unit investment trusts and mutual funds to invest in Ginnie Maes, which make available shares for as little as $1,000. They are considered almost as safe as Treasury bonds but yield somewhat more, usually 0.5 to 1.0 percent more (but less when bought through a mutual fund.) Unlike Treasury bonds, Ginnie Maes make monthly payments to investors; these payments represent both interest and part of the principal. Therefore interest payments decrease over the life of the investment, since the principal is shrinking monthly. This disadvantage can be offset by investing in a Ginnie Mae mutual fund that provides for reinvestment of either the principal payback or both interest and principal payments. Of course many investors do not hold Ginnie Maes until maturity, and they are freely traded in the open market. Also, Ginnie Mae certificates are among the financial futures traded in the futures market.

Ginnie Mae prices appear in the financial pages of some large newspapers but differ from other listings of government agency issues. No maturity date is given, because although the stated maturity of a Ginnie Mae pool is thirty years, most last only about twelve years, owing to prepayments into the pool from the sale of houses under the mortgage. Also, the stated yields in such listings are estimates based on past performance. Earier-than-expected prepayment would raise the effective yield, and later prepayment would lower it. See also PRODUCTION RATE.

global fund   See under FOREIGN INVESTMENT.

GNP See GROSS NATIONAL PRODUCT.

going public   Making an INITIAL PUBLIC OFFERING.

gold   A precious metal that has been treasured for thousands of years, its value depending in large part on its limited supply. One can invest in gold by buying bullion (gold bars), bullion or rare coins (see COIN COLLECTING), futures and options (see FUTURES CONTRACT; FUTURES OPTION; OPTION), and shares in gold mines, mutual funds, and unit trusts. Bullion can be bought from banks, brokerage firms, coin and bullion dealers, private mints, department stores, jewelers, and other outlets, but serious investors should probably deal with leading banks, brokerage firms, or established precious metals dealers that handle gold. Wholesale customers such as banks and jewelers can buy gold bars in various sizes ranging from 0.5 troy ounce to 1 kilogram. Individuals usually buy bars in multiples of 5 troy ounces. Brokerage customers usually pay the London market's opening price for the morning immediately following placement of the buyer's order. This price, called the *London Bullion Fix*, is issued at 5:30 A.M. New York time. To sell gold, the same terms hold: that is, the London price for the following morning, less any brokerage charge. Brokers must offer gold that bears a well-known assay mark, indicating the degree of purity certified by a prescribed assay office. (See also FINE-NESS.) The seller generally delivers the gold to a customer's bank for safekeeping or provides storage facilities and gives the buyer a warehouse receipt or similar document. Buyers of bullion often prefer not to take physical possession. Instead they purchase warehouse receipts or *gold* or *bullion certificates* issued by certain banks, brokerage firms, and mutual funds. These certificates are nontransferable and are for gold stored in specific warehouses in the United States or even abroad. Generally there is a minimum investment of $1,000 or $2,500, or a minimum weight purchase, such as 10 troy ounces. A similar arrangement, called a *precious metals passbook account*, is offered by some American banks. It resembles a savings account, except that the funds are in the form of gold or silver or platinum and are available for physical delivery if requested.

Generally investors in bullion are advised to buy only from reputable dealers and make sure the gold bullion bears the mark of a known refiner, assaying weight and fineness. One should ask for a written guarantee. Since the offering price reflects the seller's commission and other costs, it pays to shop around. Ask also for itemization of charges for storage, insurance, assaying.

One can also buy shares in gold-mining companies. Since South Africa supplies about 75 percent of the non-Communist world's gold, most of the available gold stocks are South African. The shares of about a hundred South African companies are traded in the U.S. over-the-counter market and in the London market. The most common method for American investors is to buy AMERICAN DEPOSITARY RECEIPTS in the U.S. or London-registered shares. Shares of some American, Canadian, and Philippine mines also are available. Like other stocks, these earn dividends as well as possibly appreciating in value.

In addition, a small number of mutual funds and unit trusts invest predominantly in gold bullion, gold-mine stocks, and other gold-related assets; these offer both experienced management and greater diversification than most individual investors can afford.

Although American dealers generally charge the London market price for gold, which is "fixed" twice a day by five member firms, a similar market is maintained in Zurich, Switzerland, where three Swiss banks maintain a market called the *Gold Pool* (and there is another major market in Hong Kong). The Zurich market is a free auction market that, like other commodity markets, is open all day. Also, in Switzerland there is no capital-gains levy on profits from gold holdings for nonresidents. Consequently some investors, larger ones in particular, prefer to confine their gold dealings to Swiss banks, which will not only execute buy and sell orders but will store a client's gold bullion and handle gold futures contracts as well.

gold fix   Another name for London Bullion Fix. See under GOLD.

good till canceled order   Abbreviated *GTC*. Also, *open order*. An order to buy or sell securities that is in effect until the customer cancels it. It may run for a day, week, month, or, in theory, indefinitely.

government bond   A BOND issued by a central government or one of its agencies. See TREASURY BOND; U.S. SAVINGS BOND. A bond issued by a state or local government is usually called a MUNICIPAL BOND. See also FEDERAL AGENCY ISSUE.

Government National Mortgage Association   See GINNIE MAE.

graduated payments mortgage   Abbreviated *GPM*. A fixed-interest mortgage involving lower initial monthly payments than would be paid with a standard mortgage, and higher monthly payments later. After five to ten years the payments become fixed, but at a higher level than with a standard mortgage at the same interest rate. GPMs are appropriate for younger households that anticipate above-average income growth.

grantor The person who endows a TRUST.

greenmail The practice of purchasing a large block of a company's stock and then threatening a takeover with the expectation that the target company will buy back those shares at a significant premium over the current market price. See also MERGER.

gross income Income derived from all sources during any accounting period. See also NET INCOME.

gross national product Abbreviated *GNP*. The total value of a nation's output of goods and services for a given period, usually a year. The growth of a nation's GNP is considered the single most important measure of its economic health. The figures for the U.S. GNP are published quarterly, both in current dollars and in a version adjusted for inflation.

gross profit The revenues from sales of goods or services after deducting the cost of the goods or services sold, but not deducting overhead and other expenses.

gross spread The difference between the underwriter's purchase and sales prices for a new security issue.

growth stock Stock in a company with great earning potential or one whose growth substantially exceeded that of the economy and/or other comparable companies in recent months or years. Such a stock often pays only a modest dividend, the company preferring to reinvest its earnings in order to expand more rapidly.

guaranteed security A bond or preferred stock on which interest and/or principal or dividend is guaranteed by some firm other than the issuer. The guarantor may be a parent company backing the issue of a subsidiary, or a company leasing property from the issuer and guaranteeing the issue as part of its lease agreement. The latter situation frequently occurred with railroad bonds, where a large company leasing track from a smaller one would guarantee the latter's bonds.

hard-money investments Investments in gold and silver in various forms. Some use the term to include currencies that are considered very stable, such as the Swiss franc. See also FOREIGN INVESTMENT.

head and shoulders See under CHARTIST.

heavy market See ACTIVE MARKET.

hedged tender Selling short a portion of the shares of a TENDER OFFER in the expectation that not all of the shares being tendered will be bought. For example, Raider Company makes a tender offer for shares of Target Company at $32 a share, which is $4 above the current market price. You would like to sell all of your 5,000 shares of Target but are not sure they will be accepted. To protect yourself, you sell short perhaps half of them once the market has risen to $32 or close to it (which happens soon after the tender offer is announced). If you were right and Raider does not want all your shares, the market will drop after the tender offer expires but your short sale has protected you and you will have sold all 5,000 Target shares at $32. If you were wrong, you still will have made a good profit on half the shares.

hedge fund A MUTUAL FUND that engages in hedging— selling short, buying and selling options, and so on—in order to limit risks for its shareholders.

hedging Also, *hedge*. Reducing the risk of loss by taking a position in futures opposite to the position one holds in the current market. In the commodity futures market, this means taking a position in futures opposite to that held in the cash (spot) market. Unlike speculators, who wish only to profit financially from price changes, the commodity hedger actually wants to buy or sell a particular physical commodity at some later date. For this reason organized futures exchanges set lower margin (down payment) requirements for hedgers than for speculators. The hedger who anticipates a rise in the price of wheat, for example, will buy wheat futures, hoping to make enough profit from selling the futures to offset the higher market price of wheat. This protection is far from foolproof. Cash and futures market prices generally tend to move in the same direction, but the magnitude of the change may be quite different. Conversely, the hedger who anticipates a price decline will sell wheat futures, hoping that the profit realized will cover the possible decline in market price of the wheat he/she already owns. Since the extension of options and futures trading to stocks, financial instruments, and stock indexes, investors have tried to protect themselves against adverse price changes by taking similar positions in these markets. See also INDEX OPTIONS; SELLING SHORT; STOCK-INDEX FUTURES.

hidden asset An asset whose value on the balance sheet is deliberately understated, for tax purposes or the like, or one that represents intangibles that cannot be accurately measured and hence are not identified as such at all.

high flyer A highly speculative stock whose price moves up very rapidly compared to that of other stocks, and presumably can move down just as fast.

holder of record See OF RECORD.

holding company A company whose principal business is the control of other companies by owning or controlling a substantial share of their voting stock. Its principal advantage is that it can exert great influence over numerous subsidiaries with combined capital much greater than its own, since it need control

only half (or less than half) of their stock. See also
CONGLOMERATE.

home run   A large return on an investment, conventionally 100 percent, in a relatively short time.

hybrid annuity   An ANNUITY that combines the traditional fixed-dollar annuity with a VARIABLE ANNUITY, either by allowing the policyholder to switch from one to another or by dividing premiums between the two kinds.

hypothecation   The pledging of securities as collateral for a broker's loan, to be used to buy securities or cover short sales (a margin loan). The broker may then use these securities as collateral for a bank loan, a procedure called *rehypothecation*. A customer opening a margin account generally signs a *hypothecation agreement* or *margin agreement*, which specifies the hypothecation and other terms of the account.

illiquid Describing an asset or investment that cannot be readily turned into cash without paying a penalty for haste. See also LIQUIDITY.

inactive Describing a stock or bond that is traded relatively seldom, either on an exchange or in the over-the-counter market, and consequently is considered ILLIQUID. On the New York Stock Exchange, some inactive stocks are traded in round lots of 10 (instead of 100) at a trading post called the *inactive post* or Post 30; for inactively traded bonds, limit orders are stored in cabinets at one side of the bond trading floor, giving rise to the name *cabinet crowd* or *inactive bond crowd* for those who trade in them.

in-and-out trader Also, *in-and-outer*. Speculator who tries to profit from quick price changes, often by buying and selling the same security in one day.

income bond Also, *adjustment bond, reorganization bond*. A bond on which interest is paid only if enough is earned by the issuer. It usually is issued in exchange for other bonds to bondholders who accept it because the issuer would otherwise go bankrupt. Sometimes, if the issuer overcomes its financial difficulties, the accrued interest is paid on redemption.

income fund A MUTUAL FUND that concentrates on minimizing risk and obtaining the highest possible income in the form of dividends and/or interest.

income share In a DUAL FUND, a class of share that entitles its holders to receive all interest and dividends on the fund's investments.

income statement Also, *earnings report, operating statement, profit-and-loss statement*. A summary of a company's or other organization's earnings and outlays during a certain period, usually a year. Basically, the costs of running the business are subtracted from what was earned from its main operations, called either *net sales* or *operating revenues*. To this figure are added nonrecurring items, such as the sale of a subsidiary or a one-time tax write-off and income received from other sources, such as dividends and interest on the firm's investments. From this total are subtracted the cost of sales (which may include raw materials and other goods, labor, factory overhead, etc.), depreciation, selling and administrative expenses, the interest on long-term debt, and taxes. The result is the firm's *net income*, which when divided by the number of shares of stock outstanding shows the company's *earnings per share*. Publicly owned companies must show results for at least the previous three years on their annual income statement, and many also summarize five to ten years' worth of operations. Among the important figures investors may derive from an income statement are the *operating margin of profit*, calculated by dividing sales into operating profit; it indicates what percentage of sales is being converted into income from operations. Another is the *net profit ratio*, found by dividing net profit for the year by net sales. Still another is a quick estimate of *cash flow*, obtained by adding to net earnings any noncash expenses and deducting any noncash revenues.

indenture Also, *trust indenture*, *deed of trust*. The written agreement between the issuer of a bond and the bondholders, which empowers a trustee to represent all the bondholders and which must be deposited with that trustee, usually a bank or trust company, before the bonds may be sold. The indenture spells out in detail the terms of the debt, including the total amount of the bonds, maturity date, coupon (interest) rate, whether or not the bond is callable and, if it is, the premium (see CALLABLE BOND).

independent broker   Also, *two-dollar broker*. A stock-exchange member who handles a transaction for another broker, who for some reason cannot do so at the time. Formerly paid at a fixed commission of $2 per 100 shares, independent brokers now receive a negotiable fee.

index   A measure of relative value compared with a base quantity for the same series. Indexes are used principally to compare changes in various phenomena over time. The United States government's Consumer Price Index, for example, tracks a basket of consumer goods' prices as compared to the base year (1967). Like many indexes, this one also weights products by their importance. Stock indexes (see STOCK INDEX/ AVERAGE) frequently are weighted according to the prices and number of shares outstanding. Some price indexes take into account other factors, such as *growth persistence*, the historic tendency of a stock to show persistent growth compared to the average stock, or *price stability*, including both sensitivity to the market (see BETA) and the stock's inherent VOLATILITY. (See also PERFORMANCE INDEX.) A *composite index* is one made up of other indexes.

index fund   A MUTUAL FUND or UNIT INVESTMENT TRUST that tries to match the performance of the Standard & Poor's 500 Composite Price Index or some other stock index by adjusting its investment in each stock to reflect the market value relative to that of the other stocks in the index. Thus, if IBM represents 7 percent of the S & P 500 Index on January 15, the index fund should have 7 percent of its holdings in IBM.

index option   An option contract on a stock or other price index. Trading in such options on organized exchanges began in 1983 with the Chicago Board Options Exchange's stock-index option based on Standard & Poor's index of one hundred stock prices. Unlike options on individual stocks or commodities, index options are settled in cash, not the delivery of stock. As with other OPTION trading, one buys a call option with the hope that the underlying stock index will move up and put option in the belief that it will go down. A number of strike prices, in five-point increments, are available for each index option, much as they are for stock options. However, the expiration dates often are for three consecutive months (March, April, May, for example) rather than three months apart as for stock options. Stock-index options are generally considered less risky than STOCK-INDEX FUTURES, since the investor can make a sizable investment with less cash and knows from the outset the maximum possible loss (the cost of the option, or premium). Among the principal stock-index options available in the mid-1980's were the Chicago Standard & Poor's 100 Index, the Major Market Index on the American Stock Exchange, the New York Stock Exchange Composite Index on the same exchange, and the Value Line Composite Index and National Over-the-Counter Index on the Philadelphia Stock Exchange. In addition, indexes that reflect the performance of stocks within a single industry have been created specifically to accommodate index traders. Among these ''sub-index'' options are computer technology index options, oil index options, and transportation index options (American Stock Exchange); transportation index options (Chicago Board Options Exchange); technology index options (Pacific Stock Exchange); and gold/silver index options (Philadelphia Stock Exchange).

By selecting the stock-index contract that most closely resembles the stocks in one's own portfolio, investors can use these options to hedge against a price decline. The investor who anticipates such a drop might buy a put option on a stock index, which gives the buyer the right to sell the index at a predetermined price, the strike price, any time before the option expires. If the index price begins to fall, one can exercise the option and earn a profit, selling it at the old, higher level, and offsetting the loss in market value of the portfolio. If stock prices rise, the index will move up as well, and if the option expires before the exercise price one will lose what one paid for it, but this this loss may be offset by the gain on the stock portfolio.

Individual Retirement Account   See IRA.

industrial revenue bond   See under REVENUE BOND.

initial public offering   Abbreviated *IPO*. Also, *going public*. The first offering of a corporation's stock to the public. It differs from a PRIMARY DISTRIBUTION in that the stock has already been held by private investors and venture capitalists.

inside price   Also, *dealer price, wholesale price*. The price quoted by dealers in the over-the-counter market to each other, as opposed to the somewhat higher prices they quote to customers. The difference between the two (the SPREAD, def. 1) constitutes the dealer's profit.

insider   An individual with access to information about corporate affairs before they are made public, usually a director or officer of a corporation or one of their relatives or anyone who owns 10 or more percent of its stock. The Securities and Exchange Commission (SEC) prohibits securities trading on the basis of such information, and insiders' decisions to buy or sell shares of their stock must by law be made public and are regularly published in *Official Summary*, a monthly SEC publication available by subscription. Reports of insider trades also are available on some of the electronic DATABASES specializing in investment information.

Instinet   Acronym for *Institutional Networks Corpora-*

tion, a computerized dealing system that offers its subscribers up-to-date stock market information, automatic execution of transactions up to 1,000 shares, and computerized negotiation and execution of other deals. It is registered with the Securities and Exchange Commission as a stock exchange. Begun in 1969 as a matching market for institutions, Instinet rapidly grew, and by the mid-1980's it was supplying quotations for 1,700 exchange-listed stocks and more than 3,000 over-the-counter stocks, as well as ADRs and stock options and currency options. Its subscribers, principally mutual funds and other institutional investors, thus can trade large blocks of securities among one another directly, without going through a broker or dealer.

institutional investor   An organization that customarily trades in very large blocks of securities—for example, a mutual fund, pension fund, bank, insurance company, labor union, or college endowment fund. Institutional investors are said to account for two-thirds to three-fourths of all trading on the New York Stock Exchange, in addition to trading among themselves without benefit of a broker or exchange (see THIRD MARKET).

insured account   A bank or brokerage account that is insured against loss. The principal insurers are the FEDERAL DEPOSIT INSURANCE CORPORATION (banks); FEDERAL SAVINGS AND LOAN INSURANCE CORPORATION (savings and loan institutions); and SECURITIES INVESTOR PROTECTION CORPORATION (brokerage accounts).

intangible asset   An asset that does not physically exist but has value to an individual or firm because it can generate income. Such assets include goodwill, franchises, and patents.

interest coverage.   See under COVERAGE.

interest rate   The price paid for the use of money, usually expressed as a percentage per year. Since the circumstances of borrowing vary widely, there are numerous interest rates for various credit instruments at any one time. Current interest rates for the most important instruments are listed in the financial pages of nearly all newspapers, under such headings as "interest rates," "money rates," or simply "money." They generally include the PRIME RATE, FEDERAL FUNDS RATE, DISCOUNT RATE, CALL LOAN rate, and the rates for different maturities of BANKERS' ACCEPTANCE, CERTIFICATE OF DEPOSIT, EURODOLLAR, LONDON INTERBANK OFFER RATE, TREASURY BILL, FREDDIE MAC, FANNIE MAE, and perhaps also a MONEY-MARKET FUND.

interest-rate futures   See FINANCIAL FUTURES.

interest-rate option   An OPTION on a debt instrument, so called because it conveys the right to buy or sell that instrument at a different interest rate from the current one. The principal instruments concerned are U.S. Treasury bills, notes, and bonds, all traded on organized options exchanges. Like the INDEX OPTION on stock indexes, the interest-rate option can be used not only to speculate but to hedge a portfolio of fixed-income securities against an unfavorable change in interest rates. Although few individuals hold enough different bonds to take advantage of hedging, they can buy bond mutual funds that do. The managers of such funds hedge by selling call options against their portfolios. Interest-rate options are quoted in the financial pages of newspapers.

interest rate swap   An agreement between two parties for the exchange of a series of cash flows, one representing a fixed interest rate and the other a floating interest rate. In return each party gets some protection against unfavorable fluctuations, one in the fixed rate and other in the floating rate. For example, in a swap involving fixed-coupon bonds issued by Company A and floating-rate commercial paper issued by Company B, Bank C may act as the intermediary, exchanging one for the other. Thus Company A makes floating-rate payments to the bank in exchange for fixed-rate payments; Company B makes fixed-rate payments in exchange for floating-rate payments.

Intermarket Trading System Abbreviated *ITS*. A computerized price quotation system that links the trading posts of the New York, American, Boston, Midwest, Philadelphia, and Pacific stock exchanges, so that the buyer or seller of a security traded in more than one of these markets may choose the best current price. A broker can place an order electronically, but the actual transaction is completed by telephone or telex.

intermediate-term Between short-term and long-term. For bonds it refers to a maturity longer than two years but usually no more than ten. For stocks it refers to earnings prospects six to twelve months in the future.

international fund, international investment See under FOREIGN INVESTMENT.

in the money Describing a call OPTION or warrant whose strike price is below the current market price of the underlying security, or a put option whose strike price is higher than the market price of the underlying investment. For example, if Red Hot stock is selling for $50 a share, a call option of Red Hot 45 would have to sell for at least $5 a share and is called an in-the-money option. In most cases in-the-money options command a premium above the price of the underlying stock. See also INTRINSIC VALUE; AT THE MONEY; OUT OF THE MONEY.

intraday Within one day, used, for example, for a loan rate, or a stock or bond price fluctuation.

intrinsic value In options trading, the value of an OPTION in relation to the value of the underlying security. In the case of a call it is the amount by which the stock price is higher than the strike price; in the case of a put it is the amount by which the stock price is lower than the strike price. For example, if Red Hot common stock were selling at 53, a Red Hot Nov 50 call would have an intrinsic value of $300; its holder could exercise the call at 50 ($5,000) and resell the stock at the market price of $5,300. The intrinsic value is often referred to as how much an option is IN THE MONEY.

inventory   General term for materials owned by a business, including raw material, work in process, and finished products not yet sold. Too much cash tied up in inventories prevents a firm from using its assets efficiently; too little inventory can hamper its productive efficiency. One measure of efficient inventory management is *inventory turnover*, calculated by dividing year-end inventory into the cost of goods sold. However, the value of year-end inventory depends on the inventory accounting system used—first-in, first-out or last-in, first-out.

inverted market   In futures trading, the situation when current cash prices and futures about to expire exceed prices of distant futures. It occurs when demand for a commodity greatly exceeds its supply.

investment adviser   Also, *investment counselor*. An individual or firm that provides investment advice for a fee. All individual investment advisers and firms in the business of giving such advice to fifteen or more clients are required by law to register with the Securities and Exchange Commission and abide by the regulations of the Investment Advisers Act. Investment advice ranges from offering tips through a newsletter sold to subscribers to actually managing a client's portfolio. The qualifications of such advisers vary widely, some being in effect self-appointed experts and others having taken many courses and passed examinations entitling them to use a title such as

Chartered Financial Consultant (ChFC), awarded by the American College in Bryn Mawr, Pennsylvania, or Certified Financial Planner (CFP), awarded by the Institute of Certified Financial Planners in Denver, Colorado. Investment advisory newsletters are periodically rated in the *Hulbert Financial Digest*, which ranks them according to how readers would have done over the past few years if they had followed their advice.

Investors also may obtain advice via personal computer programs. One such program combines fundamental and technical analysis to project stock prices and advise when to buy or sell. Another offers daily rankings of what it considers the ten most overvalued and undervalued stocks, the five best and worst industries for investors, and the most and least attractive stocks within them. There are numerous others, all of which claim to perform extremely well. See also under BROKER.

investment banking The business of selling new issues of securities to the public. The issuer sells them to the investment bank, which either distributes them to dealers or sells them directly to the public, taking a profit on the spread between the purchase price and the offering price. (See also UNDERWRITING, def. 1.) In addition to public offerings of new issues, investment banks also arrange for PRIVATE PLACEMENT, market municipal securities, help arrange corporate mergers and acquisitions, and may assist in obtaining real estate financing.

investment club A group of individuals, usually ten to twenty in number, who pool their money in order to make investments that are determined by the entire group or by a committee formed from its members. Each member puts in a certain amount of money and contributes an additional amount monthly or quarterly, which is added to the investments.

investment company Also, *investment fund, investment trust, management company.* A company or trust formed for the purpose of investing in other companies or in commodities, real estate, or other assets by pooling its members' resources. The two main kinds of investment company are the CLOSED-END INVESTMENT COMPANY, whose shares are traded in the open market just as stocks are, and the OPEN-END INVESTMENT COMPANY, which is the same as a MUTUAL FUND. Their main advantage to investors is their ability to diversify their holdings much more than the average individual could, thereby reducing risk. See also DUAL FUND; UNIT INVESTMENT TRUST, def. 1.

investment counselor See INVESTMENT ADVISER.

investment income dividend A payment to shareholders in mutual funds of dividends and interest earned on the fund's securities after operating expenses have been deducted. Such payments usually are made on a quarterly basis.

investment tax credit The deduction of a percentage of the cost of new plant and equipment expenditures from a business's taxes.

investment trust Same as INVESTMENT COMPANY.

IRA Popular abbreviation for *Individual Retirement Account,* a tax-sheltered investment plan that permits any wage earner (and spouse) to accumulate funds for retirement by making tax-deferred contributions to an account. The contributions may be made individually or through a payroll-deduction plan, but the maximum annual contribution is set by law ($2,000 per worker in the mid-1980's, $2,250 if there is an unemployed spouse; these provisions were expected to be revised). Exempt from this maximum is the transfer to any lump-sum pension payment from another source into the IRA. Should one receive such a sum and wish to avoid paying income tax on it, one may simply roll it over—a so-called *IRA rollover*—and deposit it in an IRA within sixty days of receiving it. It then earns tax-free interest like other IRA funds until they are withdrawn. The rollover provision applies to every separate IRA one owns. This means one can withdraw any or all funds from an IRA once a year provided the money is returned to the same or a different IRA within sixty days. Early withdrawal, before age 59½, carries a penalty and withdrawals must begin by age 70½. Upon withdrawal the money is taxed as ordinary income.

An IRA may be set up with a commercial bank or thrift institution, mutual fund, brokerage account, or insurance company. Each has advantages and disadvantages, and different fees. An IRA may be entirely *self-managed* but then must be administered through an intermediary, usually a broker, with the account-holder choosing the specific investments (collectibles and precious metals other than U.S.-minted gold and silver coins, are forbidden by law, however). Fees and commissions vary significantly, and small accounts may become quite expensive. IRAs with banks and thrift institutions are insured up to $100,000, just as other deposits are, and may be put in any kind of account offered by the particular institution (money-market deposit account, variable-rate certificate of deposit, fixed-rate certificate of deposit, etc.). Mutual funds that sponsor IRAs often have families of funds and permit holders to shift accounts at no charge simply by telephoning, so that funds can be moved in or out of a money-market fund, bond fund, common stock fund, and so on. When a mutual fund is used, investors are urged to pay its fees separately rather than allowing them to be subtracted from the fund account, because they are then tax-deductible. IRAs offered by insurance companies are often called *individual retirement annuities* and generally represent one of two kinds— fixed annuity contracts, in which the company guarantees a minimum specified interest rate, and variable annuities, where the interest rate depends on the type of investment chosen (see also ANNUITY). This kind of IRA tends to be the costliest in terms of fees and, as with other annuities, proceeds end upon the death of the account-holder, unless a variation such as a joint-and-survivor annuity is purchased. See also KEOGH PLAN; SIMPLIFIED EMPLOYEE PENSION PLAN.

issue   General name for securities sold by a corporation or government at a particular time. Creating a new set of securities is called *floating an issue* and is generally done to raise funds for working capital, plant and equipment, to retire debts, or some other reason. Most companies that issue securities use the services of an underwriter to sell them to the public or may sell them directly to a limited number of investors (see PRIVATE PLACEMENT). See also PRIMARY DISTRIBUTION; SECONDARY DISTRIBUTION.

ITS   See INTERMARKET TRADING SYSTEM.

J

joint and survivorship annuity   An ANNUITY that pays income through two lifetimes, the policyholder's and one survivor's. When one dies the income continues until the other's death, after which benefits usually cease. This form of annuity is required in many group pension plans for married employees.

joint-stock company   A kind of business organization that, like a corporation, is owned by stockholders who have shares in the company and exercise voting rights but, unlike a corporation, does not confer limited liability on stockholders, each of whom is legally liable for all of the company's debts.

joint tenancy   See under TENANCY.

junior   Describing a security, either debt or equity, that is subordinate to another issue in claiming assets and/or income. If a company goes bankrupt the claim of common stockholders on assets is junior to that of preferred stockholders. Some companies reward employees by giving them *junior stock* or *junior shares*, which generally have reduced dividends and voting rights and are sold to executives at a discount but are not traded on stock exchanges; after a specified period they may be converted into ordinary common stock.

junk bond   Also, *high-yield bond*. A bond with a low quality rating—BB or Ba or lower (see under BOND-RATING AGENCY)—so that it is believed to carry a much higher risk of default but consequently offers a higher yield. Originally a nickname for the bonds of troubled companies, the term is now applied to bonds of newer, unproved companies as well. A junk bond typically pays 3 to 4 percent more than a Treasury bond or high-grade corporate bond. Junk-bond prices tend to fluctuate much as those of common stock do, rising and falling with the general economic climate.

K

Kansas City Board of Trade   See Appendix A.

Keogh plan   A retirement savings plan for the self-employed. The maximum amount one can contribute annually to such a plan is set by law and is fully deductible from income tax until it is withdrawn. Early withdrawals, before age 59½, carry a penalty, and withdrawals must begin by age 70½. On retirement, the participant's funds are distributed in a lump sum or installments, whichever is preferred, and are taxed as normal income. Keogh plan funds may be invested however one chooses—in an interest-bearing bank account, money-market or other mutual fund, brokerage account, insurance policy, or a combination of these. There must, however, be a custodian for the account (usually a bank or similar institution). A Keogh plan, like a company PENSION PLAN, may be either a defined-benefit plan or a defined-contribution plan.

kicker   A bonus offered to a lender in addition to interest. For example, a borrower might offer a mortgage lender a percentage of a property's rental income in exchange for a larger mortgage or better interest rate. An *equity kicker* offers some form of ownership participation, for example, stock rights or warrants to bondholders.

Krugerrand   See under GOLD.

L

last in, first out Abbreviated *LIFO*. A method of inventory accounting in which the items acquired last are counted as those used during a given accounting period, and they are valued at their purchase prices. In a period of rising prices, therefore, inventory investment and profits under this system appear to be lower than under FIRST IN, FIRST OUT accounting.

last sale The most recent transaction in a particular security, which is not necessarily the same as the last transaction in a particular trading session. It is last sale that is referred to in price descriptions such as DOWN TICK and UP TICK.

late tape A significant delay in the reporting of completed transactions on the stock exchange tape, usually owing to unusually heavy trading. When the delay is five minutes or longer, the first digits of each price are deleted (see DIGITS DELETED).

leader See MARKET LEADER.

lease A contractual rental of land, plant, or equipment. On the balance sheet a lease must be "capitalized" (regarded as owned property) when the lessee has most of the benefits and obligations of actual ownership.

leg In options trading, colloquial term for one side of a SPREAD, def. 3; for example, when one buys a call option and a put option on the same commodity, each option is called a "leg" of a spread. If one of the options represents a commitment to buy the underlying security or commodity, it is called a *long leg*. Selling either of the two options is called *lifting a leg*.

legal list   A list of very high-quality securities chosen by a state agency in which mutual savings banks, insurance companies, pension funds and other fiduciary institutions may invest. See also PRUDENT-MAN RULE.

legal transfer   A securities transaction that requires special documentation (other than an ordinary stock or bond power) to effect the transfer of ownership from seller to buyer. Such documentation is required when the owner has died or if the securities are registered to a corporation.

letter of intent

1. A pledge to buy enough mutual fund shares in a limited period of time to qualify for a reduced selling charge that would apply to a comparable lump-sum purchase.

2. Any letter that expresses an intention to perform a particular action, such as the investment letter for a LETTER SECURITY.

letter security   Also, *letter bond, letter stock.*   A stock or bond that is not registered with the Securities and Exchange Commission and hence can be sold only directly by the issuer to the investor. The buyer, however, must sign an *investment letter* stating that the purchase is for purposes of investment and not for resale. Eventually such securities may be resold to the public provided they have been held for at least two years and certain other conditions are met.

leverage   In corporate finance, the ability of a small change to make a big difference. A company is said to have high *operating leverage* when its operating costs are mostly fixed, so that when its volume of business increases its profits rise considerably, and when business slumps it loses a great deal. For example, a 15 percent increase in air travel may increase an airline's net profits by 50 percent, since the additional travelers can be handled with virtually no increase in fixed costs (such as equipment or personnel). A company is said to have high *financial leverage* when it has a high DEBT-TO-EQUITY RATIO. Financial leverage is further described under LEVERAGED, def. 1 and 2.

leveraged

1. Describing any transaction in which borrowed funds are used to get a higher rate of return, on the principle that the interest rate paid for borrowing is lower than the return on the investment. A company is said to be *highly leveraged* when a high proportion of its capital is in the form of long-term debt (see BOND RATIO). A *leveraged fund* is a DUAL FUND in which the two classes of shareholder (income and capital) each benefit from the use of the other's equity. See also LEVERAGED BUYOUT.

2. Describing the use of a small amount of money to produce a potentially large gain or loss. Thus a *leveraged hedge* is an investment that may produce a gain far larger than its purchase price—for example, the purchase of a stock option or warrant. A *leveraged stock* is one that may produce a gain or loss far out of proportion to its purchase price.

leveraged buyout   Taking over a company by means of borrowed funds, with the company's assets serving as collateral for the loan. The term is most often used when the management of a publicly owned corporation converts it to private ownership, thereby retaining control, or when the employees of a company in financial difficulty wish to take it over as an alternative to having it go out of business entirely. In such cases the publicly owned shares are generally bought back at a premium.

liability   Any debt that gives the creditor a claim on the borrower's assets. On the balance sheet both bonds and short-term debts are regarded as liabilities, as are accounts payable, wages and salaries payable, dividends declared payable, and accrued taxes payable.

LIBO, LIBOR   Abbreviations for LONDON INTERBANK OFFER RATE.

lien   A claim on property that lasts until a debt has been discharged.

life insurance   Insurance that pays a cash benefit and/or a savings reserve upon the death of the insured or when the insured reaches a certain age. There are three main kinds of insurance: term insurance, straight or whole life insurance, and endowment. (A fourth kind is treated separately; see ANNUITY). *Term insurance* is good for a given period of time, such as one, five, or ten years, often with an option to renew. Premiums are paid throughout this time but generally become higher during the course of the term, as the policyholder grows older. *Straight* or *whole life insurance* is good for the insured's entire lifetime at a fixed premium, payable throughout the holder's life, and the face of the policy is payable at death. However, a cash surrender value builds up, against which the insured may borrow. *Endowment* is good for a specific period, during which premiums are paid, after which the benefits are paid even if the insured is still living.

Since the late 1970's a number of variations on these kinds of insurance have developed, mainly to make them more attractive to investors. Because these newer policies are investment instruments, they must be registered with the Securities and Exchange Commission, and agents who sell them must be licensed by the National Association of Securities Dealers and operate under the supervision of a registered broker dealer. The main new kinds of policy are: *variable life insurance*, a form of whole life that offers a guaranteed death benefit but ties the savings portion to investments in stocks, bonds, or money-market portfolios, so that the cash value rises or falls with the value of the portfolio; and *universal life insurance*, a form of term insurance in which the savings portion is invested in a money-market account, and in which premium and coverage can be varied by the policy-holder to fit changing life circumstances. There are also some combinations of these. Until the mid-1980's one advantage of these policies was that taxes on the investment earnings they generated were deferred. However, this special tax status was being investigated and in danger of being eliminated. A major disadvantage of these policies is the high sales charge involved, meaning that it might take ten years or so for the policy's earnings to reach the projected rate of return. Therefore investors planning to hold insurance for shorter times would do better by buying much less costly term insurance and investing the difference elsewhere.

LIFO   Abbreviation for LAST IN, FIRST OUT.

limited partnership   A form of business organization in which there are two classes of partner, one or more *general partners*, who manage the enterprise and can be held generally liable should the business fail, and *limited partners,* who own shares in the business and are liable only to the extent of their investment. A limited partnership is frequently used for attracting investors to a high-risk enterprise that qualifies as a TAX SHELTER. A private limited partnership, which is one that has no more than thirty-five limited partners, each with a net worth of $1 million or more and annual income of at least $200,000, need not be registered with the Securities and Exchange Commission (SEC). These tend to be for the very rich and to take much greater risks than public partnerships. Public partnerships, which may have thousands of limited partners, are reviewed by the SEC and the minimum investment usually is about $5,000. To benefit from the tax advantages of public partnerships, one should be in or close to the top federal income tax bracket. Information about public partnerships is published in the monthly *Stanger Register* (see also Appendix B), which provides details about each partnership's offering terms, the general partner's experience, size of fees, and minimum investment, and rates them according to risk. Investors also should carefully review the prospectus. Many brokerage firms sell limited partnerships; normally these are quite carefully screened, but it is still advisable to get a second opinion. The most popular kind of limited partnership is the REAL ESTATE PARTNERSHIP, followed by the OIL AND GAS PARTNERSHIP.

One disadvantage of limited partnerships is their lack of liquidity; there is no secondary market where one can quickly convert one's interest into cash. This drawback is overcome by a new kind of *master limited partnership,* in which a company with numerous limited partnerships, such as an oil exploration firm, allows its investors to consolidate their interests into a single master partnership. Interests in a master are sold in units that can be bought and sold through a broker and often are traded on an organized stock exchange.

limit order Also, *limited price order.* An order to buy or sell securities at a given price, the *limit price,* or better (lower for buying, higher for selling).

line of credit The maximum amount of credit a bank is willing to extend to a particular borrower during a given period.

Lipper Mutual Fund Industry Average A computation of the performance level of mutual funds, published quarterly and annually, calculated for all funds and also by type of fund (growth fund, income fund, and so on). It is compiled by Lipper Analytical Services of New York.

liquid asset Also, *quick asset.* Any property that is

cash or is readily converted into cash, such as a highly marketable security like a Treasury bill.

liquid assets account   See MONEY-MARKET FUND.

liquidating price   See REDEMPTION PRICE, def. 1.

liquidation

1. Conversion of any property, for example, securities, inventory, or accounts receivable, into cash.

2. Repayment of a loan.

3. The closing out of a company, annuity, pension plan, or other enterprise or investment through the sale of its assets and the settlement of its liabilities.

liquidity

1. The ability to turn an asset into cash quickly, without losing any of its real value.

2. The proportion of a firm's liquid assets to its liabilities. A firm with high liquidity has enough cash and marketable securities to meet its short-term cash obligations.

3. In the securities trade, the ability of the market in a particular stock or bond to absorb considerable trading without fluctuating widely in price.

liquidity ratio   A measure of a company's financial LIQUIDITY (def. 2), also called acid-test ratio and QUICK-ASSET RATIO.

listed security   Also, *on-board security*. A security that is listed on an organized exchange, having met the requirements of that exchange. To be listed on the New York Stock Exchange, for example, a corporation must have at least 1 million publicly held shares worth at least $16 million and an annual before-tax net income of at least $2.5 million. Listed securities are traded over-the-counter as well as on their respective exchanges (see THIRD MARKET).

load   Also, *loading charge*. The commission paid by investors in a mutual fund (in any but a NO-LOAD fund) to cover the fund's sales costs. It is usually much higher than a brokerage commission for trading in a listed security—typically 8.5 percent—and highest of all with a FRONT-END LOAD PLAN. Only about 25 percent of total mutual fund assets are held by load funds, which generally are bought through brokers. Another kind of charge is a *low-load sales charge,* which runs about 2.0 to 3.0 percent and is levied even by funds not sold through brokers. There also may be a *back-end charge* of 1 to 4 percent, which is levied when shareholders redeem their shares. By law all these charges must be stated in the mutual fund's prospectus.

loan value The maximum amount a lender is willing or allowed to lend against collateral, for example, the maximum percentage of the current market value of securities a broker can lend to a margin account customer.

local Another name for FLOOR TRADER, def. 2.

London Bullion Fix Also, *gold fix.* The setting of the price of gold by London dealers. See under GOLD.

London Interbank Offer Rate Abbreviated *LIBO, LIBOR.* The rate at which major international banks are willing to offer EURODOLLAR time deposits to one another, which in turn is a measure of the international cost of money. This rate also affects the coupon rate of various Eurodollar credit instruments, including certificates of deposit, notes, and bonds.

long See LONG POSITION.

long coupon An interest payment on a bond that represents interest for more than the conventional six-month period.

long hedge Buying a futures contract or call option to protect against a price increase in a commodity that will be needed in the future, or against a drop in interest rates on a security. See also SHORT HEDGE.

long leg See under LEG.

long position Any purchase of stocks, bonds, or options by an investor, in contrast to SHORT POSITION.

long-term
    1. The gain (or loss) from selling property held for more than six months, or in some cases one year, which traditionally was subject to less heavy income tax than a *short-term* gain. Though the 1986 federal income tax law eliminated this distinction, it persists in some states and may eventually be reinstated.
    2. For bonds and other debt instruments, maturity of at least one year and often more.

loss   The opposite of profit, that is, any costs in excess of income. For insurance companies the term means payments made on behalf of the insured.

lot   In the securities trade, an amount bought or sold. See ODD LOT; ROUND LOT. It also represents the basic trading unit in gold coins, for example, 20 Mexican 50-peso pieces or 20 U.S. double eagles.

maintenance margin Also, *minimum maintenance*. The margin required by a broker, exchange, or other authority for keeping open a margin account. This margin usually is lower than the initial margin required by the Federal Reserve to open the account, for example, only 25 to 30 percent of the market value of the securities in the account. Should their value decline below the minimum, the broker makes a margin call for the customer to put up more cash. If the customer cannot comply, the broker will liquidate the account by selling the securities (a *margin sale*).

make a market See MARKET MAKER.

management company Another name for INVESTMENT COMPANY.

management fee A fee charged by a MUTUAL FUND to cover the cost of managing the fund's portfolio. It typically ranges from 0.5 to 1.0 percent per year per share, a figure that may either be fixed or vary with such factors as the portfolio's total value.

manipulation In the securities trade, deliberately influencing a price by creating a false impression of unusually heavy trading, acting either alone or with a group. It is illegal. See also CHURNING; MATCHED ORDER; PAINTING THE TAPE; PEGGING; POOL.

margin

1. The customer's equity in a margin account, that is, a brokerage account whereby the broker lends the customer either cash or securities for SELLING SHORT and/or buying on margin (see MARGIN TRADING). It is often expressed as a percentage of the current market

value of the investment. The percentage of cash that must be deposited with a broker to open a margin account is set by the Federal Reserve and was, in the mid-1980's, 50 percent of market value for common stocks and convertible bonds (see also REGULATION T). Thus an investor could buy $20,000 worth of stock for $10,000 in cash, borrowing the remainder from (and paying interest on the loan to) the broker and using the securities as collateral. Should the stock's market value decline so that the loan represented 70 percent or more of the total, the broker would have to demand partial repayment. (See MAINTENANCE MARGIN.)

2. In a forward contract or futures contract, the down payment or deposit, which is set by the exchange where the contract is traded. It is sometimes expressed as a percentage of the current market value of the investment. In futures trading additional margin may be required if the contract goes against the investor. Margin requirements for speculators are higher than for hedgers, sometimes by as much as 100 percent. There is no legal limit on margin loans on commodities.

margin account See under MARGIN TRADING.

margin agreement See under HYPOTHECATION.

margin call Demand by the creditor of a margin account that the borrower put up more cash or securities (reduce the loan) so that his or her equity will be in accordance with the MAINTENANCE MARGIN required. A drop in stock price generally is the reason for a margin call. If the investor does not wish to or cannot put up more collateral or cash, some of the securities held in the margin account must be sold and the proceeds of this *margin sale* used to reduce the loan.

margin requirement See under MAINTENANCE MARGIN.

margin sale See under MARGIN CALL.

margin trading Also, *buying on margin*. Purchasing

securities by using a broker's credit to pay for part of them. The customer must first open a *margin account* by putting up some cash or eligible securities as required by the Federal Reserve Board (a minimum $2,000 in the mid-1980's), and then an *initial margin* (in the mid-1980's, 50 percent of the current market value of the securities). The respective exchanges and individual brokers may require an even higher initial margin. In a typical margin transaction, John Doe wants to increase his holdings by $100,000. He puts up $50,000 and borrows the rest from his broker, who will charge Doe the interest she herself must pay for the BROKER'S LOAN that will fund the purchase, plus a little extra (less than 1 percent) for profit. Doe buys $100,000 worth of stocks, which the broker holds as collateral and for which Doe must pay the normal brokerage commission. However, he receives whatever dividends they earn. Doe's main reason for buying these stocks is speculative, that is, he wants to profit from advances in their price. Such a profit is potentially twice what he could earn from an ordinary stock purchase, since he could only have bought half the amount of stock by paying cash. Should the stocks decline in value by 15 or 20 percent, his broker may make a MARGIN CALL, forcing him to put up more cash or risk losing his investment. See also MAINTENANCE MARGIN. For margin trading in bonds, see SPECIAL BOND ACCOUNT.

markdown   A reduction in price. In the securities industry it applies to a municipal bond issue whose price is reduced by the underwriter when there is insufficient demand; to adjustments in valuation made by banks and brokers when the market price drops; and in the over-the-counter market to the dealer's spread in a purchase from a customer (see also MARKUP).

market   1. A public place for buying and selling securities; a stock exchange; sometimes, the New York Stock Exchange.

   2. The demand for a good or service or security.

market if touched Abbreviated *MIT*. In the commodities market, the equivalent of a STOP ORDER in the securities market. In other words, an order to buy or sell a futures contract or commodity as soon as the market reaches a predetermined price.

market index Another name for STOCK INDEX.

market leader Also, *leader*.

   1. A company or product that has a large share of the market.

   2. A stock or group of stocks that is somewhat ahead of the rest of the market in a major price advance or decline.

market letter A newsletter sent by a broker to customers or written by an independent analyst and sold by subscription. The former tends to be sales literature and repeats in writing the recommendations and findings of the brokerage firm's research department concerning current market conditions and the expected future outlook. The latter reflects the interests and outlook of its author(s), for example, emphasizing some form of technical analysis, or favoring a particular kind of investment. In the mid-1980's there were at least a thousand market letters of various kinds in circulation; they are not controlled by the Securities and Exchange Commission or any other regulatory agency. The *Hulbert Financial Digest* is a market letter that tracks the record of about sixty market letters compared to established market indexes (see Appendix B).

market maker In the over-the-counter securities market, an individual who maintains firm bid and ask prices in a stock by being prepared to buy or sell that stock in round lots. These quotations must be announced through NASDAQ, which requires that there be at least two market makers in each stock listed, and the market makers must be registered with the National Association of Securities Dealers. The term is also used on organized exchanges and in commodity markets as a synonym for FLOOR TRADER (def. 1 and 2) and SPECIALIST.

market multiple   The PRICE-EARNINGS RATIO of the average stock, which can be found in numerous financial publications. It is calculated from the Standard & Poor's 500, Dow Jones averages, and similar large composite indexes and is computed by multiplying the number of shares outstanding by the price per share and dividing this figure by cumulative earnings. The market multiple is useful for comparing a company's price-earnings ratio with that of the market as a whole.

market order   An order to buy or sell a security or commodity at the best price after the order reaches the exchange floor. It obliges the broker to buy at the lowest available price or sell at the highest available price.

market price   The last reported price at which security was sold on an exchange. For over-the-counter stocks or bonds, the combined bid and ask prices available at any one time from a dealer or other market maker.

market weighting   Also, *market-value weighting.* Weighting a STOCK INDEX/AVERAGE according to the total market value of outstanding shares, so that each stock is entered with its price multiplied by the number of shares outstanding. The New York Stock Exchange Composite Index is market-weighted.

mark to the market   An adjustment in a brokerage account to make it conform to a new market price. It may involve a MARGIN CALL if the price of a stock sold short rises.

markup   An increase in price. In the securities industry it applies to the dealer's spread in the over-the-counter market in sale to a customer, and to a municipal bond issue whose price is raised by the underwriter when there is increased demand for it. See also MARKDOWN.

matched and lost The result of flipping a coin to decide which of two brokers simultaneously making an identical offer or bid for the same stock should complete the transaction, since demand or supply for that stock is insufficient for both of them to do so.

matched order Buying and selling the same stock in a flurry of orders by the same person at virtually the same price and time, to give the impression of extensive trading in hopes of driving the stock price up. This kind of manipulation is illegal.

matrix trading Another name for bond swapping; see SWAP.

maturity The date on which a loan, bond, or other debt falls due and is to be paid in full (redeemed) by the borrower.

maturity yield See YIELD TO MATURITY.

MBIA See under MUNICIPAL BOND.

medium-term bond Also, *intermediate-term bond*. A bond with a maturity of ten years or less, distinguishing it from a long-term bond. See also NOTE.

member firm (corporation) A brokerage company that has at least one officer or employee who is a member of a STOCK EXCHANGE. The exact name depends on the company's form of organization, whether a partnership (firm) or corporation.

merchant bank A type of financial institution found mainly in Europe that undertakes investment banking, portfolio management, insurance, negotiation of mergers, and a variety of other services.

merger Also, *takeover*. The combining of two or more formerly independent companies into a single one. Depending on legal, tax, and accounting considerations, a merger may take one of three forms: two companies create a new corporate entity; one company is absorbed into the operations of another; or one company becomes a division or wholly owned subsidiary of another. In the first instance there is a pooling of interests, in which the firms merely exchange common stock for common stock and add together their assets and liabilities. In the second and third forms a buyer pays cash or uses a debt instrument to acquire a company's stock or assets. The company being acquired may be in the same business (horizontal merger), a customer or supplier (vertical merger), or in a totally unrelated line (conglomerate merger). The merger may be friendly and desired by the present management of the *target company* (the one being acquired), or it may be hostile, with the buyer inducing stockholders to sell their holdings by offering a premium price, new securities in the company-to-be, or other benefits (see also TENDER OFFER). Threatened with an unwanted takeover by a *raider*, the target company's management may retaliate with a *poison pill* (make itself less attractive by altering its capital structure, selling off some desirable portion of its business, or similar means). Alternatively it may offer the raider *greenmail* (try to buy back shares at a premium price) or seek a different, more desirable company (a *white knight*) to take it over. An individual or corporate investor who accumulates 5 percent or more of the outstanding shares in a company must by law report such a purchase to the Securities and Exchange Commission, as well as to the exchange where the stock is listed and to the company itself, so a totally secret takeover is impossible to accomplish. However, investment advisers and other securities analysts carefully watch the market for potential takeover attempts in order to profit from tender offers and other side effects. Also see LEVERAGED BUYOUT; RISK ARBITRAGE, def. 2.

merger arbitrage See under ARBITRAGE; RISK ARBITRAGE, def. 2.

MidAmerica Commodity Exchange See Appendix A.

Midwest Stock Exchange See Appendix A.

minimum maintenance See MAINTENANCE MARGIN.

Minneapolis Grain Exchange See Appendix A.

minority interest The ownership of less than 50 percent of the outstanding shares of a corporation.

minus tick See DOWN TICK.

monetary policy The regulation of money and credit in a nation, which is carried out by the central bank—in the United States, the Federal Reserve. The principal vehicles of monetary policy are expansion or contraction of the reserves of commercial banks by buying and selling government bonds (through the Federal Open Market Committee). Other measures are changing RESERVE REQUIREMENTS and adjusting the DISCOUNT RATE. There are two main kinds of monetary policy, generally called *easy money* and *tight money*. The former expands the banks' reserves by reducing reserve requirements and enlarges the nation's money supply, lowers the discount rate (and other interest rates), and buys securities in the open market. It is intended to increase investment spending and demand for loans. A tight money policy increases reserve requirements, raises the discount rate, and sells government securities; these actions tend to reduce the overall money supply, reduce credit (because interest rates are higher), and curb inflation.

money market Collective name for the markets for short-term credit instruments, which are relatively safe, offer relatively low yield, and are very liquid (easily converted into cash). They include U.S. Treasury bills, commercial paper, broker's loans, bankers' acceptances, negotiable certificates of deposit, Federal funds, and repurchase agreements (repos).

Unlike the organized markets in stocks, bonds, and commodities, money-market instruments are not traded on any central exchanges. By far the majority of participants in money-market trading are commercial banks, state and local governments, large corporations, and the federal government. Individual investors participate in the money market principally through buying Treasury bills and other short-term government securities and through investing in a MONEY-MARKET FUND or a MONEY-MARKET BANK ACCOUNT.

money-market bank account   Also, *money-market deposit account*, abbreviated *MMDA*. A kind of investment account offered by commercial banks and thrift institutions since 1982 to compete with money-market mutual funds offered by brokerage houses. Such accounts are federally insured up to $100,000 but generally require a larger minimum deposit (by law until 1986; set by individual banks thereafter) and do not necessarily compound interest every day. Although customers may withdraw as much cash (above the minimum deposit) as they wish, they may write only a limited number of checks or other orders of payment to a third party.

money-market certificate Abbreviated *MMC*.   Also, *Treasury bill account, T-bill account.* A six-month CERTIFICATE OF DEPOSIT whose interest rate is tied to a six-month Treasury bill. Offered by savings banks and savings and loan associations, it requires a minimum deposit of $10,000. Although the interest rate quoted is identical to that of a six-month Treasury bill, the yield on T-bills is actually higher because it is quoted on a discount basis. Further, T-bills can be sold at any time, but closing out a money-market certificate early is generally subject to penalties. Finally, the interest on Treasury bills is exempt from state and local income tax, whereas that on MMCs is taxable.

money-market fund Also, *liquid assets account, money-market mutual fund.* A MUTUAL FUND that specializes in a portfolio of short-term high-yield securities in the money market, which are far too costly for most individual investors. Among them are Treasury bills and Treasury repurchase agreements ("repos"), Federal agency issues, short-term municipal bonds, and a host of private issues such as certificates of deposit, bankers' acceptances, commercial paper, Eurodollar issues, and Yankee dollar issues. All of these obligations are short-term, with an entire portfolio maturing (and being replaced) in as little as two days and rarely more than ninety days. Like other mutual funds, money-market funds can be invested in simply by buying into a brokerage firm's fund, although many require a minimum initial investment (usually $1,000). Interest is compounded daily and there is no redemption penalty, making them a very liquid investment. Many also offer check-writing privileges.

The first money-market fund in the United States was set up about 1974, and during the next few years, a time of high interest rates, the funds flourished because they got a much higher return than investors could get through bank accounts. From 1982 on, investment companies had to compete with commercial banks and thrift institutions, which offered similar MONEY-MARKET BANK ACCOUNTS. These had the advantage of federal insurance but the disadvantages of higher minimum investment ($2,500 was typical), sometimes lower interest rates, and not necessarily daily compounding of interest. In the mid-1980's a new kind of money-market fund, a *tax-free money fund,* developed; it invests in short-term municipal instruments, maturing in less than one year and not subject to federal income tax, but offering considerably lower interest than conventional money-market funds.

The principal money-market funds are listed in the financial pages. Such listings include average maturity (the average maturity time for the fund's entire holdings); the shorter the time, the more quickly the fund responds to changes in interest rates. The average yield is for the previous seven days, and the quotation is then annualized and calculated so as to give a seven-day compounded (effective) rate of return. Bank money funds are charted separately and show the annual effective yield based on the method of compounding interest and the rate for the lowest minimum deposit, along with the interest rate for six-month certificates of deposit.

Moody's Investors Service   A registered investment adviser that is a well-known BOND-RATING AGENCY and also supplies ratings for commercial paper, short-term municipal issues, and common and preferred stock. Its publications provide information about many corporations and securities in considerable detail.

mortgage   A long-term loan for real property (land and/or buildings), in which the property serves as security for the loan. A *first mortgage* gives the lender, called the *mortgagee,* a primary claim on the property. Sometimes the borrower, called the *mortgagor,* takes out a *second mortgage;* with home mortgages it usually is a short-term (five years or so) instrument used to allow a loan assumption (taking over an older mortgage), to reduce the necessary down payment on a house, or to allow an existing homeowner to "cash in" on his or her equity. The interest rate usually is higher than on a first mortgage, and often a BALLOON PAYMENT is involved. The conventional home mortgage, also called standard fixed-rate mortgage, calls for a fixed interest rate and is paid in equal amounts for the term of the contract, which usually is for twenty-five or thirty years. Variations on this kind of mortgage include a *renegotiable rate mortgage* (RRM), which allows the interest rate to be changed every three to five years in accordance with current prevailing interest rates, ADJUSTABLE RATE MORTGAGE, and GRADUATED PAYMENTS MORTGAGE. The growth in home mortgages has given rise to an active SECONDARY MORTGAGE MARKET, consisting of primary mortgage lenders who sell loans to investors who buy loans or mortgage-backed securities. See also OPEN-END MORTGAGE; REVERSE-ANNUITY MORTGAGE; WRAPAROUND MORTGAGE.

mortgage-backed securities Any security backed by a mortgage on real property. It includes the pass-through securities sold in the SECONDARY MORTGAGE MARKET, as well as the conventional corporate MORTGAGE BOND.

mortgage bond A bond secured by a mortgage on all or part of the property, equipment, or other real assets of the issuing corporation. A mortgage bond may be backed by a first or second mortgage, the former having prior claim on the company's assets should it fail to pay its debts. However, most American corporate bonds today are unsecured (see DEBENTURE).

mortgage market The overall demand for and supply of mortgages, that is, funds for building and real estate projects of various kinds. Buyers of mortgages choose to pay interest on a loan rather than pay for a large property outright (if indeed they have enough cash to tie up in this way). Sellers of mortgages find such long-term loans profitable, especially since they normally are collateralized by the property. The chief lenders in the primary mortgage market in the United States are insurance companies, commercial banks, and thrift institutions. See also SECONDARY MORTGAGE MARKET.

mortgage pass-through certificate Another name for

a participating certificate (PC) in a mortgage pool. See under SECONDARY MORTGAGE MARKET.

mortgage REIT   A REAL ESTATE INVESTMENT TRUST that specializes in the financing of real estate projects, with its income coming from interest earned and discounts received. REIT mortgage loans include short-term construction and development loans, first and second mortgages, WRAPAROUND MORTGAGES, and a variety of other real estate financing programs.

moving average   A statistical tool used in the securities industry by technical analysts to create forecasting systems based on the prices of individual securities or on market indexes. A moving average consists of a series of averages taken over a fixed period of time, such as ten days. The average ''moves'' because as another day's average is added to the series the first day's average is discarded. Three methods of calculating averages are commonly used: simple averages (such as a total of ten prices divided by 10); weighted averages, with prices that are considered more important being given a higher multiple; and exponential moving averages, in which a fixed weight is assigned to the current price and all of the remaining weight to the previous value of the moving average itself. Moving averages are most useful for identifying trends, which in turn can help investors better time their purchases and sales.

multiple   See MARKET MULTIPLE; PRICE-EARNINGS RATIO.

municipal bond   Also, *muni* (slang), *tax-exempt bond*, *tax-free bond*. A bond issued by a state or government unit (state, county, city, town, village), the interest on which is usually exempt from federal income tax and sometimes also from state and local taxes. There are three main categories of municipal bond: GENERAL OBLIGATION BOND, REVENUE BOND, and SPECIAL-TAX BOND. They differ in how they are backed and payable. Most municipal bonds are sold in denominations of $1,000 and $5,000. For many years they were largely coupon bonds, but any issued after June 30, 1983, must by law be registered bonds. The majority are serial bonds maturing over a period of years. (See COUPON BOND; SERIAL BOND.) Unlike corporate bonds, municipal bonds are usually quoted on a YIELD-TO-MATURITY basis.

In many cases the issuer of a municipal bond is able to redeem the issue long before it is due, but municipal revenue bonds offer the investor protection against early redemption by the Federal Savings and Loan Insurance Corporation (see under REVENUE BOND). Although municipal bonds are considered a comparatively safe investment, certain municipals may be insured to guarantee payment of both interest and principal, by either the Municipal Bond Insurance Association (MBIA) or the American Municipal Bond Assurance Corporation (AMBAC). The latter also insures mutual-bond-fund and individual-bond portfolios. Even though the issuer pays the insurance premium, insured bonds yield slightly less. Municipal bonds also are, like other bonds, rated by bond-rating agencies such as Moody's and Standard & Poor's (see also WHITE'S RATING). Municipals are widely traded, almost entirely over-the-counter (few are listed on organized exchanges). Information about municipals is published daily in Standard & Poor's BLUE LIST; another special publication, *The Bond Buyer,* compiles an index that measures the yield levels of newly issued municipal bonds. Because they are largely tax-exempt, municipal bonds yield less than taxable bonds, and therefore they are recommended principally for those investors who are in a high tax bracket. However, a law passed in 1986 limited the tax-exempt feature of municipal issues floated for nonessential purposes, such as privately owned sports centers, making some subject to the ALTERNATIVE MINIMUM TAX.

Municipal bonds can be bought through brokers, commercial banks, and investment bankers. Individual investors also can buy shares in municipal-bond mutual funds or municipal unit investment trusts. The former are managed and the bonds bought and sold so as to earn capital gains as well as interest; the latter are unmanaged and consist of an unchanging pool of bonds, so that the interest rates do not change. Shares in funds and trusts enable the individual investor to hold an interest in short-term (under one year), intermediate-term (up to ten years), and long-term municipal obligations. For municipal bond index futures, see under STOCK-INDEX FUTURES.

municipal investment trust   Abbreviated *MIT*. A UNIT INVESTMENT TRUST whose holdings consist of various kinds of MUNICIPAL BOND.

municipal lease   A short-term debt instrument used by state and local governments to finance the purchase of equipment, which serves as collateral for the loan. At the end of the lease period the equipment (fire engines, or computers, for example) usually becomes the property of the municipality. In such a transaction the local government is the lessee and a brokerage firm, bank, or other institution is the lessor. Individual investors acquire a portion of a particular lease by buying a certificate of participation from a broker for a minimum of $5,000, or shares in a mutual fund specializing in such leases for a minimum of $2,500 a share. The advantage to investors is that the investment is secured by the equipment, yields are exempt from federal income tax, and the return is usually somewhat higher than on comparable municipal bonds. Most equipment leases have terms of three to seven years, and, because they are not in large supply, they are a less liquid investment than bonds. Most are self-liquidating, so that the monthly or semiannual coupon payments include both principal and interest.

mutual fund   Also, *open-end investment company*. An INVESTMENT COMPANY that buys and sells its own shares and uses its capital to invest in the securities of other companies, or in other equity or debt instruments. Mutual funds are not listed on organized exchanges, and the price of their shares is determined by their NET ASSET VALUE, a figure that changes constantly. The principal mutual funds are listed in the financial pages of large newspapers. Such listings usually include net asset value per share (the price at which shares may be redeemed), the offer or buy price (at which shares can be bought), and sometimes the change in price between current quotation and that of the previous trading period (day or week).

The chief advantages of investing in a mutual fund are much greater portfolio diversification (through the pooling of money with thousands of other shareholders) than is possible for all but the wealthiest individuals, and professional evaluation and management of the investment. Many funds also offer other services, such as check-writing privileges, exchange privilege (enabling switching part or all of one's shares to another fund in the same group with different goals), automatic reinvestment of dividends, and retirement plans. Shares in mutual funds are sold through a stockbroker or financial planner, through some large commercial banks, through the fund's own sales force, or directly from the fund. The last method involves no sales commission; the others do. (See also LOAD and NO-LOAD.) Mutual funds often are classified according to the kind of investment they undertake: common-stock fund, bond fund, tax-free bond fund (investing in medium- and long-term municipal bonds), income fund (corporate bonds and high-yield stocks), growth fund (largely common stocks, aimed at long-term growth), balanced fund (aiming at balance between income and growth), specialty or sector fund (limits investments to a specific industry), utility fund (invests in public utilities only), money-market funds, and numerous others. A fund's investment goals and the techniques it will use to achieve them must by law be stated in its prospectus. Investors interested in a mutual fund should read either its prospectus or the Statement of Additional Information it issues, along with its latest financial statement. See also DUAL FUND; INDEX FUND; MONEY-MARKET FUND; TARGET FUND; UNIT INVESTMENT TRUST.

N

n Abbreviation

1. In newspaper stock listings, for *new issue* (issued during last 52 weeks). Therefore the "52-week high" and "low" prices for this stock refer to the beginning of trading in it rather than to a 52-week period.

2. In mutual fund listings, for a *no-load fund*.

3. In tables of Treasury bonds and notes, for *note* (as opposed to *bond*).

naked option Also, *uncovered option*. Selling (writing) an option without owning the underlying security. See under OPTION.

narrow market See THIN MARKET.

NASDAQ Abbreviation for *National Association of Securities Dealers Automated Quotation System*, a computerized system that provides its subscribers with current price information on over-the-counter securities. Its quotations are published (usually only in part) in the financial pages of large newspapers. Founded in 1971 and owned and operated by the National Association of Securities Dealers, NASDAQ grew rapidly, and by the mid-1980's was providing price quotations in more than four thousand stocks. In 1984 it began also to provide automatic execution of small orders (up to 500 shares at first). In 1982 NASDAQ added its *National Market System*, which provides more extensive trading information about the most active stocks and is published separately from other over-the-counter stock listings in newspapers. Unlike the organized exchanges, the NASDAQ stocks are traded by competing dealers, called market makers, who buy and sell for their own inventories and sell to investors. Their quotations, formerly transmitted by messengers, mail, and telephone, are now disseminated in seconds via the market makers' computer terminals to a central data center, which transmits them to subscribers' terminals.

NASDAQ Indexes Seven price indexes of the American common stocks in the NASDAQ system, except for those also listed on an exchange and those with only one market maker. Unlike the Dow Jones averages (but like most other indexes), the NASDAQ indexes are weighted according to market value, the influence of each stock being proportional to its price multiplied by the number of shares outstanding. In addition to a composite index, there are indexes for industrial, bank, transportation, insurance, utility, and other finance stocks.

National Market System See under *NASDAQ*

National Securities Clearing Corporation A clearing facility that serves the New York and American stock exchanges and the National Association of Securities Dealers; it enables brokers, exchanges, and others to reconcile accounts with one another.

NAV Abbreviation for *NET ASSET VALUE*.

NC Also, *nc*. Abbreviation for noncallable (see CALLABLE BOND).

nd In stock tables, abbreviation for next-day delivery (of a stock certificate and settlement for the transaction).

negotiable Describing a claim or right to payment that is readily transferable from one party to another, that is, can be bought or sold. Examples include a stock certificate with the stock power signed, short-term certificates of deposit, promissory notes, and checks. A *negotiable order of withdrawal* is a loan withdrawal that is negotiable (see NOW ACCOUNT).

net assets Another name for NET WORTH.

net asset value Also, *net asset value per share, NAV*.

The market value of a mutual fund's investments, after deducting liabilities, divided by the number of shares its has outstanding. In newspaper listings of mutual fund quotations, a fund's NAV appears in the first column after its name and its equivalent to the bid, or selling price, in over-the-counter market quotations, that is, the price at which shareholders can sell their shares. The second column shows the offer price (same as the ask price for over-the-counter stocks), the price at which one can buy shares of the fund. The third column, NAV Change, states the change in net asset value, in cents, from the close of the previous trading day. Funds' net asset values are calculated daily, usually just after the market has closed. See also MUTUAL FUND.

net change   In the securities trade, the difference between the final price of a stock, bond, commodity, or mutual fund on two successive trading days. For over-the-counter stocks it is usually the difference between bid prices on two successive trading days. The net change is quoted in points, just as prices are, so that + 1¼ means the stock sold for $1.25 more than in the last sale on the previous day. Both dividends and stock splits are considered in calculating net change; if a stock is trading with dividend one day and ex-dividend the next and the dividend is $1.25, a price 1¼ less on the second day would be considered unchanged. Similarly, a stock selling for $50 the day before a 2-for-1 split and trading for $26 the next day would have a net change of + 1 ($25 + $1).

net current assets   See WORKING CAPITAL.

net earnings   See NET INCOME.

net income   Also, *net earnings.* The difference between a company's income (from sales and other operations) and its costs and expenses over a given period of time, usually a year. If income exceeds costs, it represents a *net profit;* if costs exceed income, it represents a *net loss*. See also EARNINGS PER SHARE; INCOME STATEMENT; OPERATING MARGIN; RETURN ON EQUITY.

net sales Also, *operating revenues*. The proceeds of a company's main operations, that is, the sale of goods and services. See also INCOME STATEMENT.

net worth Also, *net assets* For an individual or business firm, all assets minus all liabilities. For a corporation the result is the sum of common and preferred *stockholders' equity*, which is a synonym for "net worth."

new issue An ISSUE of securities offered to the public for the first time. It may be an INITIAL PUBLIC OFFERING from a company that was previously privately owned, or an additional issue by a company already publicly owned.

New York Cotton Exchange See Appendix A.

New York Futures Exchange See Appendix A.

New York Mercantile Exchange See Appendix A.

New York Stock Exchange See Appendix A.

New York Stock Exchange Index See under STOCK INDEX/AVERAGE.

no-load Abbreviated *NL*. Describing a MUTUAL FUND that does not charge a sales commission, usually because it employs no salespersons. Shares in a no-load fund must therefore be purchased directly from the fund. In newspaper listings of mutual funds, NL indicates no-load funds, for which the NET ASSET VALUE is equal to the offer price (there is no difference between bid and ask). Shareholders in no-load funds still must pay a management fee, usually 0.5 to 1 percent per year per share. Further, some funds also levy a *12b-1 charge,* allowed by the Securities and Exchange Commission since 1980, to cover marketing and advertising expenses; it usually ranges from 0.1 to 1.25 percent of total assets per year, prorated from each shareholder's assets each month.

Neither the management fee nor the 12b-1 charge are counted as a LOAD.

nominal quote   Bid and ask prices quoted by dealer or broker as a general estimate of value but not constituting a firm offer. The National Association of Securities Dealers requires that a nominal quote be identified as such. See also FIRM QUOTE; SUBJECT QUOTE.

nominal yield   For a bond or other fixed-income security, the rate of return stated on the face of the instrument, not adjusted for changes in price levels or other circumstances. See also REAL RATE OF RETURN.

noncallable   Abbreviated *NC*. Describing a bond or other security that may not be called (redeemed) before maturity. See CALLABLE BOND.

noncompetitive bid   A bid for less than the standard amount of U.S. Treasury securities, that is, $500,000 or less for Treasury bills and $1 million or less for Treasury notes and bonds. The noncompetitive bidder will then pay the average of prices paid by those competitive bidders whose bids are accepted by the Treasury.

noncumulative   Describing a preferred stock for which unpaid dividends do not accrue. Almost all preferred stocks now carry a CUMULATIVE DIVIDEND.

nondiscretionary trust   Also, *fixed-investment trust, fixed-investment company*. An investment company that invests specific proportions of its assets in specific securities, which are set forth in the trust.

nonparticipating   See under PARTICIPATING PREFERRED STOCK.

nonrecourse loan   See under RECOURSE LOAN.

nonrefundable   See under REFUNDING.

no-par stock   Also, *no-par-value stock*. A stock with no set value stated on the stock certificate or in the issuing corporation's charter. Such stock has an implicit value derived from how it is carried on the corporation's balance sheet, either as part of the CAPITAL STOCK, or as part of PAID-IN SURPLUS, or both. Thus, if a company sells 2 million shares of no-par stock for $40 million, it may carry the stock at $15 million in its capital stock account and add $25 million to its paid-in surplus account, or it may carry it at $1 million and leave $39 million for paid-in surplus. However, since PAR VALUE has little meaning in terms of real value, and some states tax corporations on the basis of par value, many corporations today issue stock with no par value or only a very low par value.

normal trading unit See ROUND LOT.

note A written acknowledgment of a debt. The term is used in a general way to describe debt securities with a short- or medium-term maturity. Treasury notes have maturities from two to ten years; municipal notes commonly have maturities less than four years, and frequently much shorter. Some municipal notes are redeemed by long-term bonds. Unlike bonds, a note is rarely CALLABLE.

notes payable Short-term loans, coming due in a year or less, that are owed by a business. Unlike accounts payable, they usually require an interest payment as well as repayment of the principal. On the balance sheet they are listed as current liabilities.

notes receivable Short-term loans, coming due in a year or less, that are owed to a business. They include promissory notes and similar debts, and are listed as current assets on the balance sheet.

not held Abbreviated *NH*. Instruction to the floor broker on a MARKET ORDER that the customer wants the broker to obtain the best possible price but will not hold him or her responsible if this is not done. It usually accompanies an order for a large block of securities.

NOW account   Also, *negotiable order of withdrawal account*. In effect, an interest-bearing checking account. It actually is a savings account for which the withdrawal slips are negotiable, just as checks are for demand deposits. Technically the account-holder is required to give one to two months' notice before withdrawal, but this provision is rarely invoked. Like other bank accounts, NOW accounts are federally insured, and with the completion of bank deregulation there is no ceiling on the maximum interest rate paid. There is no limit on the number of monthly transactions allowed. See also SUPER NOW ACCOUNT.

numismatic coin   See under COIN COLLECTING.

o   In options tables, indication that an option, owing to a stock split or stock dividend, does not permit the holder to buy or sell 100 shares of that stock but rather a different number of shares (fewer or more than 100).

obligation   Any form of debt, such as an IOU, bond, note, or bill.

odd lot   A securities or commodity transaction for an amount less than the standard trading unit, called a ROUND LOT. For most listed stocks it means fewer than 100 shares (although 10 shares constitute a round lot for some inactive stocks), and the investor must sometimes pay a small premium, the *odd-lot differential* (typically 12½ cents per share). In over-the-counter trading there is no official minimum quantity, but in practice dealers may charge more for small purchases. Most odd-lot purchases are made by small investors who lack enough funds to buy a round lot, and it was long believed that their market judgments were invariably wrong, so that wise investors could profit by doing the exact opposite (buying when they sold, selling when they bought). Known as the *odd-lot theory*, this notion has not been reliably borne out, and in fact odd-lot investors, who tend to buy in a rising market, have frequently done fairly well.

off-board

   1. Describing a transaction in an unlisted security, that is, in the OVER-THE-COUNTER market.

   2. Describing a transaction in a listed security that is carried out away from an exchange, either over-the-counter or in the THIRD MARKET.

offer   Also, *offering price*. Same as ASK.

offering   See DISTRIBUTION, def. 1.

off-floor order   An order to buy or sell a security that originates off the exchange floor, that is, from a broker's office rather than from on-floor traders who are dealing for their own accounts. Off-floor orders must be executed before on-floor ones.

offshore   A bank or other financial institution that is located somewhere outside the United States, often on an island (hence the term), where very liberal banking laws and tax rates encourage EURODOLLAR deposits. The term is also used to describe mutual funds and other security traders so located in order to avoid the stiff regulations of the Securities and Exchange Commission.

of record   Describing shareholders who are on a company's books on the RECORD DATE.

oil and gas partnership   Investment in a share of an exploratory and/or developmental oil- and gas-drilling program for profit and, principally, tax benefits (see also TAX SHELTER). The investment is usually in the form of a limited partnership, with a general partner (sometimes called the sponsor) managing the work and the limited partners putting up the money. Exploratory programs look for oil and gas, and run the risk of finding none; developmental programs drill in proven areas but do not always produce oil. Tax deductions in a drilling program are bunched in the first year or two of operation. If and when oil or gas is found, the partnership begins to pass along smaller annual deductions for operating expenses. Partners also get income from the sale of oil and gas. Some of the cash is sheltered (from tax) by the depletion allowance, that is, depreciation allowed for certain natural resources. If enough producing wells are found, they may be sold to a large oil company and the partners receive appropriate shares of the proceeds of this sale, which are taxed as capital gains. In general, an oil and gas partnership is regarded as a much riskier investment than a REAL ESTATE PARTNERSHIP.

on the money   Another term for AT THE MONEY.

on-balance volume   In TECHNICAL ANALYSIS, a method for measuring the accumulation and distribution of a stock that was developed by Joseph Granville and is based on the assumption that volume trends lead price trends. Each day's on-balance volume figure equals the volume of trading for the day with a plus or minus sign indicating whether the stock price rose or fell on that day. The cumulative on-balance volume series is calculated by adding successive daily on-balance volume figures, the total increasing when the stock gains in price and decreasing when it declines. If cumulative on-balance volume is positive, the stock is under accumulation and, according to this theory, should rise in price; if it is negative, the stock is being distributed and, again in theory, should fall in price.

OPD   Abbreviation for *opened*. A symbol appearing on the ticker tape to indicate the first trade of the day in a stock after a delayed opening, or the first trade in a security whose price has abruptly advanced or declined considerably, 1 or more points for stocks selling below $20 and 2 or more points for stocks selling higher than $20.

open-end investment company   An investment company that continually creates new shares as they are needed, as opposed to a closed-end company that issues a limited number of shares. For all practical purposes it is synonymous with MUTUAL FUND.

open-end mortgage   Also, *open mortgage*. A mortgage that permits increasing the total amount of the mortgage loan without taking out a new mortgage.

opening   Also, *opening price*. The price at which a

security or commodity sells when trading for the day begins. It is not necessarily the same as the closing (last) price of the previous trading day, since the SPECIALIST opens trading at a price where current supply and demand can meet.

open interest In the commodity futures market, the number of futures contracts outstanding in a particular commodity at a certain time, which indicates the extent of public interest there might be in a contract. The higher the open interest, the more likely that buyers will want to find sellers, and vice versa.

open-market operations See FEDERAL OPEN MARKET COMMITTEE.

open order Another name for GOOD TILL CANCELED ORDER.

open repo Also, *continuing contract repo, open repurchase agreement*. A series of overnight loans, in the form of a REPURCHASE AGREEMENT, or repo, that are automatically renewed every day unless either the borrower or the lender decides to terminate the agreement.

operating cost Also, *operating expense*. Any expenses incurred by a company in carrying on its business.

operating leverage The proportion of a company's fixed OPERATING COST to its variable costs. For example, an airline, which has much the same fixed cost no matter how many or how few seats it sells, has very high operating leverage, whereas a building contractor, who buys materials and hires laborers only as they are needed for a job, has very low operating leverage.

operating margin Also, *operating margin of profit, operating ratio, return on sales*. Operating earnings (the difference between gross profit and OPERATING COST) expressed as a percentage of sales, or, if as a *ratio*, the proportion of operating income to the cost of goods (or services) sold. This figure, derived from the INCOME STATEMENT, tells what percentage of sales is being converted into income from operations and is most useful when compared to those of prior years, companies in similar lines, and industry averages.

operating revenues   See NET SALES.

operating statement   Another name for INCOME STATE-MENT.

opportunity cost   The return available from an alternative investment. For example, the investor who purchases stock futures instead of the underlying stocks forgoes the advantage of earning dividends in favor of possibly far greater gains from smaller investment in the futures; the "lost" dividends represent opportunity cost.

option   A contract for the right to buy (or *call* away from the owner) or the right to sell (or *put* to the buyer) a certain quantity of a commodity, security, or futures contract at a set price, called the *strike price,* by a certain time, called the *expiration date,* regardless of the market price of the commodity (security, or future) at that time. Calls and puts, as the two kinds of option are called, originally were trading vehicles mainly in the commodity market. In the early 1970's they began to be widely used by securities investors, and since 1972 they have been traded on a number of organized exchanges, which list their options in the financial pages. Such listings show the name of the underlying commodity or security, strike price, and month of expiration. Nine months is the longest period for which options are available, and they expire quarterly—for example, in May, August, November. The last day an option may be exercised (that is, the underlying security may be bought or sold at the strike price) is the third Friday of the stated contract month. After that the option is worthless. Some listings also include the volume of trading (the number of option contracts traded that day) and the open interest (the total number of outstanding contracts for that option). Each stock option is either bought or sold against 100 shares of an underlying security and gives the owner the *right* to buy that stock; it is not a down payment on the stock and carries no voting or other ownership privileges.

Options are almost always bought with the intention of reselling them before expiration rather than exercising them (buying the underlying stock). The main purpose in buying an option is to make a profit from a stock's price change while limiting the amount of possible loss to the relatively small investment in the option. Buyers of calls hope the underlying stock's price will go up; buyers of puts believe it will go down.

For example, suppose you believe Red Hot stock, now selling for $50 a share, is bound to go up in the next few months but don't want to tie up $5,000. You ask your broker to buy a call option with a strike price of $50 that will expire in three months, having seen in the newspaper that Red Hot Nov 50 is selling for $3. (This price, called the *premium*, is determined by a number of factors, including INTRINSIC VALUE, TIME VALUE, and volatility of the stock; the more volatile the stock, the higher the premium; the shorter the time until expiration, the lower the premium.) You are spending $300 for the right to buy Red Hot stock at $50 per share before the third Saturday in November, plus an estimated $25 in brokerage commission and transfer tax costs. Suppose you are right. Red Hot becomes the target for a takeover, and the stock jumps to $70 per share. You can exercise your call option, buy 100 shares for $5,000, and immediately sell them for $7,000. Your profit amounts to $2,000 minus $325 for the premium and additional brokerage costs, or about $1,500 in three months' time. Suppose, however, you are wrong, and Red Hot stock drops to $45 a share. You do nothing and have lost $325, which is far less than if you had spent $5,000 on the actual shares and now sold them for $4,500, losing $500 plus commissions. Finally, suppose that Red Hot stock rises to $55 a share within a month of your option purchase and you decide it will probably go no higher. The stock price increase, however, is reflected in a higher premium for Red Hot Nov 50, $5 instead of $3, so you can sell your call option for $500, less another $25 for commission, making a profit of $150 in a month's time. Put options work in the same manner. If you expect Red Hot stock to drop from $50 to $40 or less, you would buy a put at 50, giving you the right to sell the stock at $50 in a market where, if you were correct, it was selling at $40.

Options can be sold as well as bought. The seller of options, called the *writer*, is thereby obliged to deliver or buy the stock at the strike price. One can sell options either on stocks in one's own portfolio or on stocks not already owned; the former is called *covered option writing*, the latter *naked* or *uncovered option writing*. Covered option writing is usually undertaken to protect against loss from a drop in the stock's price, as well as to get additional income from the same investment. If you buy 100 shares of Red Hot at $50 and write a call option at $3, you get the $300 premium right away. If Red Hot goes up to $55, you can buy back the option at the current market price, which might be $5, thereby losing $200 ($500 − $300), but you will not have to sell the stock for $50 a share. Moreover, the value of your portfolio will have risen by $500. If you decide not to buy it back, you run the risk that the option's buyer will exercise it and you will have to sell your stock for $5,000 instead of the current market price of $5,500, but you still will keep the $300 you received for the option, so your loss is only $200. Naked option writing is riskier. It is comparable to SELLING SHORT stocks and is profitable only when stock prices are declining. If you sell a Red Hot 50 call for $300 and Red Hot either stays at 50 or goes down, you have the $300 premium. If Red Hot goes up to $60, however, you could either buy back the option or buy enough shares to cover, losing $1,000 minus the $300 premium.

Traders have developed numerous strategies for buying and selling various combinations of options and futures in order to maximize profit and limit risk (see COMBINATION; SPREAD, def. 3), but in the fast-moving, highly leveraged options market these are generally regarded as too complicated (and risky) for all but the most knowledgeable and sophisticated investors. See also FUTURES OPTION; INDEX OPTION; INTEREST-RATE OPTION; RATIO WRITING; STRADDLE.

option premium See PREMIUM, def. 3.

Options Clearing Corporation Abbreviated OCC. A corporation, owned by the stock exchanges dealing in options, that issues all options contracts, guarantees that their terms will be fulfilled, processes the money in such transactions, and maintains records of them. Its prospectus, which spells out the rules, risks, and ethics of options trading, is required reading for all prospective options investors.

options exchange An exchange on which listed options are traded. In the 1980's four American stock exchanges (the American, New York, Philadelphia, and Pacific stock exchanges) handled options trading and a fifth, the Chicago Board Options Exchange, handled options exclusively. In addition to the stock options handled on all stock exchanges, these five traded in stock-index options, interest rate options (on U.S. Treasury notes, bills, and bonds), foreign currency options, and futures options. See also Appendix A.

option spread See SPREAD, def. 3.

or better Abbreviated *OB*. More favorable to the customer, describing a higher selling price or lower buying price on a LIMIT ORDER.

order In the securities and commodities trade, an instruction to a broker or dealer to buy or sell a security or commodity. See LIMIT ORDER; MARKET ORDER; STOP ORDER.

order book official See under BOARD BROKER.

OTC See OVER-THE-COUNTER.

out of the money Describing a call OPTION or a WARRANT whose strike price is higher than the current market price of the underlying investment, or a put option whose strike price is lower than the market price of the underlying investment. For example, if Red Hot stock is selling for $50, a Red Hot Nov 55 call option is said to be out of the money, and the stock would have to rise above 55 for it to have any INTRINSIC VALUE.

outstanding

1. Securities that have been issued and bought, as opposed to securities that have not yet been issued or not yet publicly offered.

2. Describing any obligation that has not yet been met, such as accounts receivable (unpaid bills) or checks that have not cleared.

overbought Describing a security or a market in which vigorous buying has driven prices to an unreasonably high level, which is bound to be driven down by a CORRECTION or by PROFIT TAKING.

overlapping debt The sharing of responsibility for borrowed funds by a municipality and some portion of it, for example, by a county and one or more of its towns, or by two municipalities of equal rank, such as two towns sharing a school district. The existence of such arrangements can be important to prospective investors in municipal bonds, since they affect how much money a locality needs to raise through real estate taxes and other means in order to meet interest payments. See also UNDERLYING DEBT.

overnight repo The most common form of REPURCHASE AGREEMENT, or repo, made for one business day. See also OPEN REPO.

oversold Describing a security or a market in which excessive selling has driven prices to an unreasonably low level, which is bound to be raised by a CORRECTION or a TECHNICAL RALLY.

oversubscribed Also, *overbooked*. Describing a new issue of securities for which there are more buyers than available shares. In some instances the issuer will increase the number of shares; more often, the underwriter will allocate them so that, for example, if an issue is 15 percent oversubscribed each subscriber will receive 85 percent of his or her subscription. Usually such a security will rise sharply in price once it begins to be traded.

over-the-counter Abbreviated *OTC*. Also, *off-board*. The market for securities that are not traded on any organized stock exchange, as well as for some listed securities traded off the exchange (the so-called THIRD MARKET). They include the majority of bonds (corporate, municipal, and government), almost all new stock issues, shares in mutual funds, tax-shelter offerings, annuities and other insurance company securities, and the more than four thousand securities quoted on the nationwide electronic NASDAQ system. The principal difference between the over-the-counter market, which has no physical location, and the stock exchanges is that securities are quoted and sold by telephone or computer on a bid-and-ask basis by dealers, called *market makers*, rather than being sold by public auction as on the exchanges. The market makers buy and sell at their wholesale prices to one another and at retail prices to investors. Thus, although the quality of OTC securities may be as high as those traded on exchanges, the individual investor in effect pays a double markup on OTC transactions, the dealer's retail price and the broker's commission (unless the broker also is a market maker in that particular issue and elects to take only a single markup). Prices and other information about bonds, mutual fund shares, and OTC stocks are printed in the financial pages of large newspapers. Information about less active OTC stocks (which are not part of the NASDAQ National Market System) are available through the *National Stock Summary,* a periodically updated book published by the National Quotation Bureau in New York, and the daily PINK SHEETS to which many brokerage firms subscribe. The over-the-counter market is self-regulated by the National Association of Securities Dealers (NASD), which operates under the supervision of the Securities and Exchange Commission.

overvalued   Describing a security whose current market price is exceedingly high in terms of its price-earnings ratio or earnings forecast, and so can be expected to decline. The high price may result from unusual demand—a burst of buying by institutional investors, for example—or because investors have not yet learned that the company is in financial difficulties or has a poor earnings outlook for other reasons. See also UNDERVALUED.

overwriting   Writing a quantity of put or call options on a security on the assumption that they will not be exercised. The option writer is in effect speculating that a security is so underpriced (for puts) or overpriced (for calls) that it will change in value before the option can be exercised.

P

Pacific Stock Exchange   See Appendix A.

paid-in surplus   Also, *capital surplus, paid-in capital*. The difference contributed by stockholders who bought a corporation's stock at prices above its par value. This figure is stated on the company's balance sheet under stockholders' equity. See also RETAINED EARNINGS.

painting the tape   Frequent appearance of a particular security on the TAPE, indicating an unusual amount of trading. It may be caused by some special interest of investors in the company, or it may be the result of illegal manipulation by group trading among themselves in order to drive the price up.

panic   A wave of financial fear that the economy is going into a deep slump, seen in the securities and commodities markets as a period of frantic selling in hopes of beating all-time low prices. The selling itself can bring on the very decline that is feared. See also BUYERS' PANIC.

paper   General name for any short-term loan, such as commercial paper, bankers' acceptances, and negotiable certificates of deposit.

paper profit (loss)   A profit (loss) that would be realized if the owner or investor sold a property at a given time. Investors often keep track of the paper profits and losses in their portfolios as the market prices of their holdings change, but of course these become true profits and losses only when they sell their holdings.

par bond   A bond selling at par (face) value. See also DISCOUNT BOND; PREMIUM BOND.

parity The current conversion value of a convertible debenture, that is, what it would be worth if it were immediately converted into common stock. To obtain this figure one multiplies the current market price of the stock by the conversion rate (the number of shares into which the debenture is convertible).

partial delivery The delivery of only a portion of the security or commodity involved in a transaction.

participating preferred stock A preferred stock issue stipulating that its holders will receive dividends exceeding the stated dividend payment in the event that common-stock dividends exceed a specific limit. For example, a participating preferred might specify a dividend payment of $5 per share and, if common stock dividends exceed $5, the preferred stockholder will receive the same payout as the holder of common stock. Most preferred-stock issues, however, are *nonparticipating* (do not carry this provision).

participation certificate Abbreviated *PC*. A certificate representing an interest in a pool of mortgages; see under SECONDARY MORTGAGE MARKET.

partnership A form of business organization in which two or more individuals enter a business, pooling their resources and sharing the profits. The principal disadvantage of a partnership is that each partner is legally liable for the entire business's debts. See also LIMITED PARTNERSHIP.

par value Also, *face value, par*. The value of a stock or bond, expressed in dollars and so stated on the certificate. For debt instruments such as bonds, it also signifies the redemption value at maturity. Both term and concept are much less important for common stock, where the par value rarely is related to a stock's market value, and many corporations therefore either issue NO-PAR STOCK or deliberately undervalue the stated par value for tax purposes. For preferred stocks and bonds, however, par value tends to be closer to market value and, except in the case of FLOATING-RATE issues, is the figure on which interest and dividend payments are based.

passed dividend The omission of a dividend payment on common stock or preferred stock. If business has been poor or the company wants more funds to invest in new plant and equipment, the board of directors may vote to omit a dividend. In the case of CUMULATIVE preferred stock, passed dividends must eventually be paid, along with current dividends, before any dividend is paid on common stock.

passive income Income from businesses such as limited partnerships, in which investors do not materially participate. Losses from such investments, according to 1986 tax law, may not be deducted from other income.

pass-through securities See under SECONDARY MORTGAGE MARKET.

paying agent The bank designated in a bond indenture as the payer of bond interest and principal.

payout ratio Also, *dividend payout ratio*. The sum of common and preferred stock cash dividends declared for a year, divided by that year's net profit, expressed as a percentage.

P/E See PRICE-EARNINGS RATIO.

pegging Setting or stabilizing the price of a security, commodity, or currency at some predetermined level. Pegging security prices by heavy trading at the desired price is illegal. The only pegging permitted is that of underwriters who are authorized by the Securities and Exchange Commission to stabilize the market price of a new issue by buying shares in the open market. See also STABILIZATION.

penny stock A low-priced, highly speculative stock, traditionally one that sells for less than $1 per share initially but in practice sometimes rising to as much as $10 per share when there is strong demand for it. All penny stocks are traded over-the-counter and are considered too speculative for heavy investment by the average individual, but occasionally a penny-stock issuer makes large profits from a new venture and the stock proves both sound and profitable.

pension plan A form of investment in which regular contributions over a period of time are invested, with the earnings reinvested, and are paid out as an allowance or other series of regular payments after retirement. The term "pension plan" usually refers to a company plan offered by an employer to employees, to which both make periodic contributions. Similar retirement plans are available to self-employed individuals (see KEOGH PLAN; SIMPLIFIED EMPLOYEE PLAN) and employed individuals (see IRA), and there also are special company plans (see SALARY-REDUCTION PLAN). Company pension plans usually are one of two kinds (although a few companies establish both kinds). A *defined-contribution plan* specifies the size of the periodic contribution to be made (or a rule for determining it). The benefit (payout) will be whatever results from the investments made with the contribution. A *defined-benefit plan,* in contrast, specifies the size of the pension to be received (or a rule for determining it). Contributions to the plan are determined by estimates of what is required to produce that benefit. A major advantage of either kind of pension plan is that it serves as a TAX SHELTER. The company need not pay income tax on its contributions to the plan, and employees pay no tax on money so contributed until it is paid out to them. Earnings from investments made with funds from the plan accumulate tax-free, and payouts from the plan, if made after retirement, receive favorable tax treatment. Investments made with company pension funds, which constitute a huge source of capital, are limited by the PRUDENT-MAN RULE and the LEGAL LIST.

performance fund A MUTUAL FUND that invests primarily in fairly speculative securities in the hope of making large profits quickly.

performance index   An INDEX of investments that takes into account not only stock prices but dividends and other distributions to shareholders.

performance stock   Another name for GROWTH STOCK.

periodic-payment plan   Accumulating additional shares in a mutual fund by means of regular fixed payments, made monthly or bimonthly or quarterly. Most such plans are organized for a specific period, such as ten or twenty years, and arrange for means of withdrawing funds from the plan after a specified time. The periodic-payment plan is a version of the constant-dollar plan; see also FORMULA INVESTING.

perpetual bond   Also, *annuity bond*. A bond that has no maturity date and on which interest is payable indefinitely, without any repayment of the principal.

perpetual warrant   A WARRANT with no expiration date.

pf   In stock listings, abbreviation for PREFERRED STOCK.

Philadelphia Stock Exchange   See Appendix A.

pickup   Colloquial term for a bond SWAP in which a bond is exchanged for another with a similar maturity date but slightly better coupon (interest) rate.

pink sheet   A list of securities being traded in the over-the-counter market (OTC) that is published daily by the National Quotation Bureau and is subscribed to by many brokerage firms. Printed on pink paper (hence the name), it not only lists bid and ask prices for many more OTC securities than are listed in the financial pages but also names the market makers who are trading each stock. See also YELLOW SHEET.

pit   See RING.

plow back   To reinvest earnings in a business rather than pay out dividends. Small, growing firms tend to plow back more than large, well-established companies. See also PLOWBACK RATIO.

plowback ratio   Net profit minus all dividend payments divided by common stock equity (including intangible assets), expressed as a percentage. It shows the percentage of a firm's earnings relative to common stock and measures the extent to which it is reinvesting its earnings in anticipation of future growth. See also REINVESTMENT RATE, def. 1.

plus tick See UP TICK.

point

1. The basic unit of price for trading stocks. In American markets, 1 point = $1, and a stock selling for 36 costs $36 per share. Fractions of points—½, ¼, and ⅛—also are used, representing $.50, $.25, and $.125 respectively.

2. In bond trading, a unit of change in the market value of a bond relative to its par (face) value. Thus 1 point = 1 percent change, signifying a $10 change in market price for a $1,000 bond or a $50 change for a $5,000 bond. See also BASIS POINT.

3. In real estate, a unit of prepaid interest on a loan, 1 point = 1 percent of the amount of the loan. Points are sometimes charged to the mortgagor. In the case of FHA or VA mortgages, points often are paid by the seller at the time of closing.

point and figure chart A chart used in TECHNICAL ANALYSIS in which columns of X's and O's represent rising and falling stock prices. When a stock price moves up, its path is shown by a vertical series of X's; when it moves down, the path is shown by a downward series of O's. With each change of direction the next column to the right is used. Each square on such a chart might denote $1 per share, in which case a move from $35 to $50 would be shown by 15 X's, and a decline from $50 to $45 by 5 O's in the adjacent column to the right. Time is not taken into account at all; the price change might take a month or a year.

poison pill See under MERGER.

pool Combining the resources of a number of individuals or firms to obtain more capital or influence or both. Associations of underwriters (syndicates) to market a large new stock issue or associations of insurers organized to share the premiums and risks of very large or very risky insurance are perfectly legal business entities, as are investors who combine their resources, either informally in an INVESTMENT CLUB or through a large enterprise like a mutual fund. Pools formed for the purpose of manipulating a company's stock to control its market price or to gain a monopoly in a particular industry are illegal. For *mortgage pool*, see SECONDARY MORTGAGE MARKET.

pooling of interest   A method of drawing up the balance sheet that treats two newly merged companies as if they had always been a single entity.

portfolio   The total investment holdings of an individual or organization, including stocks, bonds, real estate, IRA funds, annuities, and similar assets. *Portfolio* or *investment* income refers to dividends and interest from such assets.

portfolio-management program   A personal computer program that keeps track of investment transactions, displays the portfolio structure, updates its market value, and records and computes other relevant information. To use it, one types in information about the portfolio—typically the ticker symbol for each security, when and how much of it was bought at what price and commission, dividends and interest as they accrue, and further purchases and sales. To keep the portfolio up to date, the computer dials a DATABASE and automatically extracts current prices for each security. Or those who prefer to do their own price research can obtain current prices from the financial pages at regular intervals and type them in.

Besides this basic information, useful for obtaining detailed records of income from a portfolio plus information about capital gains and other data that help compute tax liability, various programs offer additional options. These include the ability to calculate compound annual return for every stock owned and how price fluctuations in each holding affect the return on the entire portfolio; lists of realized and unrealized capital gains before and after taxes; reminders of when options and warrants are about to expire, or when securities are about to go long-term and when their prices have passed any limits one has specified; and margin accounts and commissions. One such portfolio-management program creates hypothetical portfolios, does commission accounting (includes commission costs), allows long-term projections of holdings, will enter fractional shares, and can handle up to twenty-six different portfolios at one time (on floppy disks; ten times that number for hard disk.) It can obtain accounting information and automatic valuation of stocks, bonds, Treasury issues, options, and mutual funds, and keeps track of tax obligations for each transaction, as well as brokerage commissions, dividends, interest, stock splits, and portfolio cash balances. Some programs also can do FUNDAMENTAL ANALYSIS and TECHNICAL ANALYSIS. A similar program for commodity futures contracts not only makes available market prices but enables traders to place orders directly by computer, without using a broker. Comparable programs are available for direct stock and options trading and are expected to capture a sizable share of the market by the 1990's.

portfolio theory   Also, *modern portfolio management, portfolio-management theory.* The theoretical bases for selecting and managing one's investments so as to minimize risk and maximize return. The simplest and most important way to reduce risk is to diversify one's holdings; in common stock most experts believe that one should spread one's interests among at least twenty stocks. An obvious way to increase reward (profit) is to use leverage, either by buying the stocks of companies themselves highly leveraged (using borrowed funds to increase their earnings) or by MARGIN TRADING. Using leverage, however, increases risk. Further, what is risky for one investor—for example, the long-term investor interested in compounding dividend income—is less so for the short-term investor. Portfolio managers frequently rely on technical analysis of one kind or another to assess the risk of specific securities against overall market performance. The calculations used have been greatly facilitated by the use of computer programs whereby one can select securities that satisfy a given set of requirements, for example, 25 percent in fixed-income securities, no more than 5 percent in a single stock, a minimum average current yield of 7 percent, and so on. (See also SCREENING.)

position   See LONG POSITION; SHORT POSITION.

position limit   The maximum amount of options in a single security allowed by the exchange to be bought or sold by any individual or group of persons acting together.

post

    1. In accounting, to transfer financial data into a ledger.

    2. See TRADING POST.

power of attorney   A written authorization to perform certain acts on behalf of the principal (signer). It may be either a full power of attorney or a limited power of attorney and must be witnessed by a notary public in order to be valid. It expires (becomes void) when the principal dies. A broker given a full power of attorney has complete discretion over the assets in question, whereas a limited power of attorney would allow only transactions in an existing account. See also DISCRETIONARY ACCOUNT; STOCK POWER.

precedence   See PRIORITY.

precious metals   Metals whose scarcity value and aesthetic appeal have made them vehicles for investment. The principal metals so regarded are GOLD and SILVER. To a much lesser extent platinum and palladium are also so regarded and traded.

precious stones   See GEM INVESTMENT.

preemptive rights   See RIGHTS.

preferred stock   A security that, like common stock, represents ownership in a corporation but has a claim ahead of common stock on the payment of dividends and on the corporation's assets in the event it is dissolved. Preferred stock is junior (subordinate) to all debt that a company owes (in the form of bonds, notes, and debentures, for example) but is senior to common stock and so is considered a senior security. The dividend paid on preferred stock usually is at a set rate, similar to the coupon rate of bonds, so preferreds are classed as a fixed-income security. Unlike bond interest, however, preferred dividends may be decreased or even omitted at the discretion of the company's directors. Most preferred stocks carry a CUMULATIVE DIVIDEND. Also, unlike common stock, preferred stock rarely gives its holders voting rights or, unless it is PARTICIPATING PREFERRED STOCK, the right to share in corporate profits. Most preferred stocks are CALLABLE at prices set when they were issued and can be redeemed in full or in part at intervals to retire the stock gradually over a period of time. Some issues are CONVERTIBLE PREFERRED STOCK, exchangeable for common stock.

If a company is liquidated, the money due to preferred stockholders is equal to the par (face) value of the stock, the price at which it was originally issued. Newly issued preferred stock is sold with a par value of $25, $50, or $100. The dividend is stated in one of two ways, either as a percentage of par or as a dollar amount per share. Thus a share of preferred with $100 par value might have an annual payout equal to 12.5 percent of par, or it may be stated as $12.50 per share. It usually is paid quarterly. Some issues of preferred stock are *guaranteed*, that is, a corporation other than the issuer guarantees the dividend payments. Another variety of preferred stock has an *adjustable-rate* (also called variable-rate or floating-rate) dividend. The dividends paid out are pegged to the current level of interest rates on various Treasury securities and are adjusted quarterly.

Most preferred stocks are listed on the major stock exchanges; the rest trade in the over-the-counter market, where spreads (the difference between bid and ask prices) can raise investors' costs. Such spreads tend to be higher on preferred than on common stock.

Both the major bond-rating agencies, Moody's Investor Service and Standard & Poor's Corporation, also rate preferred stock issues, on the basis of the likelihood that their dividends will be paid as promised. One can also invest in preferred stocks through a mutual fund specializing in them; such funds frequently favor the adjustable-rate preferred issues.

premium

1. For a fixed-income security such as a bond, the amount by which its market price exceeds its par (face) value or book value. See also CONVERSION PREMIUM; PREMIUM BOND.

2. For a common stock, the amount by which its price exceeds some other price, for example, a tender offer for it over the current market price, or the price of one stock over comparable stocks of similar firms in the same industry.

3. In trading options, the price paid by the buyer of puts and calls, and conversely, the price received by the seller (writer) of such options. This price depends on a number of factors. A strong demand for certain options will raise their premium; conversely, a large supply relative to demand will decrease it. Another factor is INTRINSIC VALUE, the difference between strike price and the price of the underlying security. A third factor is TIME VALUE; the longer the life of the option, the higher the premium. As expiration approaches, the time value decreases, and at maturity it disappears entirely. Finally, the volatility of the underlying security affects the premium as well. Although the degree of volatility is a subjective judgment, the higher it is deemed to be, the higher the premium (because there is a potentially larger chance of great price change and great profit). See also OPTION.

4. In the commodities market, the amount by which the forward price exceeds the spot price of a commodity.

5. In the coin market, the amount by which the price of a coin exceeds the value of its metallic content.

6. In insurance, the payment made to keep an insurance policy in force or to purchase an annuity.

premium bond Also, *cushion bond*. A bond selling at a price above its par (face) value. Most often it is a security that was issued when interest rates were much higher than currently, so that the fixed coupon rate of the bond attracts more buyers, causing its price to rise. The difference between the purchase price and par value affects the total return on the investment (see YIELD TO MATURITY). Generally, buyers of premium bonds do so for the extra current income (in the form of high interest payments) so generated, which can be reinvested (or spent) immediately, and are willing to accept the lower redemption price at maturity.

prepaid expense An expense paid in advance, such as rent for a year, or insurance premiums. On the balance sheet such payments appear as current assets.

prepayment Payment of an obligation before it is due.

prerefunding See under REFUNDING.

present value method See DISCOUNTED CASH FLOW.

price-earnings ratio Also, *P/E ratio, multiple*. The current market price of a stock divided by the company's earnings per share over a twelve-month period. A stock selling for $75 a share and earning $15 a share has a P/E of 5. Normally appearing with stock-price quotations in the newspaper, the P/E is widely regarded as a yardstick for investors. The higher it is, the more they are paying for a stock, and therefore they expect a greater increase in earnings. A high P/E—20 or higher—signals a more volatile stock than a low one—10 or lower. The former is typical of a young, fast-growing concern, whose stock may pay no dividends but is expected to advance in value rapidly. The latter tends to be that of a company in a mature industry, a well-established secure firm, or one that has fallen out of public favor, and generally pays a good dividend but is not expected to advance much in price. See also MARKET MULTIPLE; PRICE-SALES RATIO; RELATIVE MULTIPLE.

price gap Also, *gap*. A blank space between the prices of a security on two successive trading days, no trading having taken place at the intervening prices. A downward gap occurs when the high price of a stock on a given day is lower than for the previous day's low price, for example, a stock closing at 12, opening at 10, and continuing to decline. An upward gap signifies that the low price on a given day is higher than the previous day's high. The term "gap" is used because this situation leaves an empty space on a chart of the stock's price (see also CHARTIST).

price limit The maximum price change in one day's trading in a particular commodity that is permitted by the commodity futures exchange where that commodity is traded.

price-sales ratio Also, *market value/revenues ratio, P/S ratio*. The current market price of a stock divided by its sales per share. Thus, if a corporation has $50 million in annual sales and 2 million shares of common stock outstanding, its sales per share is $25, and if its current price is $15, it has a price-sales ratio of 15/25, or 0.60. (The number of shares outstanding can be learned from a stock guide or from the company itself.) Analysts who consider this figure significant advise buying or holding stocks with a low price-sales ratio (0.75 or less) and selling or avoiding those with a high P/S (1.5 to 3.0 or higher). They believe that the best investments are stocks in companies whose prices do not sufficiently reflect sales revenues and consequently are not in high demand, whereas those with high price-sales ratios are too popular (overpriced). Most authorities, however, believe this figure should be used only in conjunction with other information, such as a company's balance sheet, market share, management, and debt level.

price stability index See under INDEX.

primary distribution Also, *primary offering*. The sale of a new issue of stocks or bonds. It may or may not also be an INITIAL PUBLIC OFFERING. The term "primary" distinguishes it from SECONDARY DISTRIBUTION, which involves the sale of previously issued stock.

primary earnings See under EARNINGS PER SHARE.

primary market The market for new issues of securities, newly created futures contracts and options, and new mortgages.

prime paper See under COMMERCIAL PAPER.

prime rate Also, *the prime*. The rate of interest charged by commercial banks on short-term loans to their highest-quality ("prime") business customers. Rates to borrowers of less than the highest quality are correspondingly higher than the prime rate, which thus becomes the most significant bank interest rate and was, until the late 1970's, considered an important measure of the entire money market. Since then, however, large corporations have found other sources of short-term funds, such as borrowing from each other (so-called prime commercial paper) and in the Eurodollar market, and deregulation of American banks made it possible for them to adjust interest rates on their deposits. Consequently the prime rate, while still important, is regarded as only one of several measures of the cost of lending or borrowing short-term funds.

principal
   1. A person being represented in a transaction by an agent, for example, the signer of a power of attorney.
   2. The amount of capital that is being invested or lent, as distinct from dividends, profits, or interest. The amount an investor pays for securities represents principal.
   3. Also, *principal amount.* The face amount of a bond or other debt instrument; the same as its face value or par value.

principal stockholder   A shareholder who owns a significant percentage of a corporation's outstanding shares, according to Securities and Exchange Commission rules, 10 percent or more (5 percent as shown on a proxy statement).

priority
   1. The order of precedence of claims on assets. In bankruptcy various classes of creditor have priority over others (said to be junior to them) in claims on assets. With a corporation, bondholders have priority over preferred stockholders, who have priority over common stockholders in sharing earnings (in the form of interest and dividends) and, in case of liquidation,

claiming the assets. In the case of a mortgage on real estate, a *first mortgage* has priority over a *second mortgage*.

2. Also, *precedence*. The order of precedence used in an auction market such as an organized stock exchange, where the first bid or ask at a given price must be executed before other bids and offers at the same price, no matter what size of order is involved. Similarly, off-floor orders must be executed before orders originating on the exchange. See also MATCHED AND LOST.

prior lien bond A bond whose holder has a senior claim over other bondholders of the same company. Such bonds generally are issued by companies in bankruptcy or other financial difficulty.

private corporation See CLOSED CORPORATION.

private placement Also, *direct placement*. Selling a whole issue of securities directly to investors, without using an intermediary such as an underwriter. Bonds frequently are sold in this way, usually to one or more large institutional investors. Not only does this save the cost of underwriting, but private placements need not be registered with the Securities and Exchange Commission provided the investors are few in number (no more than thirty-five, not counting any qualifying as an ACCREDITED INVESTOR). A private LIMITED PARTNERSHIP is also considered a private placement.

proceeds The actual amount received by a seller after deducting expenses, commissions, etc. Similarly, the actual amount received by a borrower after interest has been deducted.

proceeds sale In the over-the-counter market, the sale of one security in order to purchase another with the proceeds. The National Association of Securities Dealers holds that this should be treated as a single transaction in terms of the dealer's profit.

produce exchange   Older name for COMMODITY FUTURES EXCHANGE.

production rate   The coupon (interest) rate of a Ginnie Mae security, which by law is always .005 (½ of 1 percent) less than the rate on the underlying mortgages.

profit   Also, *earnings*. Any excess of income over the costs of obtaining it. For investors it means the difference between a security's purchase price and its current (higher) market price. For a business the term is further refined into GROSS PROFIT, NET INCOME, and OPERATING MARGIN. See also INCOME STATEMENT.

profit-and-loss statement   Another name for INCOME STATEMENT.

profit margin   Gross profit expressed as a percentage of net sales. It is calculated by subtracting the cost of goods sold from net sales, and dividing the result by net sales. See also OPERATING MARGIN.

profit taking   The selling of securities or commodity futures by investors in response to a sudden rise in price, so they can cash in on their profit. It results in a sudden market decline.

pro forma   Latin for "as a matter of form," a phrase used on financial statements that are complete and accurate except for some small matter of detail.

program trading   The use of computer programs to place orders from institutional investors and other professional traders to buy or sell shares in large companies that are representative of the broader Standard & Poor's Index of 500 stocks. Such programs are often set in motion by ARBITRAGE opportunities when the current value of stocks reflected by Standard & Poor's 500 and the price of a STOCK-INDEX FUTURE on that index are out of line, with the index future level above or below the actual index level by an abnormal amount. When that occurs, traders quickly try to take advantage of the price difference by buying futures in one market and selling stocks in another, or vice versa. As a result, when a wave of such transactions reaches the market at the same time, the available supplies of stock are temporarily absorbed and the prices of the market indexes move sharply up or down. Thus, although such arbitrage is profitable only for very large investors who can trade very rapidly by means of computer-generated buy or sell orders sent to the exchange floor even before the trading decision is made, it affects the rest of the market, at least temporarily.

project note   Abbreviated *PN*. A short-term municipal security, usually issued by a housing authority and guaranteed by the U.S. Department of Housing and Urban Development (HUD), to finance public housing. After the housing has been constructed, the notes are redeemed by means of long-term bonds, similarly guaranteed by HUD.

proprietorship   A business that has a single owner, who is personally liable for all claims against it and solely responsible for raising capital to expand it.

pro rate   To assign a portion of a cost to a particular account according to some given formula.

prospectus   Also, *offering circular*. A formal offer to sell securities that informs potential buyers of a new issue as to the financial condition of the issuer, its history, current officers and directors, outstanding securities, past performance (in terms of profit and loss), and other factors. For a public offering the prospectus must be filed with the Securities and Exchange Commission as well as given to potential buyers. Prospectuses also are issued by mutual funds, describing the fund, offering shares for sale, and outlining investment goals, policies, services, restrictions, officers and directors, method of purchasing and redeeming shares, charges, and recent financial statements. Limited partnership offerings in real estate, oil and gas, equipment leasing, and the like similarly prepare prospectuses giving information about finances, the general partners, and so on.

protective covenant In an INDENTURE, the portion that promises to protect bondholders by setting rules that will assure payment of interest and principal.

proxy A written authorization from a stockholder to some other individual that authorizes a specific vote at a stockholders' meeting. Before proxies may be solicited, the Securities and Exchange Commission requires that stockholders be informed of the issues in a *proxy statement*. Should there be disagreement between the company's existing management and another group, there may be a *proxy fight*, in which each side tries to solicit the support of a majority of shareholders.

prudent-man rule An investment standard for pension funds, insurance companies, trustees, executors, and other fiduciary investors that is contained in the laws of many states. It states that such a fiduciary must act prudently, with discretion and intelligence, seeking reasonable income and preservation of capital without needless speculation. The Employee Retirement Income Security Act of 1974 expanded this rule to include the criterion of knowledgeability and the need for diversification in order to reduce risk. States that do not invoke the prudent-man rule usually have a LEGAL LIST.

public housing authority bond A long-term municipal bond issued by a local housing authority to finance low-income housing. The bonds are marketed through the U.S. Department of Housing and Urban Development (HUD), which also guarantees payment of interest and principal.

publicly held A corporation whose shares are freely available to the public. In the United States such a corporation is regulated by the Securities and Exchange Commission.

public offering Another term for DISTRIBUTION, def. 1.

purchase and sale statement Abbreviated *P & S*. A statement sent by a commission house (commodity broker) to a customer to show that the purchase and sale of a contract has been wholly or partly offset. The statement generally shows the quantities and prices of the commodity contract in question, gross profit or loss, commission charges, and net profit or loss.

put An option contract for the right to sell a certain security, commodity, or futures contract at a certain price within a certain time. Investors in puts expect the price of the underlying security to go down. They can use puts in a number of ways, for example, to protect against price declines in the stocks they already own, or to protect their business against a sharp decline in the overall economy. See under OPTION for further information.

putable bond Also, *put bond*. A long-term bond with a PUT option, which allows the holder to redeem the bond early, as in three or four years, at various prices. Holders usually are notified of the approaching put date (when they may exercise their option), but they generally must notify either their broker or the tender agent if they wish to sell their bonds at the agreed-upon price.

pyramid Also, *pyramiding*. The use of paper profits

in a margin account as collateral for additional MAR-
GIN TRADING. For example, one can buy 300 shares
of a $20 stock on margin, putting up $3,000, the
required 50 percent, in cash. If the stock advances to
$22, one has a 10 percent greater equity in the mar-
gin account, or $3,300, and can buy $300 worth
more shares without putting up more cash.

quasi-public corporation A corporation whose stock is publicly owned and traded and which is privately operated, but which has some kind of government backing. For example, FANNIE MAE and SALLIE MAE, which both were founded to encourage secondary loan markets, are quasi-public corporations.

questioned trade Abbreviated *QT*. Also, *don't know*. A discrepancy in the comparison sheets brokers exchange with one another to verify transactions.

quick asset Another name for LIQUID ASSET.

quick-asset ratio Also, *acid-test ratio, quick ratio.* A measure of financial liquidity, calculated by dividing liquid assets (current assets minus inventories) by current liabilities. A ratio of 1:1 is considered satisfactory. See also CURRENT RATIO.

quotation Also, *bid and asked quote.* In the securities trade, the highest price offered by a buyer and the lowest price acceptable to a seller at any given time. For example, a quotation of 13½ to 13 ⅞ means that $13.50 is the highest price offered for this stock by a buyer and $13.925 is the lowest price the seller will accept. A quotation is assumed to be for a round lot (100 shares of stock).

quote terminal An electronic device that displays a summary of detailed information, on demand, for any specific stock requested. The data include high and low transaction prices for the year, the daily opening price, current bid and ask prices, price-earnings ratio, dividend information, and the like. There are several brands of quote terminal, among them Quotron and Bunker Ramo, and their arrangement and the information they contain vary. Some can be used by over-the-counter traders to enter bid and ask prices for NASDAQ securities; others are limited to obtaining stock quotations. Quote terminals have become increasingly available in brokerage offices, banks, and other public places, and scaled-down models are available for home use.

R

r
> **1.** In stock tables, indication that this amount was declared or paid in dividends in the preceding twelve months, plus a STOCK DIVIDEND.
> **2.** In bond tables, abbreviation for *registered bond*.
> **3.** In options tables, indication that this option was not traded during the period covered.

raid   See *bear raid*, under BEAR.

raider   An individual or firm that wants to take over a company. See MERGER.

rally   Also, *upturn*. In the securities and commodity markets, a brisk rise in prices, usually following a decline. See also TECHNICAL RALLY.

RAN   Abbreviation for *revenue anticipation note*.

random walk   The hypothesis that security and commodity prices are no more predictable than the walking pattern of a casual stroller, so that studying past prices (technical analysis) or the issuing companies (fundamental analysis) will be of no use to investors. Provided one diversifies sufficiently, one can profit from choosing a number of stocks at random and holding them for a long enough time.

range   The high and low price of a commodity or security over a given period of time. Technical analysts follow these figures closely, watching for a marked change (see BREAKOUT). The financial pages of newspapers report annual high and low price ranges of stocks traded on the New York and American stock exchanges, as well as over-the-counter.

rate base   The total investment on which a public utility is allowed to earn a return. The investment usually is calculated as the net original cost of plant and equipment plus some allowance for working capital, materials, and supplies, and the total is called *value* or *fair value*. The profit that the utility is permitted to earn on this amount, which is determined by federal, state, or local regulators, is called the *fair rate of return*. Ideally, it is set high enough for the company to maintain service and attract sufficient capital investment but not so high that it exploits customers.

rate covenant In a municipal REVENUE BOND, the portion of the bond agreement that resolves to set user rates for the facility being financed so as to assure payment of bond interest and principal.

rate of return The rate of profit relative to the amount of capital invested. For investments it is a synonym of YIELD.

rating

1. Also, *credit rating*. An evaluation of a borrower's financial trustworthiness. See under CREDIT, def. 1.

2. A comparative evaluation of the safety and profitability of various investments, provided by a BOND-RATING AGENCY or an investment service. Current leaders in this area in the United States are Fitch Investor's Service, Moody's Investor Service, Standard & Poor's Corporation, and Value Line Investment Survey. Although their publications are available only by subscription, many public libraries are among their subscribers.

3. Also, *rate-making*. In insurance, setting rates for various kinds of protection, based on estimates of risk of loss. There are three principal kinds of rating: *class rate,* for many homogeneous clients; *schedule system,* a base rate adjusted for higher or lower risk in particular clients (such as for life insurance, a history of cancer; for fire insurance, presence of a

warning and sprinkler system); and *experience rating,* based on the particular experience of the insured (such as past automobile accidents for car insurance).

ratio writing   Writing (selling) one covered call OP-TION, for which one owns the underlying security, and one or more naked calls, for which one does not own the security.

reacquired stock   Another name for TREASURY STOCK.

real estate, investing in   Purchasing an interest in land and/or buildings in order to realize a profit. Real estate investment ranges from direct personal investment, such as the purchase of a house, condominium, or cooperative dwelling for the investor's personal use, to such indirect means as a savings account in a savings bank or savings and loan association, whose deposits are largely invested in home mortgages. Other means of real estate investment include the purchase of mortgage-backed securities, issued either by federal agencies or private institutions (see SECONDARY MORTGAGE MARKET), or of shares in a REAL ESTATE INVESTMENT TRUST or REAL ESTATE PARTNERSHIP. The advantages of indirect over direct real estate investment are considerable: One need put up only a few thousand dollars (or even a few hundred) and one avoids the costs of direct ownership (such as property taxes, insurance, maintenance and repairs, and management). Nevertheless, direct real estate investment appeals to many because the potential yield is huge compared to other investments. Real estate purchases are nearly always heavily leveraged; most buyers borrow as much as 80 to 90 percent of the purchase price of a house. Therefore every $1 of cash can be matched by $8 or $9 of mortgage money. During a period of inflation, the interest paid on a mortgage or other debt is offset by a decline in purchasing power of what is still owed. Therefore interest becomes equivalent to repaying the principal. Moreover, interest payments are deductible from taxable income. If a mortgage finances an investment that appreciates in value but produces little or no income, the investor's tax payments are pushed off to the future, when they can be paid with depreciated dollars (which buy less owing to inflation). Of course, some real estate investors are seeking income as well as appreciation in value, and buy property that yields generous rental income. Such income is taxed as regular income. Apart from the costs of ownership, which can be large enough to offset both rental income and property value appreciation, there are other disadvantages to direct investment in real estate other than one's own primary residence. Inflation may end and property values drop. Changes in tax law may work to the owner's disadvantage. Finally, real estate is not liquid. It may be extremely difficult to get rid of a property one no longer wants, especially if the general economic climate has become less favorable. Consequently most experts suggest that most investment real estate is not suitable for those who cannot afford to tie up a sizable amount of money for a long period of time.

real estate investment trust   Abbreviated REIT. A trust, association, or corporation that is established for investing in and managing real estate and mortgages. In order to qualify for exemption from corporate income tax, it must distribute 95 percent of its ordinary income to beneficiaries (shareholders), and at least 75 percent of its assets must be real estate, cash or cash items, and government securities. REITs are similar to mutual funds in that they sell shares to investors and use the proceeds to invest in real estate, either in income-producing properties or in mortgages for construction and development projects. As with mutual funds, capital gains are passed through to the individual investor and these are taxed at lower rate than ordinary income. See also MORTGAGE REIT.

real estate partnership A group formed to invest in real estate—commercial and industrial properties, such as hotels, shopping centers, and warehouses, as well as residential property—for profit and/or tax benefits. (See also TAX SHELTER.) Typically it is a LIMITED PARTNERSHIP. The returns come in three forms: tax advantages, income from rentals, and appreciation in property value. For example, suppose a group of forty limited partners puts up $5,000 each, or a total of $200,000, and borrows an additional $170,000. After sales fees of $30,000, the remaining $340,000 is used to buy an apartment building. The $170,000 borrowed is a twenty-five-year mortgage at 13 percent interest, the building will be sold after six years, and there will be a 5 percent increase each year in operating expenses, rental income, and property value. In six years, each investor could expect a total of $1,707 in nontaxable cash flow from operations (no tax is paid because it is offset by deductions). Then there are additional tax deductions for interest and depreciation (the declining value of the building allowed under tax laws) totaling $534; Finally, after giving some profit to the general partner, each limited partner would receive $2,221 after taxes at the time of the sale. The return on the initial investment thus would be about 9 percent per year.

The advantages of real estate over other tax-sheltered partnerships are that it is easily understood, it can be leveraged (financed by debt, usually in the form of mortgages), there is a steady cash flow from rent, its value may appreciate considerably, and partners are not liable for more than their investment. The disadvantages or risks are rising interest rates, problems with occupancy and financing, and the 1986 tax law provision that losses be deducted only from PASSIVE INCOME. Some real estate partnerships are income-oriented rather than sheltered, that is, they concentrate on generating a stream of cash. These may be appropriate for investors who wish to diversify their portfolios by adding real estate to their stock and bond holdings. In contrast, tax-sheltered partnerships are mainly for those in high tax brackets who want to take advantage of tax write-offs.

In general, any real estate partnership is considered riskier than a money-market fund. Among the issues a prospective investor is advised to investigate are: whether the property in question has been resold several times during a short period for ever higher amounts in a possible attempt to overinflate its value and thereby increase depreciation benefits; the fees involved, which go to the general partner, the broker selling the partnership, real estate brokers, and other middlemen (they probably should not amount to more than 25 percent of the investor's money); the general partner's past record and experience with similar projects; who will be paid when the project is sold; and the economics of the particular project (Is it in a growing locality? Is there a need for the buildings proposed? and so on). Partnerships that borrow as much as 80 percent of the purchase price of their property are considered risky; 60 percent is normal. Also, the partnership should not confine itself to three or fewer properties in a single region. Buying properties under construction is riskier than buying those already built and renting, and fully occupied ones carry the least risk. In order of risk some authorities list properties as follows, from least to most risk: shopping malls, large office buildings, small office buildings, apartment buildings, hotels.

real rate of return The return on investments adjusted for inflation. In the case of a fixed-income security such as a bond, it is calculated by taking the annual yield and reducing it by the yearly rise in the cost of living.

recapitalization Altering the capital structure of a corporation by exchanging the securities outstanding, such as preferred stock for common stock, bonds for stock, or debentures for some other kind of bond. Bankruptcy may force a company to recapitalize, the bondholders either receiving common stock or some kind of INCOME BOND. Recapitalization also may be a means to improve a company's credit rating, by replacing bonds with stocks to reduce the debt on the balance sheet and enabling more borrowing, or to reduce its tax liability by exchanging bonds for preferred stock and thereby deducting bond interest. It also has been used as a device to prevent an unfriendly takeover; the target company reduces the floating supply of common stock by increased borrowing, which finances buying back shares of its own stock. See also CORPORATE RESTRUCTURING.

recapture The amount of gain on the sale of a depreciable property that represents depreciation charges previously taken for tax purposes. Recapture taxes must be paid on investment tax credits taken at the time of purchase if the assets are sold before a sufficient holding period has elapsed.

receivables Short for ACCOUNTS RECEIVABLE and NOTES RECEIVABLE.

receiver A court-appointed person who takes charge of the property or funds involved in a legal dispute or bankruptcy. The receiver conducts the business as directed by the court and collects rents and other income from it but does not take title to the property. A company so administered is said to be *in receivership*.

recession An extended, widespread decline in overall economic activity, characterized by a rise in unemployment, and decreased general output (GROSS NATIONAL PRODUCT). See also BUSINESS CYCLE.

record date Also, *date of record*. The date on which a shareholder must be registered on a company's books in order to be entitled to a dividend or voting rights. See also EX-DIVIDEND.

recourse loan A loan entitling the lender to collect from the guarantor or endorser in the event the borrower defaults. Under a *nonrecourse loan*, which is common practice in financing real estate projects, the lender's sole security for repayment is the mortgage on the property, and the lender expressly disclaims any right to proceeds against the borrower. In the case of a REAL ESTATE LIMITED PARTNERSHIP, the lender therefore cannot call the assets of the general or the limited partners to repay the debt or interest on the loan.

recovery
   1. A rise in economic activity following a recession. The term is applied to the economy as a whole and to the securities market, where it is synonymous with RALLY.
   2. In accounting, the absorption of cost through assigning depreciation.

redeemable bond Another name for CALLABLE BOND.

redemption
   1. The repurchase of a security by its issuer.
   2. Another term for call (see CALLABLE BOND).
   3. The conversion of a currency into gold or silver by the currency's issuer.

redemption price
   1. Also, *bid price, liquidating price*. The amount per share paid to an investor in a mutual fund when the shares are cashed in, which depends on the market value of the fund's portfolio at that time. It

usually is equal to the NET ASSET VALUE per share, but some companies charge a small fee for redemption. With a closed-end investment company the redemption price is equal to the highest price offered in the exchange market.

2. Also, *call price*. The price at which a CALLABLE BOND or preferred stock can be redeemed by the issuer.

red herring   A preliminary PROSPECTUS for a new issue of securities given to brokers to attract new investors before the completed prospectus comes out. It is so called because on the front page, in red ink, it announces that the information therein is subject to change and therefore does not constitute a firm offer to sell.

rediscounting   Discounting again a negotiable instrument, such as a bankers' acceptance or commercial paper, that has already been discounted. The bank, which has exchanged the instrument for cash minus interest at the current rate (deducted in advance; see DISCOUNT, def. 3) then may discount the instrument again with another bank or with its Federal Reserve bank. For this reason the Federal Reserve interest rate, or DISCOUNT RATE, is also called *rediscount rate*.

refinancing

1. Exchanging one loan for another at a lower interest rate or a more favorable maturity date or both. Homeowners, for example, may decide to exchange an existing long-term mortgage for a new shorter-term one when interest rates drop. Although they will have to make higher monthly payments owing to the shorter term of the loan, the total payments over the life of the loan will be considerably less.

2. Synonym for REFUNDING.

refunding   Also, *refinancing*. Floating a new bond issue in order to retire an existing one. It most often is done to take advantage of a decline in interest rates but sometimes simply to extend the term of the loan. If the new issue is floated before the older issue can be called in (see CALLABLE BOND), the process is called *prerefunding*. Similarly, *advance refunding* refers to the practice of allowing bondholders to exchange bonds that are due to mature soon for a new issue on exceptionally favorable terms. Advance refunding is done principally with Treasury bonds. A bond indenture may carry a provision forbidding refunding at any time, until some specified future time, or only at a specific coupon rate. Such a bond issue is said to be *nonrefundable*.

regional stock exchange Basically, an American exchange outside New York City; see under STOCK EXCHANGE.

register A corporation's listing of all its shareholders, which is maintained by the firm itself or by a transfer agent.

registered bond A bond whose owner's name is recorded with the issuer (or its proper agent). Interest payments are made to the holder automatically, without the submission of coupons (see COUPON BOND). To transfer ownership, the registered holder must endorse the bond. All municipal bonds issued after June 30, 1983, have by law been registered bonds.

registered coupon bond A bond that is registered for payment of the principal (upon redemption) but not of interest, which is payable to whoever submits the coupons when they come due (see COUPON BOND).

registered (competitive) trader See FLOOR TRADER, def. 1.

registered representative Also, *account executive, customer's man*. Employee of a brokerage firm who takes customers' orders and passes them on to the firm's floor broker on the exchange for execution. To qualify, one must pass a series of tests concerning the

securities business (see under BROKER), entitling one
to be "registered" and to "represent" floor brokers
in accepting customers' orders.

registrar   An individual charged with keeping track of
the owners of a corporation's securities and making
sure that it issues no more than are authorized. He or
she works with the TRANSFER AGENT in keeping up-to-
date files of bondholders and stockholders.

registration   A system of review of securities to be
sold to the public by the Securities and Exchange
Commission (SEC). A firm marketing a new issue
must first file a *registration statement* with the SEC,
giving detailed financial information about itself, its
history, and the issue, including its purpose. See also
BLUE-SKY LAWS.

regression analysis   A statistical technique for estimating the relationship between a dependent variable
and one or more other independent variables, in order
to predict the future value of the dependent variable.
The degree to which the dependent variable responds
to changes in the independent variable—for example,
the amount of coffee that is sold relative to changes
in the price of tea—is called the *regression coefficient*
or *correlation coefficient.* A correlation coefficient of
1 means that coffee purchases are directly related to
tea price and move together; − 1 means they move in
opposite directions (the more tea costs, the less coffee is bought); 0 means there is no relationship. The
regression coefficient between the rates of return on a
stock and that on the market as a whole is called the
BETA coefficient. The mathematics involved in regression analysis is performed much more readily by
computer, and there are a number of programs available for personal computers that will help determine,
for example, the relation between a stock's yield and
its price appreciation over a given time. Using such a
program, one enters for a group of twenty or so

stocks in the same industry the yield and price change for each over one year. The program can chart the relationship between these two sets of figures and create a *regression line,* whose slope shows how the numbers relate to one another. It may indicate, perhaps, that stocks with a higher yield appreciate more in price over the year. The regression line then can be used to predict future performance based on the known variable.

regular dividend A DIVIDEND that is declared and paid at regular intervals, such as quarterly, semiannually, or annually.

regular way delivery Standard delivery and payment terms for exchange-traded securities, which for the New York Stock Exchange means the buyer must pay cash and the broker deliver stocks by the fifth business day following the transaction. For money-market instruments and government securities, however, settlement must be made on the next business day.

regulated investment company An INVESTMENT COMPANY that meets certain requirements of the Internal Revenue Service so that it need not pay income tax on either income or capital gains. Instead, it passes its profits on to its shareholders, who then pay whatever taxes are required.

Regulation A

1. A provision of the Securities and Exchange Commission for simplifying the registration of smaller issues of securities, involving a shorter registration form and a brief offering circular instead of a lengthy prospectus.

2. A provision of the Federal Reserve Board concerning the conditions under which Federal Reserve banks make loans to members and other banks at the discount rate.

Regulation G Ruling of the Federal Reserve Board

concerning persons or organizations other than banks, brokers, or dealers who extend or maintain credit for margin trading, including provisions for corporations and credit unions that extend credit for employee stock option and purchase plans. The regulation covers in detail the kind and amount of collateral to be put up for such purposes.

Regulation T   A Federal Reserve Board rule governing the extension of credit by and to security brokers and dealers. It imposes, among other obligations, initial margin requirements and payment rules on securities transactions. It sets forth the required margin—that is, what a customer must put up in cash—for margin trading. In the mid-1980's the initial margin was 50 percent of the current market value of the security, except for exempted securities, registered nonconvertible debt securities (bonds), or over-the-counter margin bonds. (Exempted securities are all U.S. government securities, municipal bonds, and bonds of the International Bank for Reconstruction and Development.) Different rules applied to short sales on stock options. Regulation T does not preclude the imposition of still stricter rules by stock exchanges or brokerage houses.

Regulation U   A Federal Reserve Board rule concerning the amount of credit banks may extend for margin trading that is secured by margin stock.

Regulation X   A Federal Reserve Board rule applying its credit restrictions for margin trading to Americans and foreigners acting on their behalf who obtain credit outside the United States to carry U.S. securities or within the United States to carry any securities.

Regulation Z   Federal Reserve Board rule that reenforces the Consumer Credit Protection Act of 1968 (also known as the Truth in Lending Act), which requires that lenders must spell out to borrowers the annual percentage rate of interest, possible total cost, and other details of lending terms.

rehypothecation See under HYPOTHECATION.

reinvestment privilege The automatic reinvestment of dividends paid by a mutual fund.

reinvestment rate

1. The proportion of a firm's earnings that it reinvests in the business, expressed as a percentage of equity capital. See also PLOWBACK RATIO.

2. The interest rate at which the proceeds from a fixed-income investment can be reinvested.

REIT Abbreviation for *real estate investment trust*.

relative multiple Also, *relative price-earning ratio, relative P/E*. The proportion of a particular stock's price-earnings ratio to that of the market as a whole (see MARKET MULTIPLE). Thus, a stock with a P/E of 24 when the market multiple was 12 would have a relative multiple of 2.0, suggesting that it might be overpriced.

remargining Putting up more cash or eligible securities in response to a MARGIN CALL.

renegotiable rate mortgage See under MORTGAGE.

reorganization bond See INCOME BOND.

repo See REPURCHASE AGREMENT.

repurchase agreement Abbreviated *repo, RP*. A contract whereby an investment is sold with the stipulation that the seller will buy it back (repurchase it) at a specified price and, normally, on a specified date. It is, in effect, a loan in which the investment serves as collateral and the difference between selling price and repurchase price represents interest. The investment may consist of bonds, notes, certificates of deposit, or other securities, but most often is U.S. government securities. Repos were long used only by the Federal Reserve in its open-market operations and by large banks dealing with one another to fulfill their short-term needs for cash, and as such they are freely traded in the money market. Since the 1970's repos have been increasingly used by banks and thrift institutions, which sell an interest in a pool of securities to individuals. While such an investment, called a *retail repurchase agreement*, may offer more interest than a bank deposit, it is not federally insured (as bank deposits are) and is only as safe as the underlying securities and the bank itself. Most repos involve short-term Treasury or federal agency securities, which in themselves carry little risk. To be safe, however, the lender or some third party should have physical possession of securities equal in value to the amount of the loan. While large securities dealers usually require this provision, smaller ones may not. The cautious investor therefore should investigate the status of the collateral. See also OPEN REPO; REVERSE REPO.

reserve   Also, *reserves.*

   1. In banking, assets from which debts can be paid. See RESERVE REQUIREMENTS.

   2. Also, *allowance.* In accounting, funds taken from retained earnings in order to pay future expenses such as dividend payout, long-term debt retirement (see also SINKING FUND), taxes, operating expenses, depletion, replacement of fixed assets.

   3. Also, *valuation reserve.* An allowance for changes in the value of a firm's assets, owing to depreciation or some other shrinkage or loss. It is not an actual fund but a balance-sheet item (see also under DEPRECIATION).

   4. In insurance, funds set aside to meet claims on policies and other debts. Most U.S. insurance companies must not only maintain loss reserves (to pay claims) but unearned premium reserves (meaning they may not spend all the premiums paid in advance).

reserve requirements   The percentage of their deposits that U.S. banks must by law set aside to meet the demands of depositors. The Federal Reserve sets this percentage for its members, and the different states set it for nonmember state banks. Such reserves must either be in cash held in bank vaults or in deposits with a regional Federal Reserve bank; most member bank reserves are in the latter form. Besides protecting depositors, reserve requirements enable the Federal Reserve to control how much money banks can lend, thereby regulating the nation's money supply and economic growth. High reserve requirements mean tight money and slow growth; low requirements mean easy money and rapid expansion.

resistance level The level above which a security or commodity price does not, for the time being, rise. When this top price is reached, enough investors sell, depressing the price (or at least keeping it from rising higher). A stock that finally breaks through the resistance level, indicating that demand for it is exceeding supply, is showing an upside BREAKOUT. See also SUPPORT LEVEL; TREND.

restricted account A margin account in which the equity does not meet the minimum requirements set by the Federal Reserve Board's REGULATION T, meaning the account-holder may make no further purchases and must allocate part of the proceeds of security sales to the margin account to restore it to required levels.

restrike A coin that was minted after the date marked on it. It may or may not be otherwise genuine.

restructuring See CORPORATE RESTRUCTURING.

retained earnings Also, *earned surplus, retained income, undistributed profit*. The total net income left to a company after it has paid taxes and dividends, which it may use to expand its operations. The amount so used may not be entirely discretionary. Bond indentures frequently stipulate minimum levels of retained earnings, thereby limiting dividend payouts.

retained earnings statement Also, *statement of changes in earned surplus (retained income) (financial position).* A more detailed analysis of changes in the RETAINED EARNINGS account of a company's balance sheet, which often is presented, either separately or within the balance sheet or income statement, in a company's annual report. It analyzes profits or losses from sales, dividends declared, proceeds and payments on long-term debt, and other items affecting the amount of retained earnings.

retirement The withdrawal of a security from circulation, either through redemption (payment of principal and accumulated interest, if any) or through exchange for another security.

return Another name for YIELD. See also the next four entries and TOTAL RETURN.

return on assets The percentage of new profit earned on total assets.

return on equity Abbreviated *ROE*. The net income earned by a firm expressed as a percentage return on stockholders' equity, calculated by dividing the stockholders' equity into net income. Some analysts calculate the return on common stock equity only, first subtracting preferred dividends from net income and excluding the par value of outstanding preferred shares from stockholders' equity.

return on invested capital Also, *return on investment.* Abbreviated *ROI*. The ratio of a company's total earnings (before it pays interest, taxes, and dividends) to its total capital (common and preferred stock plus debt). Usually expressed as a percentage, it is a useful figure for comparing different firms in terms of operating profitability. The higher the figure, the higher the profitability. A highly and consistently profitable company is less vulnerable to market fluctuations.

return on sales See OPERATING MARGIN.

revenue The gross (total) income of a business or government. For a government the chief source of revenue is taxes; hence the name Internal Revenue Service for the U.S. government's tax collection agency. Accountants use the term somewhat differently for various businesses. For railroads revenues mean gross income from all sources, including passenger, freight, and mail services. For utilities it usually means the total amounts billed for utility services rendered. In real estate it refers to the total income not only from rents, construction, and land sale but also interest.

revenue anticipation note Abbreviated *RAN*. A short-term municipal debt instrument that is issued to finance current expenses with the almost certain knowledge that funds from sources other than income tax will be available to pay it off. For example, a RAN might be issued in anticipation of revenues from a sales tax or recreation facilities rentals.

revenue bond A MUNICIPAL BOND that is payable from the revenue of a particular department or special authority for a facility built with funds from the sale of the bond issue. The revenues include tolls, taxes, and charges or rents paid by the users of the facility, for example, a turnpike, civic center, hospital, or public utility. A *leased revenue bond* is backed by the government's lease to a special authority that constructs the project; an *industrial revenue bond* is backed by the municipality but is secured by lease payments made by the corporation using the facility financed by the issue. For either, it is the special authority or the user corporation, not the community, that is responsible for both interest and principal payments on the bond.

reverse annuity mortgage A mortgage loan that allows elderly homeowners to live off the equity in their fully paid-for homes. The loan is in the form of fixed monthly payments over a period of years or for life, in return for gradually relinquishing equity in the home. When the owner dies the lender, usually a bank, takes title to the home, which it may then sell. If the home is sold before the owner dies, the loan must be repaid. A similar contract may be made between a child and elderly parents, the child paying them a fixed monthly stipend in exchange for depreciation and other tax write-offs available through owning real estate.

reverse a swap Restore one's original position following a bond SWAP. For example, one may wish to sell a bond at a loss near year's end for tax purposes but then reinvest in the same security. (However, see WASH SALE.) Similarly, one may wish to purchase a certain bond with a historically attractive yield relative to similar issues or groups of issues and, when the bond moves back to its historical relationship, "reverse swap" to one's original investment or an equivalent.

reverse hedging Selling short a convertible security that can be exchanged for a common stock in which one already owns shares. The investor does so with the expectation that the premium for the convertible (the difference between its market price and the stock's market price) will fall. The name comes from the fact that it is the exact opposite of hedging (where the investor would own the convertible and sell short the stock).

reverse repo Also, *reverse repurchase agreement*. Basically, a REPURCHASE AGREEMENT in reverse. With an ordinary repo, the borrower sells an investment in order to acquire funds and buys it back at a specified time (maturity). In a reverse repo, the lender purchases an investment and resells it at maturity. Reverse repos are generally negotiated by large banks and securities dealers who wish to obtain Treasury or

Federal agency securities to use in ordinary repurchase agreements.

reverse split Also, *split down*. A reduction in a company's outstanding shares of stock without any change in the total stockholders' equity. In a 1-for-3 split, for example, a stock selling for $5 a share will sell for about $15, at least initially. The principal purpose of reverse splits is to raise the stock price and attract new investors. If the strategy succeeds the price will rise again soon after the split, perhaps to $16 or higher, as more buyers are attracted to it. Like a stock SPLIT, a reverse split is voted by the board of directors and must be approved by the stockholders.

rigging See MANIPULATION.

rights Also, *stock rights, subscription rights*. Abbreviated *rt, rts*. The right for stockholders to buy newly issued stock in the same company at a somewhat lower price than the market price. Usually rights are offered in proportion to the amount of stock held, such as one right for each five shares; thus five rights plus a cash payment will purchase one new share. Suppose five rights and $27 in cash will buy a share of new stock and the market price of the stock, after rights distribution, is $32. Each right is now worth $1 or more (because when new shares are acquired with rights the margin terms tend to be more favorable). Rights are transferable and have a value of their own, so they are actively traded, occasionally on stock exchanges as well as in the over-the-counter market. However, rights have a very short life—as short as two weeks in some cases—after which they expire and are worthless. Rights may be *preemptive*, that is, the certificate of incorporation of some companies requires them to give current shareholders first choice at buying new stock. See also SUBSCRIPTION.

ring Also *pit, trading ring*. A location on the trading floor of a commodity futures exchange where brokers and traders specializing in a particular commodity stand as they trade.

risk The possibility of financial loss. Technical analysts differentiate risk, which they consider measurable, from uncertainty, which they consider a random variable. The risks most often faced by investors include credit failure, the chance that a borrower (issuer of bonds and other debt instruments) will not be able to pay interest or repay principal; insufficient earnings, that a company will not earn enough to give stockholders much of a share and that the stock price will fall; inflation, that purchasing power and profit will be eroded by a general rise in prices; interest rate change, that interest rates will rise so that a fixed-interest security will lose value; and market risk, that the overall market will decline. The principal means of minimizing risk is diversification, spreading one's investments among different kinds of security and industry, and, sometimes, using different investments to hedge against one another and against changes in the world at large. See also SAFETY.

risk arbitrage

1. In the FUTURES OPTION market, a method of minimizing market risk. One technique involves the simultaneous purchase of a futures contract and put option and the writing (selling) of a call option; it is known as a *long conversion*. Another, called *reverse conversion*, involves a short future and put option and a long call option.

2. Also, *acquisition arbitrage*, *merger arbitrage*. Acquiring the shares of a company involved (or rumored to be a prospect) in a merger, takeover bid, leveraged buyout, or liquidation, with the expectation of reselling them at a higher price when one of these transactions takes place or when a better offer is presented; also, selling short shares of the acquiring firm, which are expected to drop. When a takeover

bid is made, a target company's shares usually rise in price immediately, but rarely as high as the final bid. There is always the chance that the deal will fall through, particularly in the case of a hostile bid (see MERGER). Many shareholders of the target company sell their stock soon after a deal is announced but before it is completed, realizing an immediate profit but forgoing the extra profit they might realize if the bid were successful. It is this spread between market price and actual bid that is sought by the arbitrager. If the deal does not go through, the price of the stock will drop, sometimes precipitously, so the arbitrager risks a substantial loss.

ROE See RETURN ON EQUITY.

ROI See RETURN ON INVESTED CAPITAL.

roll down (forward) (up) Closing out an option and immediately taking out another in the same underlying security with a lower strike price (down), later expiration date (forward), or higher strike price (up).

rollover A form of REFUNDING, that is the replacement of short-term Treasury bills at maturity with new short-term bills, or the replacement of maturing bank certificates of deposit with the proceeds of new certificates of deposit. For IRA rollover, see under IRA.

round lot The minimum size of an investment transaction that does not incur special charges, for example, 5,000 bushels in wheat futures, 100 shares in most stocks, $1,000 or $5,000 for most corporate bonds. See also ODD LOT.

round turn Also, *round transaction, round trip*. The purchase and resale of the same amount of a security or commodity within a short period of time. For traders who frequently make short-term transactions in a particular security or commodity, the commissions may be quoted in terms of total purchase and sale rather than separately. See also PROCEEDS SALE.

round up (down) Rounding off a price to the nearest

conventional unit. For example, when a stock goes ex-dividend, the specialist will round off the dividend to the nearest multiple of 1/8, since 1/8 point (.125 cents) is the traditional price differential of the market. A dividend of 85 cents, for example, might be rounded up to 7/8, or $.875.

rt, rts   In stock tables, abbreviations for RIGHTS.

run

1. A market maker's list of currently available securities, with bid and ask prices for stocks, par value and ask prices for bonds, and sometimes only a price range for Treasury and Federal agency issues and money-market instruments.

2. Also, *bank run, run on the bank*. A sudden increase in withdrawals by a bank's depositors, usually because they have lost confidence in the bank. It taxes the bank's reserves to the utmost and may cause it to fail entirely. However, deposit insurance (by the FEDERAL DEPOSIT INSURANCE CORPORATION) has greatly decreased the number of bank runs. Further, in most cases a bank in financial difficulties is assisted by state and federal banking authorities, who may arrange a merger or some other means of bolstering the bank's assets.

S

s Abbreviation

1. On the consolidated tape, for 100 shares; thus "6s" means 600 shares.

2. In stock tables, appearing with the company name, for stock split; thus "IBM s" means there was a stock split or dividend of 25 percent or more in the past year.

3. In options tables, for an option series not offered, meaning that a particular put or call, strike price, and expiration month are not being offered for trading.

4. In bond tables, sometimes used to separate the coupon rate from the year of maturity, so that in effect "s" means "percent."

safety To stock analysts, a measure of the potential risk of an individual stock rather than a large diversified portfolio (for which the BETA coefficient is sometimes considered an adequate risk measurement). In assessing a stock, analysts consider the stability of its price in the past adjusted for such individual company factors as financial leverage, overall balance sheet, and earnings, as well as the overall market for the company's products. The Value Line Investment Survey, a well-known investment advisory service, ranks hundreds of stocks on the basis of safety from 1 to 5 and advises conservative investors to limit purchases to stocks ranked 1 (highest) and 2 (above average) for safety.

salary-reduction plan Also, *401(k) plan, 403(b) plan*. A plan that allows employees to set aside part of their earnings each year into a company pension fund, where it accumulates tax-free until withdrawn. It is similar to an IRA but must be employer-sponsored and participation is through payroll deductions. Like an IRA, money can not be withdrawn prematurely from the plan without penalty, and therefore it is subject to tax. As with IRAs there is a legal limit on the maximum contribution per year, although the amount is substantially larger. Some such plans involve investment in a company's own shares. With some plans employers also make contributions; with others they do not.

sales The total income earned from selling goods and/or services. From this sum, called *gross sales,* one usually deducts returns, discounts, and allowances, resulting in a figure called *net sales* (see also INCOME STATEMENT). Security analysts also calculate a company's *sales per share,* meaning net sales divided by the number of shares of common stock outstanding. They may also examine the ratio of annual sales to the value of property, plant, and equipment, which helps show whether a company's funds are productively invested. If an expansion in facilities from one year to the next does not produce larger sales volume, there may be a weakness in marketing or some other area of management.

Sallie Mae Popular name for the *Student Loan Marketing Association* (abbreviated *SLMA*), a government-chartered, private corporation created in 1972 to provide a secondary market for trading previously created insured student loans. Sallie Mae buys such loans from financial and educational institutions, state agencies, and other lenders, which are insured by state agencies and/or the federal government, and issues a variety of securities, including adjustable-rate preferred stock, discount notes, floating-rate notes, and fixed-rate securities such as bonds. These securities are not guaranteed by the U.S. government but are considered comparable in safety to Fannie Maes and other Federal agency securities.

same-day substitution In a margin account, the purchase and sale of securities with the same dollar value on a single day, or a similar change in the account owing to the rise in market value of some holdings offset by the fall in value of others. It results in neither a margin call (to put up more cash) nor a credit to the SPECIAL MEMORANDUM ACCOUNT. It is used when an account is expanded to the limit and the investor must balance every purchase with a sale in order to avoid a margin call.

savings and loan association Abbreviated *S and L*. A specialized financial institution that offers depositors numerous kinds of savings account and invests these funds primarily in home mortgages. In the United States some S and L's are organized as mutual associations. Most of these are federally chartered and thus known as federal savings and loan associations; they are supervised by the FEDERAL HOME LOAN BANK BOARD and insured by the FEDERAL SAVINGS AND LOAN INSURANCE CORPORATION (FSLIC). Other savings and loan associations are organized as corporations and issue common stock. Most of these were, until the early 1980's, state-chartered, but the bulk of them qualified for FSLIC insurance. In the early 1980's banking deregulation made it easier for S and L mutual associations to convert into corporations, which allowed them to raise funds by selling stock, and a sizable proportion chose to do so. The major source of funds for S and L's still is savings accounts of individuals and families, which earn interest (called "dividends" in the case of mutual associations). S and L's also may offer NOW accounts; super NOW accounts; non-interest-bearing demand-deposit (checking) accounts for commercial enterprises; trust accounts such as the KEOGH PLAN and INDIVIDUAL

RETIREMENT ACCOUNT (IRA); and MONEY-MARKET BANK ACCOUNTS.

The mortgage loans made by S and L's include not only conventional home mortgages but adjustable-rate mortgages (with periodic interest-rate adjustments pegged to current market rates), graduated-payment mortgages (requiring higher payments over the years), reverse-annuity mortgages, growing-equity mortgages (in which payments increase gradually to pay off the principal as well as interest), FHA-insured mortgages, and VA-guaranteed mortgages. S and L's are active participants in the SECONDARY MORTGAGE MARKET, buying, selling, and trading already existing mortgages. They also make commercial, construction, and consumer loans, but 80 percent of their funds are invested in home mortgages.

savings bank In the United States, a financial institution that generally is state-chartered and most often is organized as a mutual association (hence *mutual* savings bank) rather than a corporation. Formerly savings banks differed from savings and loan associations in that they offered a wider range of services and invested in more diverse enterprises, and from commercial banks in that they could not serve commercial enterprises. Since banking deregulation in the early 1980's, these distinctions are no longer clear-cut. Moreover, some commercial banks have always called themselves savings banks in their official names, and since 1982 any federal SAVINGS AND LOAN ASSOCIATION also may call itself a savings bank. Strictly speaking, state-chartered savings banks, which make up the majority of such institutions, are regulated by their respective state banking laws. However, in many states banking deregulation on the federal level has been duplicated, so that in these states savings banks may deal with corporations and other businesses and offer a wide variety of accounts.

In addition to the traditional time deposit, many savings banks now offer checking accounts, NOW accounts, credit cards, telephone-bill payment and other third-party payment services, IRA's and KEOGH PLANS, and special loans to consumers and students. As in the past, however, the bulk of savings bank investment is in home mortgages.

savings bond   See U.S. SAVINGS BOND.

savings certificate   A short- or intermediate-term time deposit sold to small investors by commercial banks, savings banks, and savings and loan associations. It is relatively low in risk but offers correspondingly low interest rates. See also CERTIFICATE OF DEPOSIT.

SBA-guaranteed loan   See under SMALL BUSINESS ADMINISTRATION.

scale order   An order to buy or sell a specific number of shares of a security at a series of different prices. In a falling market, for example, one might place a scale order to buy 3,000 shares of Red Hot common stock, 500 at the current market price, and another 500 with each ¼-point price decline. Because scale orders involve considerable clerical work, many brokers will not accept them.

scalper

   1. In the over-the-counter market, a dealer who places excessive markups or markdowns on transaction, a practice considered unethical by the National Association of Securities Dealers, which regards 5 percent as a maximum fair spread.

   2. An investment counselor who buys a security that he or she subsequently recommends to many customers, driving up the price, and then sells at a considerable profit. This practice is illegal, since investment advisers are required by law to disclose their own holdings when there is a potential conflict of interest.

screening   Also, *stock screening*. Using a computer to search through all the stocks in a database in order to find those that meet certain defined investment goals. Screening software enables the investor with a personal computer to search various databases—at least four were available in the mid-1980's—to find stocks that, for example, have a high return on equity, strong earnings growth, a relatively low price-earnings ratio, and not too high a debt ratio. Some computer programs not only produce such screens but can print out detailed financial data for each issue and produce bar charts comparing the issues. Experts point out, however, that screening should not be the only basis for selecting stocks, but rather should be a starting point for more detailed research.

scrip A written claim on currency or shares of stock, which can be redeemed for cash or stock. In the securities industry it frequently is used for fractional shares of stock that result from a stock split, spinoff, or similar deal. Accumulated scrip can then be exchanged for full shares, or if necessary the remaining fraction can often be purchased to make up a full share or shares.

seat A membership on a stock or commodities exchange. The number of seats is usually set by the exchange, as are rules for membership, and seats are bought and sold by eligible members at prices depending on supply and demand. An exchange member may be a partner or holder of voting stock in a MEMBER FIRM, and member firms may have more than one member representing them on the exchange floor (see FLOOR BROKER). The SPECIALIST and FLOOR TRADER, (def. 1), also must be exchange members.

SEC Abbreviation for *Securities and Exchange Commission*.

secondary distribution The sale to the public of previously issued securities by large institutional investors, such as pension funds and mutual funds, or by private individuals who hold large blocks of stock in a company (such as family members in a family-founded corporation). Such a sale generally is handled by an investment bank or other intermediary, just as a PRIMARY DISTRIBUTION is. See also SPECIAL OFFERING.

secondary market Any market in which securities, financial instruments, or debt instruments such as mortgages are traded, subsequent to their original issuance. The term thus includes the stock exchanges, over-the-counter market, money market, and secondary mortgage market.

secondary mortgage market The buying of previously created mortgages, or of securities backed by mortgages, by investors from mortgage bankers or another intermediary. To serve this market, Congress over the years created three federal agencies, the Federal National Mortgage Association (see FANNIE MAE), Government National Mortgage Association (see GINNIE MAE), and Federal Home Loan Mortgage Corporation (see FREDDIE MAC). Fannie Mae and Freddie Mac buy mortgages, bundle similar ones into pools, and sell securities called *participation certificates,* or *PCs*, which represent a fractional interest in such a pool and which in turn finance the agencies' purchases. Ginnie Mae guarantees the securities, for a fee. The securities, also called *mortgage-backed* or *pass-through securities* (because monthly interest and principal payments are passed through directly to investors), are sold with a return that reflects the interest rates being paid by individual homeowners. In addition to these agencies, private mortgage insurance companies, mortgage bankers, commercial banks, and thrift institutions (savings and loan associations, credit unions, and savings banks) all participate in the secondary mortgage market, arranging for the sale of mortgages and creating pass-through securities.

secured bond A bond that is backed by some kind of collateral, such as a mortgage on the issuer's property (MORTGAGE BOND), securities deposited with a trustee (COLLATERAL TRUST BOND), or some other assets on which the bondholder has claim if the bond issuer defaults on payment.

Securities and Exchange Commission, U.S. Abbreviated *SEC*. An independent federal agency that regulates the securities and financial markets. It supervises all national securities exchanges and associations, registers issues of securities, registers over-the-counter brokers and dealers, and regulates mutual funds, investment counselors, and just about all other individuals and firms engaged in investment. It administers a number of federal laws affecting the investment industry and formulates and enforces hundreds of rules designed to protect against malpractice and provide the fullest possible disclosure to investors.

Securities Investor Protection Corporation Abbreviated *SIPC*. A nonprofit corporation, funded by brokers and dealers who are required by law to be its members, that insures the cash and securities of customers of brokers and dealers against financial failure. If a brokerage firm fails, SIPC may ask a federal court to appoint a trustee to liquidate the firm or may, in cases of some small firms, carry out liquidation itself. Customer accounts of a failed firm will be transferred to another SIPC member firm with as little disruption of trading activity as possible. The claims of each customer will be satisfied, up to a maximum of $100,000 in cash and $500,000 in securities. All nonbank broker-dealers registered with the Securities and Exchange Commission are automatically SIPC members except for those firms engaged exclusively in the insurance business or in distributing mutual fund shares, selling variable annuities, or furnishing investment advice to investment companies and insurance companies.

securities loan   Also, *stock loan*. The practice of brokers lending securities to one another, principally to cover a short sale (see SELLING SHORT). The proceeds of the sale serve as collateral.

security   A written instrument that shows evidence of equity (ownership) or debt or rights to equity in a corporation, government, or other enterprise. Equity and the rights to it are represented by stocks, options, rights, and warrants; debt is represented by bills, notes, and bonds.

self-directed   Term describing an IRA or KEOGH PLAN that is actively managed by the account-holder, who decides how the funds will be invested and designates a broker or other custodian to carry out his or her instructions and keep custody of the stock certificates and other assets. Such an account is subject to the same conditions as other IRAs and Keogh accounts. A self-directed IRA permits investment in individual stocks or bonds, mutual funds, unit trusts, annuities and limited partnerships, but not in collectibles or precious metals other than U.S.-minted gold and silver coins. Costs of such accounts vary significantly. Some brokers charge a one-time set-up charge and then a minimum annual fee. In addition, one must pay ordinary brokerage fees when trading in the account.

self-liquidating   Also, *self-supporting*. Referring to a loan or investment that will pay for itself within a reasonable time span. The term is often used for a municipal debt such as a revenue bond for which the revenues—in terms of tolls, taxes, etc.—are sufficient to pay both interest and principal on the loan.

seller's option   A securities transaction in which the seller may deliver the securities to the buyer at a later date than the five days allowed by REGULAR WAY DELIVERY, usually within sixty days.

selling against the box Also, *short against the box*. A form of SELLING SHORT that is also a form of hedging, that is, a protection against an undesirable price change. It requires owning the same number of shares of the same stock that one will sell short. (The "box" stands for those shares actually owned and refers to the safe-deposit box in which securities traditionally are held for safekeeping.) For example, suppose Jones buys 200 shares of General Auto at $10 a share and the stock then trades at $15. Jones wants to cash in on the $1,000 profit but does not want to pay taxes on it until next year. Therefore in November or December, Jones tells the broker to sell short 200 shares of General Auto at $15. If the stock price has fallen by January, Jones can cover by buying 200 new shares at the lower price, which offsets the loss in market value of the stock still owned. If General Auto should go up, Jones can sell the 200 shares in her portfolio to offset the loss on the short sale or simply deliver the shares to close out the short position.

selling climax A sudden sharp drop in the price of a security or commodity, caused by widespread selling. It is more dramatic than a downside BREAKOUT, in terms of both price decrease and increased selling volume. Technical analysts view a selling climax as the beginning of a gradual price rise.

selling short Selling a futures contract for a commodity or financial instrument or a stock one does not own, with the intention of buying it at a later time when, it is hoped, its price will be lower. The transaction itself is called a *short sale*. With commodities and financial instruments, the sale is a futures contract and in most cases the seller *covers* the sale— that is, buys the item in question—before the contract expires. With stocks the seller borrows the stock from the broker, who either borrows it from another broker or stockholder or obtains it from a margin account. Short sales are used to make a relatively quick profit through a price decline or to protect a profit in a security or commodity one already owns (see SELLING AGAINST THE BOX). Short selling is regulated by the Securities and Exchange Commission's SHORT SALE RULE.

sell plus An order to sell a security on an UP TICK, that is, a price higher than the immediately preceding transaction.

sell stop order A STOP ORDER to sell.

serial bond One of a series of bonds issued at the same time but maturing at specific intervals over a period of time. For example, an issue of $10 million may be in four series of $2.5 million each, maturing at two-year intervals beginning the tenth year after issue. Municipal bonds often are serial bonds. See also SERIES BOND.

series bond An identification for bond issues that carry identical provisions concerning coupon, maturity, and other terms. U.S. savings bonds are always issued in this form. Corporations sometimes use it to designate bonds with the same terms offered during a single year (Series 1982, for example). See also SERIAL BOND.

series of option A class of option on the same underlying security or commodity with the same strike price and expiration date, for example, all IBM April 40 puts.

settlement date In the securities market, the date by which a completed order must be settled, with the buyer paying for the securities and the seller delivering them. For stocks and bonds the settlement date is the fifth business day following the execution of the order; for listed options and government securities it is the next business day after execution.

settlement price Also, *settle*. In commodity futures markets, a theoretical closing price for the trading day that is established by the commodity futures exchange. In such markets the CLOSE includes a period of time—usually less than two minutes—during which transactions may still be executed. The listed close is actually a range of prices that includes the high and low during this brief period. To obtain a single price, therefore, each exchange has devised its own system for calculating a theoretical last price, and, when a commodity is not traded in every delivery month during the closing period, for estimating a settlement price. With infrequently traded contracts, the settlement price is sometimes higher than the day's high price.

share The smallest unit of STOCK in a corporation. The number of shares a firm may issue is stated in its corporate CHARTER. See also FRACTIONAL SHARE.

shareholder See under STOCK.

shark repellent Also, *porcupine provision*. A provision in a company's articles of incorporation or bylaws that is designed to protect it against an unfriendly takeover. Such provisions include staggering the terms of the board of directors or requiring approval of a large majority of shareholders for a proposed merger.

shelf registration A ruling by the Securities and Exchange Commission, issued as Rule 415, that permits some of the largest corporations, which have a very high credit rating, to prepare a registration statement and then issue securities as they wish over a period of up to two years. It avoids the costly and time-consuming practice of preparing a registration statement for each new offering, which then can be put on the market when conditions are favorable.

short against the box See SELLING AGAINST THE BOX.

short coupon An interest payment on a bond that represents interest for less than the conventional six-month period.

short hedge Buying a futures contract or put option or

SELLING AGAINST THE BOX to protect against a price decrease in a commodity or security. See also LONG HEDGE.

short interest The total number of short sales in listed securities, a figure compiled monthly by the stock exchanges from statistics provided by member firms. This figure indicates both how many investors believe that prices will decline and a potential rise in buying volume when the short sales must be covered (see also SELLING SHORT). Some newspapers, including the *New York Times* and *Wall Street Journal*, publish not only the total short positions but a listing of those securities with the largest short interest.

short interest theory The idea that a high ratio of total short sales to total trading volume signals a general rise in the market. See also CUSHION THEORY.

short position The condition of having sold a stock, bond, or option that one does not own. Same as SELLING SHORT. See also LONG POSITION.

short sale See SELLING SHORT.

short sale rule Also, *up tick rule*. A Securities and Exchange Commission rule that a short sale in a listed stock (see SELLING SHORT) may be made only in a rising market, that is, if the last sale was at a higher price than the sale immediately preceding it (up tick), or if the last sale was at the same price as the preceding one but higher than the last preceding *different* price (zero-plus tick). The purpose of this rule is to prevent manipulation of a stock's price by heavy short sales, which would drive down the price, so that speculators could then buy the shares cheaply and make a large profit. The rule does not apply to unlisted stocks.

short-term

  1. The gain (loss) from selling property held less than six months (or one year), traditionally subject to heavier tax. See LONG TERM, def.1.

  2. Describing a debt instrument that is due in a

year or less. Short-term debts range from overnight loans and repos to 30-day or 60-day commercial paper to 12-month Treasury bills, and most are traded in the MONEY MARKET. From an investment standpoint, the most popular are (in order of lowest return and least risk to highest return and most risk:) Treasury bills; certificates of deposit; money-market bank accounts; money-market funds specializing in government securities; money-market funds; bankers' acceptances; prime commercial paper.

sight draft A DRAFT payable when it is presented ("on sight"). See also TIME DRAFT.

silent partner A person who invests in a PARTNERSHIP and is liable like the other partners but takes no active part in the business although legally entitled to do so. In family businesses various relatives may be named silent partners in order to spread the profits and reduce individual tax liability. The participants in a LIMITED PARTNERSHIP other than the general partner, who manages the enterprise, are similar to silent partners but do not have the same powers as the active general partner.

silver A precious metal that has been valued for thousands of years. One can invest in silver by buying silver bars; silver bullion coins (usually sold by the BAG); silver certificates, futures, and options (see FUTURES CONTRACT; FUTURES OPTION; OPTION); and shares in silver mines, mutual funds, and unit trusts. About two-thirds of all mined silver is a by-product of copper, zinc, lead, and other base metals. Therefore the supply of and demand for the base metal influence silver production more than the supply of and demand for silver itself. Silver prices tend to be very volatile, with wide swings, and therefore silver is considered to be a much more speculative investment than GOLD. Silver coins and bars may be bought directly through banks or brokers. American dimes, quarters, and half-dollars dated 1964 or earlier are 90 percent silver, and Kennedy half-dollars dated 1965 through 1970 are 40 percent silver. Most Canadian coins issued between 1920 and 1966 are 80 percent silver. Because silver coins are no longer in circulation and are decreasing in supply, silver coin prices are tied less strictly to the value of metal content than those of gold coins; normally they sell for 2 to 5 percent below the value of silver but occasionally, when the supply is large, the discount can be higher. In both the United States and Canada they are traded in bulk, usually in $1,000 bags. Silver bars (also called *bricks*) are available in weights ranging from 1 to 1,000 ounces. Since, as with gold, safe storage of the physical commodity can present problems, investors sometimes prefer to buy silver certificates for bars stored in special facilities in the United States or abroad. Silver options and futures are traded in major options and commodity futures markets.

simplified employee pension plan Abbreviated *SEP*. A retirement plan in which an employer contributes to an IRA to which the employee is also making contributions. Both kinds of contribution are tax-exempt up to a certain maximum until withdrawal. In some cases the employer contributions are linked to company profits; in others they are not.

sinking fund Abbreviated *SF*. A sum of money set aside by a corporation or other organization to extinguish an indebtedness, usually a bond or preferred stock, as specified in the indenture or charter. The term applies both to funds to be used to retire an issue prior to maturity and to funds to be used to repay the principal at maturity. Most sinking funds are placed in very low-risk investments, such as Treasury bonds.

sld Abbreviation for *sold*. It appears on the consolidated tape, following the symbol for a security, to designate a transaction that was out of sequence. It also appears as *sld last sale*, designating a transaction in which there is a considerable price change from the previous transaction (2 points or more in high-priced issues, 1 point or more in low-priced issues).

sleeper A security for which there suddenly is great demand, with a consequent large price advance.

slump See RECESSION.

Small Business Administration Abbreviated *SBA*. A federal agency that provides guaranteed, direct, or immediate participation loans to small business firms to help them finance plant construction, acquire equipment, and/or obtain working capital. Rather than making direct loans, the SBA guarantees up to 90 percent of the principal and interest of certain loans made by commercial banks to small firms. A bank in turn may sell the guaranteed portion of the loan to investors. SBA-guaranteed loans, backed by the full faith and credit of the government, are not as liquid as Treasury securities and therefore carry a higher interest rate (typically 2 to 3 percent higher), partly offset by a small service charge to the bank (typically .75 percent per year). SBA-guaranteed loans are available principally through a large broker that deals in government securities. Because such loans are not a well-known investment, purchasers are cautioned to make sure they are buying the correct instrument, which always includes the word "guarantee" in its name (SBA Guaranteed Loan, SBA Guaranteed Loan Participation).

soft market Also, *buyer's market*. A market in which supply exceeds demand and consequently prices are declining. It is marked also by inactive trading, and in the over-the-counter market, considerable spread between bid and ask prices.

source and application of funds statement Also, *flow of funds statement*. A financial statement summarizing a company's CASH FLOW during a given accounting period. The sources of cash (or working capital) include earnings, interest from loans, and sale of fixed assets and stock; they are applied to (used for) purchasing equipment or other capital assets, paying off debts, paying out dividends, and so on.

South African gold share See under GOLD.

special arbitrage account A kind of margin account for transactions in which the customer buys and sells the same security in different markets (see ARBITRAGE). Since the customer's risk is hedged, both the initial margin and maintenance margins are considerably lower than for ordinary margin trading.

special bid Buying a large block of stock on the New York Stock Exchange by matching one brokerage client's buy order with sell orders from numerous other customers. The bid, at a fixed price, is announced in advance on the consolidated tape, and the buyer of the stock pays all commissions and other transaction costs. For the reverse procedure, see EXCHANGE DISTRIBUTION.

special bond account A margin account that permits MARGIN TRADING in government, municipal, and nonconvertible corporate bonds. Both the initial and maintenance margin requirements for bonds are less strict than for stocks, the former being set by the broker or dealer and the latter usually by the exchange or the National Association of Securities Dealers.

specialist A stock exchange member who trades only in one or a few stocks and is charged with maintaining an orderly market in them, buying or selling for his or her own account in order to prevent large price swings or when there are no other order takers. A specialist must have considerable capital in order to make a market in a stock and must obey strict exchange rules to prevent taking unfair advantage. The specialist also executes any LIMIT ORDER a floor broker cannot execute (and collects part of the floor broker's commission for this service). Such orders must be executed in the order they are received; they are written down in the *specialist's book,* one for each stock dealt in, which also includes a record of the specialist's own inventory, market orders to sell short, and other orders that exchange members place with the specialist. Each specialist works at a specific trading booth on the exchange. On the New York Stock Exchange in the mid-1980's there were some 410 specialists grouped into 57 trading units with about 27 stocks per unit; on the American Stock Exchange there were 200 specialists grouped in 27 units, with each unit trading about 35 stocks. Although orders were often received through computers, they were still executed manually.

special memorandum account Also, *special miscellaneous account.* Abbreviated *SMA.* A memorandum of the EXCESS MARGIN in a customer's margin account. It consists of dividend and interest payments, cash deposited to make a margin call, proceeds of a sale of securities or cash no longer required on an expired or liquidated securities position, and any margin excess the broker wishes to transfer to it. Such an account keeps the broker informed as to how much margin a customer has, without incurring a margin call; withdrawals from it by the customer may be made only with the broker's approval.

special offering A SECONDARY DISTRIBUTION of a large block of stock made by a New York Stock Exchange member for a customer or for its own account. The seller must announce the sale on the consolidated tape and specify the number of shares involved and the price asked, which usually is the current market price. The seller must pay all brokerage commissions and other costs, and also must obtain approval of the sale from the Securities and Exchange Commission.

special situation

    1. An UNDERVALUED security that appears to be about to rise in price owing to some unique event—such as a takeover bid, licensing of a new product, or change of management—that seems sure to change its fortunes.

    2. Describing a SWAP between different kinds of security, such as a convertible security and the underlying common stock, or one between convertible and nonconvertible bonds of the same or similar firms, or from a preferred stock to a bond, or from one type of industrial into a utility bond with different rating, coupon rate, and maturity.

special-tax bond   A MUNICIPAL BOND that is payable from the revenues of a particular tax, such as a gasoline tax or liquor tax. It is known as a *special-assessment bond* when the tax affects only the users of the facility that the loan is financing, such as new sidewalk construction or street paving.

speculation   An investment made principally with the hope of profiting from a change in price, usually in a fairly short time. It differs from conservative investment mainly in that it tends to involve more risk, is less concerned with current income or the preservation of principal, and seeks to achieve larger profits. Since these considerations are relative, a particular investment can be described as being "more speculative" or "less speculative."

spin-off   The sale of a subsidiary so that it becomes a separate company. Most often, the corporation distributes shares in the subsidiary to its own stockholders, who then become the new company's owners. However, a company can be acquired by its employees through an EMPLOYEE STOCK OWNERSHIP PLAN, or through a LEVERAGED BUYOUT by the subsidiary's managers.

split   Also, *split up, stock split.* The division of a company's outstanding shares of stock into a larger number of shares, without any change in the total stockholders' equity. As a result, the price of each share declines, and dividends per share fall proportionately. For example, in a 2-for-1 split of a stock selling for $50 a share, the 5 million outstanding shares are doubled in number to 10 million, the stock price falls to about $25, and the owner receives half the dividend per share he or she received before the split. However, the chief purpose of most stock splits is to reduce the stock price and attract new investors, and if the strategy succeeds the price will rise again shortly after the split as more buyers are attracted to it. In most instances a stock split is voted by the board of directors and must be approved by the shareholders. See also REVERSE SPLIT.

split funding A program that combines the purchase of mutual fund shares with a life insurance contract or other form of investment.

split offering A bond issue that includes both serial bonds and long-term bonds with a single maturity date. Municipal revenue bonds are frequently offered in this way.

split rating See under BOND-RATING AGENCY.

spot Also, *actual, cash, physical*. Describing a purchase or sale involving immediate cash payment, as opposed to future payment, and a physical commodity, such as potatoes or gold or Treasury bonds. See also SPOT MARKET.

spot market Also, *actual market, cash market, physical market*. A market for commodity transactions for immediate (or almost immediate) delivery and cash payment, as opposed to the futures market. The price paid in this market, representing the current market price, is called the *spot price* or *cash price*.

spread The difference between two prices.

　1. In the securities trade, the difference between a

SPREAD

bid (buyer's) price and an ask (seller's) price. In the over-the-counter market this spread constitutes the dealer's profit. The National Association of Securities Dealers has a guideline called the *5 percent rule* suggesting that this figure represents a maximum fair spread (and commission). A difference in price for the same item (such as stock or currency) in two different markets makes possible ARBITRAGE.

2. Also, *straddle*. In the commodity futures market, a price difference resulting from taking opposite positions in two or more futures contracts. An example is December wheat versus corn futures, which are purchased in late spring and removed in late fall. This spread often works because it takes advantage of the different harvest times of the two crops. In late spring wheat is in process of being harvested, creating large supplies and depressing prices; in fall corn is harvested, but until then it is not plentiful. The hedger therefore buys December wheat futures and sells corn futures. Under normal harvest conditions (not affected by untimely drought, for example) one can make a profit with relatively little risk.

3. In the options market, a price difference resulting from the simultaneous purchase of one option and sale of another involving the same underlying security but different strike prices and/or different expiration dates. If the spread involves only different expirations, it is called a *calendar* or *horizontal spread*. A *vertical* or *money spread* involves the same option and expiration but different strike prices. A *diagonal spread* involves both different expirations and different strike prices. In a *bull call spread* or *bull spread* the trader buys a call option with a low strike price and sells another call with a higher strike price. In a *bear call spread* the trader buys a call option with a high strike price and sells a call with a lower strike price. With these strategies the trader hopes to profit from a rising (bull) or declining (bear) stock price. See also COMBINATION; RISK ARBITRAGE; STRADDLE, def. 1; STRAP; STRIP.

4. See YIELD SPREAD.

spreadsheet A computer program in which the user enters and manipulates numerical data in a form resembling that of an accounting tablet. The rows and columns contain data in fixed relationships to one another, which are maintained no matter what new figures are entered. For example, an entire investment portfolio can be entered on a spreadsheet, including such information as the name of the security, the price at which it was bought, the number of shares bought, the brokerage commission paid, current market price, current price-earnings ratio, current beta coefficient, and the percentage value of the total portfolio it represents. Changing just one of these figures—for example, updating the current market price for a stock—will change all the relevant figures in the other columns. Electronic spreadsheets have long been used by professional analysts and since about 1980 have become increasingly popular with individual investors who own a personal computer.

ss Symbol on the consolidated tape, usually appearing as ', indicating that a security trades in units of 10 shares and that the number of units represented on the tape is not in round lots. Thus the indication 40 ⁚ 15½ means that 40 shares of a security sold at $15.50 a share.

st Symbol on the consolidated tape, usually appearing as ', indicating that a transaction took place at a guaranteed price, that is, it was STOPPED OUT by the specialist.

stabilization Preventing wide price swings in a commodity, security, or currency. On organized stock exchanges the SPECIALIST is charged with maintaining an orderly market without large price fluctuation.

Underwriters also may temporarily stabilize the price of a distribution by actively buying and selling it.

Standard & Poor's   A corporation that provides a large number of investment services. For Standard & Poor's Index, see under STOCK INDEX/AVERAGE; for Standard & Poor's rating, see under BOND-RATING AGENCY.

stated value   A book value assigned to NO-PAR STOCK.

statement   General name for any financial report of transactions taking place over a particular period, or the status of accounts at a given time. Brokers are required by law to send customers quarterly *statements of account* that summarize their balance and list securities transactions; they usually also send out monthly statements in active accounts. Similarly, banks send monthly statements to their account-holders. The term is also used for the monthly, quarterly, or annual statements describing the financial condition of business firms, including the balance sheet and income statement.

statutory voting   The system of allowing stockholders one vote per share for each position open on the board of directors. Thus, if you own 100 shares and there are nine candidates, you may use 100 votes for each candidate of your choice, but you may not, as in CUMULATIVE VOTING, give any one candidate more than one hundred of your votes.

stock   A share in the ownership of a corporation, which represents a claim on its earnings and assets. There are two main kinds of stock, COMMON STOCK and PREFERRED STOCK. Each owner of stock, called a *stockholder* or *shareholder*, receives a *stock certificate*, which shows the number and kind of shares held. Stock certificates are negotiable instruments when endorsed and hence are generally best stored in a safe deposit box or other place of safekeeping.

stockbroker   See under BROKER.

stock certificate Printed evidence of a stockholder's holdings in a corporation, showing the number of shares held, their par value if any, the class of stock, and voting rights. If registered in the holder's name and signed, a stock certificate is a negotiable item, and to prevent theft investors usually store the certificate in a safe deposit box or with their broker. In order to minimize risk of loss or theft when mailing a stock certificate, one can send it unsigned and send a signed STOCK POWER (or bond power) along with it to the broker. The paper used for stock certificates is usually both watermarked and finely engraved with special markings to discourage forgery.

stock dividend A DIVIDEND in the form of stock rather than cash. The company thus issues additional shares of common stock to common stockholders, with no change in the total common equity. From an accounting standpoint, the payment of stock dividends reduces retained earnings and increases the stated value of the common-stock equity account.

stock exchange Also, *securities exchange*. An organized market where member brokers and traders buy and sell securities for their customers and themselves. In the United States there are ten stock exchanges registered with the Securities and Exchange Commission. By far the largest is the New York Stock Exchange, accounting for nearly 80 percent of all shares traded over exchanges, followed by the American Stock Exchange, also in New York and accounting for another 12 percent. Seven others are known as *regional exchanges*: the Boston Stock Exchange, Cincinnati Stock Exchange, Intermountain Stock Exchange (Salt Lake City), Midwest Stock Exchange (Chicago), Pacific Stock Exchange (Los Angeles and San Francisco), Philadelphia Stock Exchange, and Spokane Stock Exchange. The Chicago Board of Options Exchange is registered to trade stocks and bonds but confines itself to options trading, which also are traded on the American, Philadelphia, and Pacific stock exchanges. (See also CINCINNATI STOCK EXCHANGE; Appendix A.) Each exchange has its own rules concerning membership and listing securities. Trading takes place among the exchange members by means of oral agreement in an open auction; the price is established by competitive bidding between brokers, and all bids and offers are made out loud. Identical securities may not be listed on both the New York and American stock exchanges, but they often are listed on one of these plus one or more of the regional exchanges, a system facilitated by the INTERMARKET TRADING SYSTEM whereby prices of a security being traded on several exchanges are displayed on a screen. Securities not listed on stock exchanges are traded in the OVER-THE-COUNTER MARKET.

stockholders' equity   See under EQUITY, def. 1.

stock index/average   A statistical grouping of prices of selected stocks that tracks changes in their value for purposes of analysis, investment, and hedging. The construction of such groupings varies. Some consist of an arithmetic AVERAGE; others represent a true INDEX, that is, an average expressed in terms of a base quantity. Some include only a small number of stocks—30 in the Dow Jones Industrial Average— and others a large number—500 in Standard & Poor's Composite Index; the former are said to be *narrow-based*, and the latter *broad-based*. Some indexes are price-weighted, with high-priced stocks having more influence than low-priced ones; others are market-weighted (see MARKET WEIGHTING). Some of the indexes and averages are used as the underlying security in STOCK-INDEX FUTURES and INDEX OPTIONS, which can be used either for investment purposes or to hedge one's position in the current market.

Of the numerous stock averages and indexes, the

best-known and most influential is the Dow Jones Industrial Average, despite the fact that many experts consider it seriously flawed because it includes so few stocks and ignores the volume of trading. Appendix C describes the most important indexes and averages. For comparable statistics for bonds and mutual funds, see BOND BUYER'S INDEX; LIPPER MUTUAL FUND INDUSTRY AVERAGE.

stock-index futures Futures contracts on various stock indexes, which began to be traded on organized commodity futures exchanges in 1982. Hedgers use such futures to protect themselves against changes in stock market prices; speculators use them to make profits. In the first two years of trading six different stock indexes became involved. The first three were the Value Line Composite Average Index, which covers 95 percent of the dollar volume of U.S. stocks traded and gives each of its issues equal weight; the Standard & Poor's Composite Index of 500 Stocks, which is a slightly smaller version of the New York Stock Exchange Composite Index, representing about 75 percent of the market value of stocks listed on the New York Stock Exchange, with a heavy proportion of blue chips and weighted by capitalization against fixed base periods; and the New York Stock Exchange Composite Average, similarly weighted, and covering most blue chips but also many more infrequently traded stocks. Futures contracts in these three indexes can be settled only in cash at expiration. Each point of change in the index is worth $5, but the minimum move is 5 points. Thus, an S & P 500 future closing 1.40 higher, at 163.30, would mean the contract is worth $81,650 (500 times the index price) and the 1.40 price change is worth $700. The original cash margin (minimum down payment required by the exchange) was $6,500. Otherwise trading is the same as for commodity futures (see FUTURES

CONTRACT; COMMODITY FUTURES EXCHANGE.) The delivery months are spaced three months apart, extending to nine months in most cases.

The introduction of stock-index futures was followed some months later with the introduction of stock-index FUTURES OPTIONS, that is, options on stock-index futures. This in turn gave rise to new stock-index futures, the Chicago Board Options Exchange Index of 100 Blue Chip Stocks, the Standard & Poor's 100, American Major Market Index and Market Value Index, and numerous others. It also prompted a rise in options on other regulated futures contracts. See also OPTION.

In mid-1985 trading began in two other kinds of index future. One was in municipal bond futures, based on the Municipal Bond Index, constructed from 40 fixed-rate long-term municipals and published daily in *The Bond Buyer*. The other was in futures based on the Consumer Price Index, which in effect asks investors to bet on the amount of future price inflation (or hedge their other investments against estimated inflation).

To hedge against a drop in stock prices in one's portfolio, one can sell a stock-index futures contract, which in theory commits one to sell the underlying index at a predetermined price on a future date. Thus, even if the prices of stocks in the portfolio fall, one can earn a profit on the sale of the futures contract, which allows the sale of the stock market index at the old, higher level even though it currently has declined along with stock prices. If stock prices rise, one loses money on the futures contract but has offsetting gains on the stocks in the portfolio. Such hedging works best if the stock index selected closely matches the makeup of the portfolio, which is most readily done with a broad-based portfolio (since most indexes reflect prices of a wide range of stocks).

The stock-index futures market is also used by arbitragers who try to profit whenever the level of an index future differs significantly in price from the actual index level. Theoretically, the future and the current index should be quoted at the same price since current stock prices reflect futures expectations. A futures contract, however, is usually higher, and the exact spread (price differential) largely reflects the interest charges on money that would otherwise be tied up by owning stocks. This difference is somewhat reduced by the fact that the owner of a futures contract collects no dividends on stocks. As the futures contract nears expiration, this difference diminishes, and upon expiration, the value of the futures contract is exactly equal to that of the underlying stocks. Occasionally, however, the spread during the life of the contract is greater or less than normal because the futures market is more bearish or bullish than the actual stock market. When the futures contract seems higher (bullish), the arbitrager sells the futures contract and simultaneously buys a basket representing the underlying stocks on the stock exchange. If enough traders engage in such arbitrage, it can alter stock market prices considerably in a very short time.

stock-index option See INDEX OPTION.

stock market

1. An organized market for the trading of stocks. See STOCK EXCHANGE.

2. General term for the trading of all securities and commodities, including stocks, bonds, futures, options, warrants, and rights. It may also refer to one or another price index or average, most often the Dow Jones Industrial Average.

stock option See OPTION.

stock power Also, *stock/bond power*. A form that permits the transfer of ownership of a stock or bond to a buyer. It is separate from the security certificate and duplicates the transfer form appearing on the reverse side of the certificate. Once signed, witnessed, and guaranteed, it empowers the TRANSFER AGENT to transfer ownership to the new owner.

stock record   A record kept by brokerage firms of the securities they hold and their owners.

stock rights   See RIGHTS.

stock split   See SPLIT.

stop-limit order   An order to a broker to buy or sell securities at a given price, called the *limit price,* or better, but only after another price, called the *stop price*, has been passed. It actually is a combination of a STOP ORDER and a LIMIT ORDER, and is designed to avoid the risk with a plain stop order that the market will move up or down so fast that the purchase price is far in excess of the stop price. However, it may never be executed because the limit price may never be reached, and further, some exchanges, notably the American Stock Exchange, do not permit stop-limit orders unless the stop and limit prices are the same. This is how it works: Smith places a stop-limit order to buy 100 shares of Red Hot at "32 stop 33 limit." When the market price of Red Hot reaches 32 the broker enters a limit order for 100 shares at 33 or better (less).

stop order   Also, *stop loss order*. An order to a broker to buy or sell securities if the market reaches a given price, called the *stop price*. A stop order to sell, always at a price lower than the current market, is often used to protect an investor's profit in a stock. For example, if Jones bought XYZ at 10 and it is now selling at 50, she may put in a stop order to sell at 45. When XYZ drops to 44⅞ her broker will sell at 45 (if XYZ is traded on an exchange, where the rules say that stop orders to sell must be executed on an up-tick in order to prevent a selling panic; in the over-the-counter market the order is executed when the stock reaches 45). A stop order to buy, always at a price above the current market, is generally used to protect a short sale if the security in question rises in price. When the market reaches the stop price, the broker should buy at the lowest obtainable market price. Should the market price rise rapidly, the actual purchase price may be well above the specified stop price. See also LIMIT ORDER; STOP-LIMIT ORDER.

stopped out   Describing a STOP ORDER that has been executed at the stop price or at a guaranteed price offered by a specialist. It is marked on the tape with the symbol '.

straddle

　　1. Also, *double option, double spread*. In options trading, purchasing (or selling) a put and a call on the same underlying security with the same strike price and expiration date. Either option can be exercised or sold separately.

　　2. In commodity futures trading, same as SPREAD, def. 2.

straight life insurance   See under LIFE INSURANCE.

straight-line method   An accounting method that charges the same amount of depreciation to each year of a fixed asset's service life.

strap   In options trading, a contract that combines two calls and one put on the same underlying security with the same strike price and expiration date.

Street   Abbreviation for *Wall Street*, referring to the New York financial community, and, by extension, to the financial world in general.

street name   Describing a stock or bond registered and being held in the name of a broker instead of the customer, either for safekeeping or as collateral for margin trading. Such securities are said to be "carried in street name." This practice also facilitates transfer when the securities are sold. The broker legally acts as nominee for the securities and the customer is the beneficial owner, that is, benefits from all the rights pertaining to ownership (such as collecting dividends).

strike price Also, *exercise price, striking price.* The price for which an OPTION must be exercised, that is, what the owner of a call option must pay for the underlying security (and at which its writer must sell), and what the owner of a put option must charge for the underlying security (and at which the writer must buy it). On options exchanges the strike price for stock options is set in increments of $5 for stocks under $70 and of $10 for those over $70. As a security's price in the market goes up or down, the exchange will set up new options for it, and the option buyer can select the strike price he or she prefers, depending on his or her judgment as to what the stock price will do. The term "exercise price" is more often used for warrants.

strip An options contract that combines two puts and one call on the same underlying security with the same strike price and expiration date.

Student Loan Marketing Association See SALLIE MAE.

subject quote A bid or ask price that is subject to further negotiation or review. See also FIRM QUOTE; NOMINAL QUOTE.

subordinate debenture A debenture (unsecured bond) that has claim on a corporation's assets only after senior debts have been met. It carries a higher risk, therefore, than an ordinary DEBENTURE.

subscription An agreement to buy a newly issued security. The RIGHTS to buy a new issue are sometimes called *subscription rights;* the price in a rights offering to existing shareholders, usually below the public offering price, is called the *subscription price;*

and the number of rights needed to buy a share of a new issue is known as the *subscription ratio*.

subsidiary A firm of which the majority of the voting stock is controlled by another company, called the *parent company*.

sum-of-digits method Also, *sum-of-the-years-digits method*. An accounting method that charges more depreciation in a fixed asset's early years and less later. The amount of depreciation charged each year is based on the sum of the digits of the asset's total life (for example, for a machine with an expected life of five years, $5 + 4 + 3 + 2 + 1 = 15$), with 5/15 charged the first year, 4/15 the next year, and so on. See also DECLINING BALANCE METHOD.

Super NOW account Also, *Super Negotiable Order of Withdrawal*. Basically, an interest-earning checking account offered by banks and other depository institutions to compete with money-market mutual funds. Like other bank accounts, it is federally insured, offers somewhat lower interest than money-market rates but more than ordinary NOW accounts, and until 1986 required a specific minimum balance. It imposes no limit on the number of monthly transactions (withdrawals or checks).

support level The level below which a security or commodity price or price index does not, for the time being, fall. When this low price is reached, enough investors decide to buy, keeping up the price (or at least keeping it from falling more). A stock that finally sinks below the support level, indicating that supply is exceeding current demand for it, is showing a downside BREAKOUT. See also RESISTANCE LEVEL; TREND.

surplus

1. The equity of shareholders over and above the par value or stated value of their stock. See PAID-IN SURPLUS; RETAINED EARNINGS.

2. In insurance companies, the amount by which assets exceed liabilities on a statutory (state-regulated) accounting basis.

swap   Colloquial term for selling one security and buying another in order to gain a small advantage, most often higher interest but sometimes a higher-rated bond, more favorable maturity date, or the like. With municipal bonds, a swap may establish a loss for tax purposes without damaging the overall value of the portfolio. However, investors must be careful to avoid a WASH SALE, which carries a tax penalty. A common tactic in fixed-income investing is to buy short-term securities if interest rates are expected to rise and long-term ones if they are expected to fall. Because of higher transaction costs and related charges for executing small trades, however, most authorities recommend that investors with a small or moderate-size portfolio do not undertake much swapping. Swap transactions on a large scale are common internationally, in the EUROBOND market as well as with currencies. See also INTEREST RATE SWAP; REVERSE A SWAP.

sweetener   A bonus offered to make a security more attractive to purchasers, for example, the feature of convertibility added to an issue of preferred stock, or a RIGHTS offering permitting the purchase of additional shares at a lower price. See also KICKER.

Swiss bank account   An account in a Swiss bank, which may be one of several kinds. A *current account* is equivalent to an American checking account and generally pays no interest. A *deposit account* is similar to an American savings account and pays interest at a fairly low rate, about half the comparable U.S. rate. Its purpose for an American investor, therefore, is appreciation in the dollar value of Swiss francs or to hide funds obtained illegally. A *custodial account* serves as a depository for investments, such as stocks, bonds, or gold. In such an account the bank purchases investments under its own name and registers them in the account-holder's account. It sends out a statement of holdings once or twice a year, invoking a small storage and insurance charge (0.5 percent is typical). The Swiss government withholds as tax a percentage of all interest earned on Swiss franc accounts. As a foreign national, an American investor can apply for a refund of that amount, and apply most or all of the foreign tax paid as a credit on his or her U.S. tax return.

switch order

1. Also, *contingent order*. An order to buy (or sell) one security and sell (or buy) another, with a stated difference between their prices.

2. In commodity futures trading, selling a future in one delivery month and buying a future of the same commodity in another delivery month.

syndicate Also, *purchase group*, *underwriting syndicate*. A group of investment bankers who join together to buy and market a new ISSUE.

t In stock tables, indication that this amount was paid in stock dividends in the preceding twelve months, and the value calculated is for the stock on the EX-DIVIDEND date.

take a position Buy a security, usually in a substantial amount. See also LONG POSITION; SHORT POSITION.

take down Also, *takedown*.

  1. In underwriting, the proportionate share of the total distribution for which each syndicate member is responsible.

  2. The price at which securities are allocated to syndicate members in a distribution, particularly of municipal securities. It is always lower than the public offering price, to allow for a small profit.

take out Also, *takeout*.

  1. Withdrawing cash from a brokerage account, usually as a result of selling securities.

  2. In real estate, a long-term mortgage that is taken out to finance a short-term construction loan.

takeover See MERGER.

tape Also, *ticker, ticker tape*. Today, an electronic device that reports the prices and volume of securities traded on major exchanges throughout the United States and Canada within a minute after they occur. Formerly, a telegraphic device was used, which made a ticking sound as it printed the information on a continuous paper tape. The present-day system uses a video screen to project the transactions, which have passed through a computer. See also BROAD TAPE; CONSOLIDATED TAPE.

target company A company threatened with an unwanted takeover. See under MERGER.

target fund A MUTUAL FUND that invests in bonds of a fixed maturity, for example, a portfolio consisting entirely of bonds that mature in 1990, 1993, and 1996. Its chief advantage to investors is that the net asset value tends to fluctuate less over such a relatively short period.

tax anticipation security A short-term credit instrument (bill or note) sold periodically by the U.S. Treasury and by some municipalities, principally to business firms but sometimes also to individual taxpayers, which they may then use to pay their taxes. The Treasury bills mature several days to a week after the due date for corporation income tax but are accepted at par on the due date, thereby giving the corporation a few extra days' interest. For both the Treasury and local governments, they offer the advantage of bringing in tax revenues at regular intervals.

tax-deferred annuity See under ANNUITY.

tax-exempt security Also, *tax-free security*. Describing an interest-bearing investment on which none or only some of the return is subject to federal income tax, and which is sometimes also exempt from state and/or local taxes. The most important kinds are municipal and U.S. Treasury securities.

tax-loss carryback (carryforward) A U.S. tax provision that permits businesses to apply a net capital loss to a previous or future year or years.

tax selling Selling securities that have gone down in price, usually done near the end of the year, in order to reduce income-tax liability.

tax shelter An investment whereby one can not only earn a return but postpone or avoid making income-tax payments within the limit of tax law. Pension plans and life insurance policies, where income is not paid out until retirement or after death, are tax shelters, as are IRAs and Keogh plans (see IRA; KEOGH PLAN). Tax-exempt securities such as municipal bonds also avoid tax payments. However, the term "tax shelter" often is used more specifically for a LIMITED PARTNERSHIP in real estate, oil and gas drilling, equipment leasing, cable television, research and development projects, or some other high-risk enterprise in which profits, losses, and related tax benefits are passed on to the partners in proportion to the size of their investment. Typically such an investment will generate losses in its early years; these losses are used to shelter each of the partners' incomes. The losses come from tax credits and write-offs that are allowed for cash expenses such as interest (most such partnerships are highly leveraged, that is, borrow heavily) and for noncash deductions for depreciation or depletion, which the tax laws allow on the premise that a property will wear out (or a resource will be used up).

Some tax shelters are publicly offered through major brokerage firms; these, like stocks, must be registered with the Securities and Exchange Commission (SEC) and may be sold in units as small as $5,000. Unlike stocks, they generally are not transferable and in effect must be kept for the life of the enterprise (or until it is sold). Private placements do not have to be registered with the SEC. They generally are available in denominations of $50,000 or higher and are intended for small groups of high-income investors.

Prospective investors are advised to investigate any offering, public or private, carefully, since abuses abound. In general, only investors in the upper tax brackets who can afford to tie up money in a tax shelter for a long period (up to ten years for some) should consider doing so. The main advantages are direct tax savings and/or postponing taxable income.

The chief drawbacks, besides illiquidity, are that tax rates and rules could easily change over the time of the investment, reducing its tax advantages, the limited partners may be liable for heavy penalties in cases of abuses or illegal acts by the enterprise, and large deductions can make one subject to the ALTERNATIVE MINIMUM TAX. In addition, each kind of tax-sheltered investment has its own pros and cons. The Internal Revenue Service (IRS) can audit shelter programs, as well as individual tax returns, and heavily penalizes abuses. A danger signal inviting IRS scrutiny is a shelter that promises deductions that total two, three, or more times one's initial investment in the first year. Experts believe that limited partnerships should be one's last method of lowering taxes, after such means as opening an IRA or Keogh plan and investing in tax-exempt securities. See also OIL AND GAS PARTNERSHIP; REAL ESTATE PARTNERSHIP.

T-bill See TREASURY BILL; for *T-bill account* see MONEY-MARKET CERTIFICATE.

technical analysis A system of analyzing investments that considers mainly the historical price and volume data of a company's stock and relies heavily on charts, trendlines, and other graphic representations of data (see also CHARTIST). In recent years computer programs, such as Standard & Poor's Trendline II, have been devised to assist such analysis and help individual investors prepare charts for individual stocks, selecting time frames, moving averages, oscillators, and other technical indicators. In order to use such charts, a personal computer requires a printed circuit board called a graphics adapter to display the charts. Since typing the raw data needed for technical analysis into a computer is tedious if done manually and costly when done electronically (using a DATABASE), some investors prefer to use a program tied to an information service that offers prepackaged technical and fundamental analysis. Critics of technical analysis say that stock prices are influenced by more than other people's investment decisions and that basic data about a company (see FUNDAMENTAL ANALYSIS) are far more revealing.

technical rally A temporary rise in the price of a security or commodity that is generally heading downward. For example, at a certain price the stock or future may become attractive to a limited number of investors, whose demand drives the price up somewhat before it resumes its downward trend. See also CORRECTION.

tenancy, joint A form of co-ownership of both real and personal property (for example, a house, bank account, or brokerage account) in which each tenant owns an equal share of the entire property. When one joint tenant dies, the survivor(s) automatically become owners of his or her share; this share cannot be bequeathed to some other person(s), nor is it subject to probate. In some states there is a form of joint tenancy called *tenancy by entirety*, in which the tenants are a married couple. Neither spouse can alter the survivorship features of the tenancy, which can be changed only by mutual agreement or if the marriage terminates. Both forms of joint tenancy thus differ from *tenancy in common*, in which each tenant owns a specific portion of the whole and can freely sell it during life or bequeath it as desired after death.

tender offer Also, *tender*. A method of taking over a company by asking stockholders to sell their shares at a higher price than the current market price and by a particular date. (See also MERGER.) Since 1968 the law has required anyone making a tender offer to file with the Securities and Exchange Commission and with the target company a statement describing the terms of the offer, the bidder, the source of funds being used to pay for the shares, and the bidder's plans if the takeover succeeds. The offer must be good for at least twenty days and shareholders must have a fifteen-day period in which they may change their minds. A company sometimes employs a tender offer to use up excess cash to reduce its capitalization and thereby increase earnings per share.

10-K form A detailed annual report that all publicly owned U.S. corporations are required to file with the Securities and Exchange Commission (SEC) within ninety days of the end of their fiscal year. It must include all pertinent information about the company, its business, and its financial condition, including a considerable amount of detail not contained in the ordinary ANNUAL REPORT, such as the names of principal stockholders, the security holdings of its management, and more detailed financial schedules. Included are a description of a company's main markets and means of distribution; for a manufacturer, the availability of raw material, any significant patents, licenses, or franchises it owns, estimated cost of research, and effects of compliance with environmental laws; if in more than one business, a breakdown of total sales, net income, and identifiable assets by business segments; and detailed data on its securities. Most companies also file *10-Q reports,* quarterly updates to the 10-K that are filed three times a year, within forty-five days after the end of the firm's first, second, and third fiscal quarters. Unlike the 10-K report, the financial statements in the 10-Q do not have to be audited but must contain details of any material changes in the status of outstanding securities, defaults under debt agreements, and any matters to be submitted to shareholders for consideration. A company must send its 10-K report free of charge to any shareholder who requests it. Other sources are a broker or one of several reporting services that provide them for a fee. They also are available to the public in the libraries of the SEC regional offices (Atlanta, Boston, Chicago, Denver, Fort Worth, Los Angeles, New York, Seattle, and Washington, D.C.).

10 percent guideline   A rule of thumb for evaluating municipal bonds, according to which a municipality's total bond debt should be 10 percent or less of the total value of the real estate within its bounds.

term   The period of time between a bond's issue and its date of maturity (or redemption if that precedes maturity). A *term bond* is a bond issue that has a single maturity date (as opposed to a SERIAL BOND).

term certificate   A CERTIFICATE OF DEPOSIT that matures in one to ten years (most often two years). It earns a fixed rate of interest, usually paid semiannually.

term insurance   See under LIFE INSURANCE.

thin market   Also, *inactive market, narrow market*. In the securities and commodities trade, a market in which trading volume is light and consequently price fluctuations are greater than normal because with fewer transactions each tends to affect the price more. The term is used for the market as a whole, a particular industry or market sector, or an individual stock.

third market   The market for trading listed stocks in the over-the-counter market by brokers who are not exchange members as well as by any other investors. The term comes from the fact that the "first" market is the exchanges and the "second" market the ordinary over-the-counter market for unlisted securities.

thrift institutions   Also, *thrifts*. A general term for savings banks, credit unions, and savings and loan associations, which are the principal holders of savings accounts (time deposits) in the United States. They invest their holdings principally in home mortgages. See also SAVINGS BANK; SAVINGS AND LOAN ASSOCIATION.

thundering herd Nickname for Merrill Lynch and Company, the largest American brokerage firm.

tick Upward or downward change in a stock price. See DOWN TICK; UP TICK.

ticker See TAPE.

tight market A market characterized by active trading and a narrow spread between bid and ask prices, the opposite of a SOFT MARKET.

tight money See under MONETARY POLICY; also FEDERAL OPEN MARKET COMMITTEE.

time deposit An interest-bearing deposit in a financial institution such as a bank that must remain on deposit for a specified period of time, or cannot be withdrawn without advance notice (usually thirty to sixty days). In practice, banks rarely require notice for withdrawals from individual savings accounts, which are the most common form of time deposit for individuals. A CERTIFICATE OF DEPOSIT, however, is issued for a specific time period and carries a penalty for early withdrawal.

time draft A written order by one party upon another party to pay, at a specified future time, a sum of money to a third party. The third party does not have the use of the money until the date specified. A *sight draft*, in contrast, is payable as soon as it is received.

time value In options trading, the difference between an option's premium (market price) and its INTRINSIC VALUE. For example, if a call option for Red Hot Nov 50 is selling for $5 (the premium), and Red Hot stock is selling for $51 a share, the option has an intrinsic value of 1 (its holder could exercise the call at 50, or $5,000, and resell the stock at the market price for $5,100) and a time value of 4 (5 − 1). An option that is AT THE MONEY or OUT OF THE MONEY has no intrinsic value, and time value accounts for the entire premium.

tip Advice to buy or sell a security, usually or purportedly based on information not generally available to the public. See INSIDER.

tombstone   An advertisement placed in newspapers that gives basic information about a new issue of securities, mainly the name, price, and size of the issue and the names of underwriters and/or dealers from whom it can be bought. It is not an offer to sell but calls attention to the PROSPECTUS and points out to future clients the services the underwriter and dealers have performed.

total return   Also, *total rate of return*. The capital gain (or loss) plus the sum of dividends or interest received on an investment. Analysts often calculate the annual total return, that is, capital gain and dividends expected over the next five years or so, divided by the recent market price and expressed as an average annual rate of growth. In this calculation individual investors must also take into account their current and estimated future tax obligations.

total volume   Also, *volume of trading*. The sum of the number of shares or contracts that changed hands in a stock, bond, future, or option in a single day. For listed stocks and bonds it is the sum of transactions that took place on organized stock exchanges; for over-the-counter securities it is the volume announced by the NASDAQ index; for commodity futures and options it is the sum of transactions worldwide.

trade   In the securities and commodities business, synonym for a transaction, that is, a purchase or a sale. Also, to engage in such transactions. Thus one can say there was a trade in IBM yesterday, Tom is trading today, and Red Hot Stock traded at 32½. See also TRADER.

trader   An individual who buys and sells goods, commodities, or securities. In the securities business the term means the same as DEALER, that is, a person buying for his or her own account rather than acting as an agent for others. It often carries the implication of being a speculator, interested in quick profit (see also IN-AND-OUT TRADER). See also FLOOR TRADER.

trading floor A large room where all the transactions of a stock exchange take place. On the New York Stock Exchange each stock is traded at its particular TRADING POST.

trading limit In the commodity futures market, the maximum amount of futures that may be purchased by a trader in one day. See also PRICE LIMIT.

trading pattern See under TREND.

trading post A horseshoe-shaped counter on the floor of the New York Stock Exchange where specialists trade in specific stocks. There are eighteen trading posts on the exchange floor, each with computer screens that display bid and ask prices for the stocks traded there.

trading ring See RING.

trading unit The conventional amount traded. See also ROUND LOT.

transaction

1. In the securities and commodities industry, the execution of a buy or sell order; a purchase or a sale. Commissions and other costs incurred in buying and selling investments are known as *transaction costs*.

2. In accounting, an event or condition that is recorded in the books in the form of a debit or credit.

transfer agent A person assigned to keep track of a corporation's stockholders and bondholders and to issue certificates to new owners and cancel certificates when securities are sold. Some corporations employ their own personnel in this capacity, but most employ a bank or some other institution.

transfer tax A tax on the sale of securities, deeds to property, or licenses. The federal government imposes a small tax on the sale of all corporate bonds and all stocks, payable by the seller, and a number of states tax the sale of stocks, based either on selling price or par value. Most states and some local governments tax the transfer of deeds and licenses.

Treasury bill Also, *T-bill.* The shortest-term U.S. government obligation, issued on a discount basis and maturing in thirteen, twenty-six, or fifty-two weeks. An extremely safe short-term investment, T-bills yield the difference between issue price (discount) and face value at redemption (or market price if sold before maturity). T-bills are sold for a minimum of $10,000 and in multiples of $5,000 above that minimum. They are offered at a weekly auction held at Federal Reserve banks and their branches around the nation and in Washington, D.C., and also can be bought by mail or phone from commercial banks and stockbrokers (the latter two sources usually charge for the service). The yield from T-bills is exempt from most state and local income taxes but is subject to federal income tax. The listing of Treasury bills in the financial pages shows their maturity date, bid (amount one would sell for) and ask (amount one would pay) prices, and yield to maturity. For example, a bid price of 8.47 means $8,470 for a $10,000 T-bill, and yield of 9.02 means 9.02 percent.

Treasury bill account, T-bill account See MONEY-MARKET CERTIFICATE.

Treasury bond A long-term debt instrument of the United States Treasury, maturing in ten to thirty years, and backed by the full faith and credit of the U.S. government. It may be purchased direct from the Treasury or any of the Federal Reserve banks or their branches without charge, or from brokers and commercial banks, which usually invoke a service charge. Treasury bonds usually are available in denominations of $1,000, are issued in either registered or bearer (coupon) form, and carry a fixed interest rate. They usually are not redeemable prior to maturity. However, some thirty-year issues have a call provision (see CALLABLE BOND), permitting the Treasury to redeem them before maturity (after twenty-five years). Interest is payable twice a year and is exempt from state and local income tax, but not from federal income tax. Treasury bonds are freely traded in the over-the-counter market. Their prices, listed in the financial pages, are quoted in 32nds of a point (see under TREASURY NOTE for explanation). Older issues, originating when interest rates were low and with a coupon rate of only 3 or 4 percent, may sell at a deep discount (that is, for much less than par value).

Treasury note Also, *T-note*. A medium-term debt instrument of the United States Treasury, maturing in one to ten years and backed by the full faith and credit of the U.S. government. It may be bought direct from the Treasury or any of the Federal Reserve banks or their branches without charge, or from brokers and commercial banks, which usually invoke a service charge. The minimum purchase for notes maturing in less than four years is $5,000; for longer-term notes it is $1,000. T-notes are issued in either registered or bearer (coupon) form and bear a fixed interest rate. Most Treasury notes are not redeemable prior to maturity. Interest is payable twice a year and is exempt from state and local income tax, but not from federal income tax. Treasury notes, along with Treasury bills and Treasury bonds, are freely traded in the over-the-counter market. Treasury note prices, listed in the financial pages, are quoted in 32nds of a point. A bid of 93.8, therefore, means a dollar price for a $1,000 note of $932.50 (1 point = $10 and each 32nd = $.3125). The yield quoted is the YIELD TO MATURITY based on the ask price.

treasury stock Also, *reacquired stock, treasury shares*.

Common stock that has been issued by a company,
which then buys it back. It may then be either resold
to the public or retired. Until resold, however, it
earns no dividends and carries no voting rights. Companies buy back their own stock for a variety of
reasons, such as to provide for the conversion and/or
exercise of convertible securities, warrants, and options; to change their financial structure and become
more highly leveraged by issuing bonds; or to protect
against a takeover.

trend Also, *market trend*. The general direction of
price changes of a commodity, security, or the entire
market. Analysis of trends, which involves charting
prices on a graph, is based on the belief that price
movements tend to continue in whatever direction
they are already headed. Even if conditions change,
prices take some time to react to such changes. An
uptrend is a series of gradually ascending peaks and
troughs; a *downtrend* is a series of gradually descend-
ing peaks and troughs; a *sideways trend* shows peaks
and troughs that are essentially horizontal. A trend
may be major, lasting for years, intermediate, or
minor (short-term). Technical analysts draw *trendlines*—
straight lines connecting the highest or lowest points
that a price has reached in a given time span—in
order to determine its past trend, from which they try
to predict the future direction. Lines connecting both
the highest and the lowest points a price reaches over
a longer period (usually several years) indicate that
price's *trading pattern*.

trendline See under TREND.

triple exempt Describing a municipal bond or other
security whose yield is exempt from local, state, and
federal income tax.

trough The lowest point of the business cycle or of a
price series or other economic series.

troy ounce A unit of weight used for gold and silver,

especially in the United States and Great Britain. One troy ounce is equal to 1.097 avoirdupois ounces; 12 troy ounces are equal to 1 pound; 32 troy ounces are equal to 1 kilogram.

trust A legal transfer of property to one person, called the *trustee*, who holds it for the benefit of another person, called the *beneficiary*. The trustee usually is expected to invest the property so that it yields income and generally has the power to sell, mortgage, or lease it as the need arises.

turnover ratio A measure of the extent to which an investment company's portfolio is turned over during the course of a year. To obtain this figure for a closed-end investment company, divide the total purchases and sales of securities (except U.S. government obligations and short-term notes) by 2 and then divide by the company's average assets. For a mutual fund, divide the total of either portfolio purchases or portfolio sales (whichever is less) by the company's average assets. The turnover ratio alone is not particularly meaningful, but it enables comparison among different investment companies and also year-to-year comparisons for the same company.

twisting Another name for CHURNING.

two-dollar broker Older name for INDEPENDENT BROKER.

U

u In stock tables, indicating a new 52-week high.

uncovered option Also, *naked option*. Writing (selling) an OPTION without owning the underlying security.

underlying debt The debt of a lesser municipality for which a larger municipality is also partly responsible, for example, the debt of a county for which the state it is in is partly obligated. Such an arrangement can be of interest in evaluating municipal bonds. See also OVERLAPPING DEBT.

underlying security The stock that must be delivered when a stock option or warrant is exercised, a rights offering is subscribed to, or a convertible debenture or preferred stock is converted. Similarly, the futures contract that must be delivered if an option on that future is exercised.

undervalued Describing a security whose current market price is exceedingly low in terms of its price-earnings ratio, book value, or potential future earnings, and so can be expected to rise. The low price may result from various factors—for example, the company is out of favor with institutional investors, or it has an erratic history, or a new and untried management. An undervalued company may become a target for a takeover, since it may be acquired relatively cheaply. See also OVERVALUED.

underwriting

    1. In the securities trade, buying an issue of bonds or other securities from the issuer in order to resell them to investors. The underwriter, usually an investment banker or group of investment bankers (called a *syndicate*), purchases the issue at an agreed-on price less a discount, which represents its fee for accepting the risk that it cannot resell all the securities at that price and for its expenses in selling them. Sometimes, in the case of a small or new company, the underwriter only agrees to help sell a new issue, without guaranteeing the issuer a fixed sum of money for the entire issue; this practice is called *best-efforts selling*.

2. In insurance, the assumption of all or part of the risk of fire, theft, accident, illness, death, or other hazards stipulated in a policy, in exchange for a payment called a *premium*. In most cases the underwriter is the insurance company itself. However, the term ''underwriter'' also is used for the expert who determines what risks a company should accept, and under what terms, and the term may also extend to the company's sales personnel and other staff.

unearned income

1. Income that has been received but not yet earned, for example, insurance premiums and rents. See also PREPAID EXPENSE.

2. Income from sources other than goods or services produced, such as interest on investments and rent on land. See also PASSIVE INCOME; PORTFOLIO.

Uniform Gift to Minors Act   A law enacted in many U.S. states that spells out how assets may be transferred to and administered for children. Investors use it to transfer securities holdings to their children, who, if they are over 14, can benefit from lower tax rates; either a parent or a trustee administers such an account until the child reaches adulthood.

Uniform Securities Agent State Law Examination   A test that in many states must be passed before a broker may become a registered representative entitled to solicit clients and give investment advice. In addition to this state test, all registered representatives, whether they work for stock exchange member firms or over-the-counter brokerage firms, must pass the General Securities Representative Examination (also called Series 7 Examination) given by the National Association of Securities Dealers. See also BROKER.

unissued stock Stock that is authorized in a corporation's charter but has not been issued and cannot pay dividends or be voted. It differs from TREASURY STOCK, which has been issued but is not outstanding.

United States savings bond See U.S SAVINGS BOND.

unit investment trust Also, *fixed investment trust, unit trust*. An INVESTMENT COMPANY that purchases a fixed portfolio of securities, such as municipal bonds, which it deposits with a bank trustee, and which it sells to investors in units of $1,000 (or some similar amount), each of which represents a portion of interest in the entire portfolio. The unit holder receives a proportionate share of the interest earned and, as the securities mature, a return of the principal. The units can be sold at any time without penalty. Although the majority invest in tax-exempt state and municipal bonds, unit trusts have been formed with portfolios of many other kinds of security, including common and preferred stocks. The chief advantages of investing in a unit investment trust are professional selection and diversification of the underlying portfolio, low unit price, periodic income payments (monthly, quarterly, or semiannually, depending on the trust), and ease of redemption. Unit investment trusts are sponsored by major brokerage firms and firms specializing in tax-exempt securities, and brokers usually invoke an initial sales charge of 3 to 5 percent. Their prices fluctuate with interest rates, just as those of the underlying securities. If interest rates rise after original purchase, their value declines, and if rates drop their value rises. They differ from municipal bond mutual funds in that their portfolio remains intact until the bonds mature or are called.

unit leverage Another name for OPERATING LEVERAGE.

unit trust Term used by some as a synonym for MUTUAL FUND. To prevent confusion with UNIT INVESTMENT TRUST, this book avoids that usage entirely.

universal life insurance See under LIFE INSURANCE.

unlisted security A security that is not listed on an organized stock or commodity exchange and is largely traded in the OVER-THE-COUNTER MARKET. However, regional stock exchanges (see under STOCK EXCHANGE) often obtain permission from the Securities and Exchange Commission to trade a particular corporation's stocks on an unlisted basis, meaning the company does not have to make a formal application for listing or pay fees to be listed.

up tick Also, *plus tick*. A security price that is higher than that of the immediately preceding transaction, designated by a plus sign just before the price shown on the screen. See also SHORT SALE RULE; ZERO-MINUS (PLUS) TICK.

U.S. savings bond Also, *savings bond*. A United States government bond that is nonmarketable, that is, cannot be sold to someone else, and can be purchased only from the government and held until the time of redemption or maturity. It is considered one of the safest investments that exists and also yields much less than other bonds. Savings bonds, which are registered in the purchaser's name, must be held for at least six months, after which they can be redeemed. They are issued as SERIES BONDS, and in the 1980's two series were available. EE bonds are bought at a 50 percent discount from par (face) value and, if held for at least five years, earn a variable interest rate that changes every six months and is based on 85 percent of the return on five-year Treasury bonds during the preceding six months. HH bonds are bought at par value and earn interest payments twice a year. Series EE bonds can be bought at most commercial banks, savings banks, and other financial institutions. No commission is charged for their sale, and they are available in denominations as low as $50. Series HH bonds are available only in exchange for the older Series E or Series EE bonds. The minimum denomination is $500 and they are issued and redeemed only at Federal Reserve banks and their branches and at the Treasury. The interest on all U.S. savings bonds is exempt from state and local income tax, and for EE bonds federal income tax may be deferred until time of redemption or maturity (if the holder wishes).

V

VA-guaranteed loan A home-mortgage loan that is guaranteed by the Veterans Administration (VA). According to a program set up after World War II, the VA guarantees 60 percent of a loan or $27,500, whichever is lower, for eligible veterans, who must obtain a certificate of eligibility from the VA. VA loans may be assumed by subsequent buyers, either veterans or nonveterans, but somewhat different regulations apply to each. The interest rate is set by the VA, and the borrower's ability to pay is evaluated on an individual basis.

variable annuity An ANNUITY in which the insurer invests the premiums in common stock and securities whose prices reflect inflation more than traditional fixed-income investments in bonds and mortgages. Payments to the annuitant therefore are not in fixed-dollar amounts but in units representing shares of stock, whose value presumably has kept pace with the cost of living. Such an annuity is regarded as far riskier than the traditional fixed-dollar policy, since the yield will depend on how well the portfolio is managed and other unpredictable factors.

variable life insurance See under LIFE INSURANCE.

variable-rate mortgage Abbreviated *VRM*. See ADJUSTABLE-RATE MORTGAGE.

venture capital Also, *risk capital*. Funds invested in a new or high-risk enterprise, with a potential for extraordinary profit or complete loss. The borrower may offer common stock, preferred stock, royalties, or other profit-sharing incentives. Providers of venture capital include rich individuals, banks, investment banks, and companies that pool investments in venture capital in special funds or in limited partnerships set up for that purpose.

vertical spread See under SPREAD, def. 3.

vj Symbol used in newspaper stock listings to indicate that a company is in bankruptcy proceedings. It is often misprinted *vi*.

volatility The sensitivity of a security price to changes in the market as a whole (other prices), which is measured by its BETA. Technical analysts consider such volatility an unavoidable risk, and in a perfectly efficient portfolio it represents the only such risk. A stock price may be volatile owing to internal factors as well—because the issuing corporation is exceptionally profitable or unprofitable, because there are only a small number of shares outstanding, or similar reasons. These are measured by its ALPHA. See also RISK; SAFETY.

volume Also, *volume of trade*. The amount traded in a particular security or commodity in a given period of time. Analysts regard volume as an important indicator, since rising volume frequently is succeeded by rising prices and declining volume often is followed by falling prices. Institutional traders, who routinely deal in large blocks of stock, naturally have a significant effect on overall volume. See also TOTAL VOLUME.

voting rights A stockholder's right to vote on corporate decisions. Normally each share of common stock is allotted one vote. Direct participation in decisions affecting a firm's day-to-day operations is rare except in the case of very small companies. In most large corporations stockholders elect the members of the board of directors, who in turn select the firm's officers. See also CUMULATIVE VOTING; PROXY.

voting trust A trust set up to give control of a corporation to a few individuals, called voting trustees. In exchange for their common stock, the stockholders receive voting trust certificates, which entitle them to all the rights of the stock except voting rights. Such an arrangement is usually made for a company in bankruptcy that is forced to reorganize and wishes to prevent anyone from obstructing reorganization. It also may be used in a proxy fight. The trust usually has a limited life, such as five years.

warrant A form of convertible security that represents an option to buy a given amount of stock at a
specified price called *exercise price* and usually over
a specific number of years. A warrant has no claim
on either the equity or profits of a company. Unlike
RIGHTS, warrants are not necessarily issued only to
stockholders. Their life is usually longer, and they
may even be perpetual. However, many do have
expiration dates, after which they are worthless. The
exercise price is usually above the market price when
they are issued, and they tend to react to price increases in the common stock much as convertible
bonds and preferred stock do. If the common stock
price declines, however, warrants have no investment
value to cushion their own decline. Warrants are
sometimes attached to bonds or other securities in
order to make them more attractive. When distributed
in this way, the warrants can usually be detached and
traded separately. Those traded on organized stock
exchanges are listed in the financial pages (often with
the abbreviation *wt.*). Similarly, *ww* is used to sig-
nify "with warrants" and *xw* "without warrants."
Also, some bonds can be purchased with a warrant to
buy more bonds.

wash sale The simultaneous purchase and sale of large
amounts of a security, either by one person or a
group acting together, in order to create the appearance of high volume and thereby drive the price up.
One way of profiting is to sell the stock short and
then buy it back; today this method is difficult to
effect because of the SHORT SALE RULE requiring a

short sale on an up tick. Another method, which involves taking a loss in order to avoid tax liability and then buying back the security, is circumvented by the Internal Revenue Service's *thirty-day wash rule,* which states that losses on a sale of stock may not be used for tax purposes (to offset capital gains) if the same or equivalent stock is purchased within thirty days before or after the date of the sale.

wasting asset A property that eventually loses all its value. For example, options and warrants are worthless after they expire. A Ginnie Mae certificate similarly becomes worthless, because principal and interest are periodically repaid. A *wasting assets corporation* is a business formed specifically for exhausting a given resource (such as a coal mine) or liquidating another business (such as a bankrupt company) and will pay out practically all of its cash in the form of dividends.

watered stock Stock with an inflated value, created by issuing additional shares of stock without a corresponding increase in corporate assets.

wd In stock and bond tables, abbreviation for *when distributed,* meaning that a stock or bond has been issued but certificates are not yet available.

when issued Short for *When, as, and if issued.* Abbreviated *WI.* A conditional trade in a stock or bond in which the price is set but the settlement date is to be determined because the security has not actually been issued. It occurs not only for new issues of stocks, bonds, and Treasury securities but also for stock splits, which can begin to be traded soon after they are announced.

white knight See under MERGER.

White's rating A system of rating municipal bonds made by White's Tax-Exempt Bond Rating Service. It classifies bonds on the basis of current market factors rather than on the credit rating of the issuer, and tries to estimate appropriate yields. It is available by subscription.

whole life insurance See under LIFE INSURANCE.

widow and orphan stock A safe, high-income stock, appropriate for those who need regular dividends and cannot afford much risk.

windfall A sudden, unexpected profit, such as that earned by the domestic oil industry in the 1970's when Arab producers quadrupled their prices.

wire house A brokerage firm whose offices and branches are linked to each other by means of its own communications network and also with the stock exchange. Until about 1980 only the largest brokerage houses could afford this, but more sophisticated and less expensive equipment has given smaller firms access to similar service, which permits rapid transmission of information concerning prices, markets, and similar data.

working capital Also, *net current assets*, *net working capital*. Total current assets minus total current liabilities; the result indicates whether a company is solvent and what it has in liquid assets for running on a day-to-day basis. The higher a firm's sales, the more working capital it tends to need.

working control The control of a corporation's operations by minority stockholders (that is, they own less than half its stock). Because ownership of many companies is very widely dispersed, a holding of 25 or 30 percent of the common stock often can be a controlling interest.

wraparound mortgage A larger mortgage that includes the amount of an original mortgage and adds to it, usually at a higher interest rate. The borrower treats it as a single loan and makes regular interest payments to the lender responsible for the second loan.

write-down (write-up) Reducing (or increasing) the

recorded value of an asset to adjust to the current market, allow for depreciation, make the company's position look better, and so forth.

write-off Removal of a bad debt or a worthless asset, such as an obsolete machine, by reducing its book value to zero.

writer The person who sells or creates an OPTION contract.

wt In stock tables, abbreviation for WARRANT.

ww In bond tables, indicating a bond sold with a WARRANT.

X

x

1. Also, *xd.* In stock tables, abbreviation for EX-DIVIDEND, that is, the day *after* dividends are awarded.

2. In bond tables, abbreviation for *ex-interest,* or without interest, meaning the day on which the new buyer of a bond that normally trades FLAT will not qualify for interest payment.

x-dis In stock tables, abbreviation for *ex-distribution,* the day after the distribution of stock dividends, so that the new purchaser does *not* get the dividend.

xr Abbreviation for EX-RIGHTS.

xw Abbreviation for EX-WARRANTS.

y In stock tables, indication that a figure means EX-
DIVIDEND and sales in full (the actual number of
shares traded is shown).

Yankee bond Also, *dollar bond.* A bond issued by a
foreign government, agency, or corporation that is
denominated in U.S. dollars, that is, both interest
and principal are payable in dollars.

Yankee CD A CERTIFICATE OF DEPOSIT that is issued
or payable in the United States by a branch of a
major foreign bank. Yankee CDs are traded in the
money market.

year-end dividend An EXTRA DIVIDEND paid at the
end of the year.

yellow sheet A list of unlisted corporate bonds published every business day by the National Quotation
Bureau, printed on yellow paper (hence the name).

yield Also, *rate of return, return.* The rate of return
on any investment, expressed as a percentage. For
example, a stock purchased for $30 that pays a divi-
dend of $2 per year is said to yield 6⅔ percent (2 ÷ 30);
this is also called its *dividend yield*, and it is independent of the stock's market price at year's end. (See
also TOTAL RETURN.) A bond purchased for $5,000
that pays $25 interest per year yields 5 percent (25 ÷
5,000). However, the return on bonds is normally
calculated in terms of their current market price (see
CURRENT YIELD) or in terms of their return until maturity (see YIELD TO MATURITY).

yield curve A graph showing the yield from various
fixed-income securities that are essentially the same
except for their maturity dates. The yields (in per-

centages) are shown on the y-axis (vertical axis) and
the maturities (in years) on the x-axis (horizontal
axis). An upward-sloping curve shows higher yields
on longer-term investments, indicating that demand
for short-term funds is low; a downward-sloping curve
shows higher yields on short-term investments, indicating more demand for them than for long-term
ones; a flat curve shows that the demand for securities is the same regardless of maturity.

yield spread The difference in returns from various
issues of securities. It may refer to the yield from the
same kind of security—for example, from bonds of
different quality—or from different securities, such
as the dividend yield from stocks versus the current
yield from corporate bonds.

yield stock Another name for income stock, that is,
one paying a high dividend.

yield to maturity Also, *maturity yield*. The rate of
return on a bond or other long-term investment, calculated on the basis of purchase price, redemption
price, the total interest payments, and the number of
months or years until maturity. This calculation assumes that the bond will be held until it matures and
that the interest it earns will be reinvested at the same
market rate. It does not take into account taxes on
interest and capital gains (see AFTER-TAX YIELD). The
yield to maturity is larger than CURRENT YIELD when
the bond is selling at a discount (below par value)
and less when it is selling at a premium (above par
value). The easiest way to determine yield to maturity is to consult a bond-yield table, which can be
found at most brokerage offices, banks, and in financial literature concerning the bond market; for this
one need know only the coupon rate, purchase price,
and date of maturity. For a CALLABLE BOND it may be
more practical to determine the *yield to call*, which
assumes the bond will be redeemed at the earliest call

date specified. The same calculations are used except that date of maturity is replaced by the call date.

For municipal securities, price quotations often are on a yield-to-maturity basis rather than a percentage-of-par basis. Thus a 5 percent coupon municipal bond with fifteen years to maturity would be quoted as 5.40 percent bid, 5.30 percent offered. To calculate the bond's dollar price, one needs to look in a *basis book*, found in the same places as a bond-yield table.

z

1. In newspaper listings of stock prices, indication that a volume figure designates sales in full (the actual number of shares traded), and not some multiple of the figure; thus *z 400* means that 400 shares were traded, not 40,000 shares.

2. In newspaper listings of mutual fund quotations, indication that the fund did not report bid-ask prices for that day.

zero-coupon issue A deep-discount fixed-income security that pays no interest prior to maturity, the return on it resulting entirely from the considerable difference between purchase price and redemption price. If the underlying security is taxable, the investor must pay taxes each year on the amount of implied interest accrued, even though that interest has not been paid out. Therefore taxable zero-coupon issues are considered most suitable for tax-sheltered accounts, such as IRAs and pension funds. Zero-coupon issues exist in numerous forms, including corporate bonds, municipal bonds, Treasury issues, certificates of deposit, and mortgages. Some carry call provisions, which if invoked can reduce the yield considerably. Corporations issue zero-coupon bonds directly, but the federal and local governments generally do not. Treasury issues are available through brokers or other financial intermediaries that buy large blocks and sell investors a part interest in them (see COUPON STRIPPING). Buyers of zero-coupon securities generally plan to hold them until maturity. Although they can be redeemed early, it is through a secondary market that will pay somewhat less than their worth. They are more suitable for meeting a specific investment goal, such as money for college tuition or for retirement. However, because they do not pay interest they are not a low-risk investment; their yield is locked in with their purchase price and does not change with changing economic conditions.

zero-minus (plus) tick Also, *zero-down (up) tick*. A security price that is the same as that in the preceding transaction but lower (higher) than the preceding different price. Thus, if ABC sells at 32, 31½, 31½, the last 31½ represents a zero-minus tick; if KXR sells at 14½, 15, 15, the last 15 represents a zero-plus tick.

Appendix A

U.S. STOCK
AND COMMODITY EXCHANGES

Stock Exchanges	*Location*	
American Stock Exchange (AMEX) (formerly Curb Exchange)	New York, NY	Second largest U.S. stock exchange; also trades options and many foreign stocks
Boston Stock Exchange	Boston, MA	Regional exchange
Cincinnati Stock Exchange	Cincinnati, OH	Regional exchange, first to be wholly automated, with bulk of trading electronically executed
Midwest Stock Exchange	Chicago, IL	Regional exchange
New York Stock Exchange (NYSE) ("Big Board")	New York, NY	Oldest and largest U.S. exchange; also trades options
Pacific Stock Exchange	Los Angeles CA San Francisco CA	Regional exchange with two trading floors; also trades options
Philadelphia Stock Exchange	Philadelphia, PA	Regional stock exchange, also trades options

Commodity Exchanges Location

Chicago Board of Trade (CBOT)	Chicago, IL	World's largest and oldest commodity futures exchange; trades commodity futures, futures options, index options
Chicago Board Options Exchange	Chicago, IL	Largest options exchange; stock options, interest rate, and index options
Chicago Mercantile Exchange, includes International Money Market (IMM)	Chicago, IL	Commodity and financial futures, futures options, index options
Coffee, Sugar and Cocoa Exchange	New York, NY	Commodity futures and futures options
Commodity Exchange, Inc. (COMEX)	New York, NY	Metal futures and futures options
Kansas City Board of Trade	Kansas City, KS	Commodity futures, index and futures options
MidAmerica Commodity Exchange	Chicago, IL	Commodity and financial futures, futures options
Minneapolis Grain Exchange	Minneapolis MN	Commodity futures and futures options
New York Cotton Exchange, includes Citrus Associates and Financial Instrument Exchange (FINEX)	New York, NY	Commodity futures and futures options, stock index futures
New York Mercantile Exchange	New York, NY	Commodity futures
New York Futures Exchange (part of New York Stock Exchange)	New York, NY	Financial futures and futures options

Appendix B

SOURCES
OF FINANCIAL INFORMATION

General Newspapers and Periodicals

American Association of Individual Investors Journal (10 issues per year), for annual dues to this nonprofit association, 612 N. Michigan Ave., Chicago, IL 60611.

*Barron's National Business and Financial Weekly (weekly), Dow Jones, 22 Cortlandt St., New York, NY 10007.

Better Investing (monthly), National Association of Investors, 1515 E. Eleven Mile Rd., Royal Oak, MI 48067.

*Business Week (weekly), 1211 Avenue of the Americas, New York, NY 10020.

Byte (monthly), McGraw Hill, Inc., 70 Main St., Peterborough, NH 03458.

*Changing Times (monthly), 1729 H St., NW, Washington, DC 20006.

Citicorp Report to Investors (quarterly), 399 Park Ave., New York, NY 10022.

Computerworld (weekly), 375 Cochituate Rd., Box 9171, Framingham, MA 01701.

*Dun's Business Month (monthly), 875 Third Ave., New York, NY 10022.

*Economist, The (weekly), London, England (U.S. subscription address: P.O. Box 904, Farmingdale, NY 11737).

Fact Magazine (monthly), 305 East 46th St., New York, NY 10017.

Financial Analysts Journal (bimonthly), 1633 Broadway, New York, NY 10019.

Financial Planning Strategist (monthly), 10076 Boca Entrada Highway, Boca Raton, FL 33433.

*Financial World, News Magazine for Investors (biweekly), 1450 Broadway, New York, NY 10018.

*Very widely used

Forbes (biweekly), 60 Fifth Ave., New York, NY 10011.

Fortune (monthly), Time & Life Building, Rockefeller Center, New York, NY 10020.

Insiders, The (semimonthly), 3471 North Federal Highway, Fort Lauderdale, FL 33306.

Insiders' Chronicle (weekly), 1111 E. Putnam Ave., Riverside, CT 06878.

Institutional Investor (monthly), 488 Madison Ave., New York, NY 10022.

Investment Dealers' Digest (weekly), 150 Broadway, New York, NY 10038.

Investor's Daily (daily), Box 25970, Los Angeles, CA 90025.

Journal of Buyouts and Acquisitions (bimonthly), 7124 Convoy Ct., San Diego, CA 92111.

Journal of Commerce and Commercial (daily), 110 Wall St., New York, NY 10005.

Journal of Portfolio Management (quarterly), 488 Madison Ave., New York, NY 10022.

Kiplinger Washington Letter (weekly), 1729 H Street NW, Washington, DC 20006.

Lynch International Investment Survey (weekly), 1010 Franklin Ave., Garden City, NY 11530.

Market Logic (semimonthly), 3471 N. Federal Highway, Fort Lauderdale, FL 33306.

Media General Financial Weekly (weekly), Box C-32333, Richmond, VA 23293.

Merrill Lynch Market Letter (semimonthly), 165 Broadway, New York, NY 10080.

Money (monthly), Time & Life Bldg., New York, NY 10020.

Nation's Business (monthly), U.S. Chamber of Commerce, 1615 H St. NW, Washington, DC 20062.

New Issues (monthly), 3471 N. Federal Highway, Fort Lauderdale, FL 33306.

News for Investors (monthly), 1319 F St. NW, Washington, DC 20004.

Personal Finance Letter (fortnightly), 1221 Ave. of the Americas, New York, NY 10020.

Professional Tape Reader (semimonthly), P.O. Box 2407, Hollywood, FL 33022.

Smart Money (monthly), Six Deer Trail, Old Tapan, NJ 07675.

*Very widely used

Stock Market Magazine (monthly), 16 School St., Yonkers, NY 10701.

*Value Line Investment Survey (weekly), 711 Third Ave., New York, NY 10017.

Wall Street and U.S. Business News (monthly), 5000 N. U.S. Highway 1, Box 1116, Mainland Sta., Ormond Beach, FL 32074.

*Wall Street Journal, The (daily), 22 Cortlandt St., New York, NY 10007.

Wall Street Letter (weekly), 488 Madison Ave., New York, NY 10022.

Wall Street Reports (monthly), 54 Wall St., New York, NY 10005.

*Wall Street Transcript (weekly), 120 Wall St., New York, NY 10005.

Weekly Insider Report (weekly), Box 59, Brookside, NJ 07926.

Wright Bankers' Service (weekly), 500 State St., Bridgeport, CT 06604.

Zweig Forecast (semimonthly), P.O. Box 5345, New York, NY 10150.

Bonds, Convertibles, and Other Fixed-Income Securities

Blue List, The (daily), 345 Hudson St., New York, NY 10014.

Bond Buyer, The (weekly or daily), 1 State St. Plaza, New York, NY 10004.

Bond Market Research, Currencies, and International Interest Rates (quarterly), Salomon Bros., 1 New York Plaza, New York, NY 10004.

Bondweek (weekly), 1 State St. Plaza, New York, NY 10004.

Creditweek (quarterly), published by Standard & Poor's, 25 Broadway, New York, NY 10004.

Eliot Sharp's Muni Newsletter (daily), on municipal issues, 150 Broadway, New York, NY 10038.

Fitch Corporate Bond Review (semimonthly), 12 Barclay St., New York, NY 10007.

Goldsmith-Nagan Bond and Money Market Letter (biweekly), 1545 New York Ave., NE, Washington, DC 20002.

KV Convertible Fact Finder (weekly), Kalb, Voorhis & Co., 27 William St., New York, NY 10005.

Moody's Bond Record (monthly), 99 Church St., New York, NY 10007.

*Moody's Bond Survey (weekly), 99 Church St., New York, NY 10007.

Moody's Municipals and Government News Reports (fortnightly), 99 Church St., New York, NY 10007.

Reporting on Governments (weekly), 2 Fifth Ave., New York, NY 10011.

Spectrum Convertibles (quarterly), 11501 Georgia Ave., Silver Spring, MD 20902.

*Very widely used

Standard & Poor's Bond Guide (monthly), 345 Hudson St., New York, NY 10014.

Coins

Coinage Magazine's Smartmoney (quarterly), 2600 E. Main St., Ventura, CA 93003.

Consultant's Coin Report (monthly), Box 8277, Fountain Valley, CA 92728.

Hard Money Digest (monthly), 3608 Grand Ave., Oakland, CA 94610.

Profit Report (National Hard Asset Reporter) (semimonthly), Box 7212 Main P.O., Chicago, IL 60680.

Commodities and Futures

COMEX Weekly Market Report (weekly), Commodity Exchange, Southeast Plaza Bldg., 4 World Trade Center, New York, NY 10048.

Commodity Journal (monthly), American Association of Commodity Traders, 10 Park St., Concord, NH 03301.

Commodity Trading Digest (semimonthly), 10076 Boca Entrada Highway, Boca Raton, FL 33428.

CRB Futures Chart Service (weekly), 75 Montgomery St., Jersey City, NJ 07302.

Dunn and Hargitt's Commodity Service (weekly), 22 N. Second St., Box 1100, Lafayette, IN 47902.

Futures (Chicago) (monthly), also options, 250 S. Wacker Dr., Chicago, IL 60606.

Futures Market Service (weekly), 75 Montgomery St., Jersey City, NJ 07302.

*Green's Commodity Market Comments (biweekly), Box 174, Princeton, NJ 08542.

Journal of Futures Markets (quarterly), 605 Third Ave., New York, NY 10016.

Rosten International Commodities Report (quarterly), 1413 Thayer Ave., Los Angeles, CA 90024.

Wholesale Commodity Prices (weekly), Dun & Bradstreet, 99 Church St., New York, NY 10007.

*Very widely used

Gold, Silver, and Strategic Metals

Aden Analysis (semimonthly), 4425 West Napoleon Ave., Metairie, LA 70001.

Gold Newsletter (monthly), 4425 West Napoleon Ave., Metairie, LA 70001.

*Green's Commodity Market Comments (biweekly), P.O. Box 174, Princeton, NJ 08540.

The Metals Investor (monthly), 711 West 17th St., G-4, Costa Mesa, CA 92627.

Mining Journal (weekly), 15 Wilson St., Moorgate, London EC2M 2TR, England.

Precious Metals Performance Digest (monthly), 10076 Boca Entrada Blvd., Boca Raton, FL 33433.

Silver and Gold Report (semimonthly), P.O. Box 325, Newtown, CT 06470.

Limited Partnerships and Tax Shelters

Limited Partners Letter (monthly), Box 1146, Menlo Park, CA 94026.

*Stanger Register (monthly), 1129 Broad St., Shrewsbury, NJ 07701.

Tax Shelter Blue Book (semiannually), Mill Hill Rd., Box 888, Woodstock, NY 12498.

Tax Shelter Insider (monthly), 10076 Boca Entrada Blvd., Boca Raton, FL 33433.

Tax Shelter Monitor (monthly), Box 512, Grand Central Sta., New York, NY 10017.

Tax-Sheltered Investments Law Report (monthly), Clark Boardman Co., 435 Hudson St., New York, NY 10014.

Money Market (See also listings under Bonds and Mutual Funds

Moody's Commercial Paper Record (monthly), 99 Church St., New York, NY 10007.

Standard & Poor's Commercial Paper Ratings Guide (monthly), 25 Broadway, New York, NY 10004.

*Very widely used

Mutual Funds

Donoghue's Money Fund Report (weekly), Box 540, Holliston, MA 01746.

*Donoghue's Moneyletter (fortnightly), Box 540, Holliston, MA 01746.

Fact Book, The (updated annually), published by Investment Company Institute (national trade association), 1600 M. St. NW, Washington, DC 20036.

Growth Fund Guide (monthly), Growth Fund Research Building, Box 6600, Rapid City, SD 57709.

Handbook for No-Load Fund Investors, P.O. Box 283, Hastings-on-Hudson, NY 10706.

*Investment Companies Service, also called *Wiesenberger Investment Companies* (annually, with monthly and quarterly updating), 210 South St., Boston, MA 02111.

Management Results (also called *Wiesenberger Investment Companies Service: Management Results*), supplement to *Investment Companies Service* (quarterly), 210 South St., Boston, MA 02111.

Money Fund Safety Ratings (monthly), 3471 N. Federal Highway, Fort Lauderdale, FL 33306.

Mutual Fund Letter, The (monthly), 205 W. Wacker Dr., Chicago, IL 60606.

Mutual Fund Performance Review (monthly), 11501 Georgia Ave., Silver Spring, MD 20902.

Mutual Funds Current Performance and Dividend Record (monthly), published by Wiesenberger, 210 South St., Boston, MA 02111.

Mutual Funds Guide (biweekly), 4025 W. Peterson Ave., Chicago, IL 60646.

Mutual Fund Specialist, The (monthly), Royal R. Lemier & Co., Box 1025, Eau Claire, WI 54701.

No-Load Fund Investor (quarterly), P.O. Box 283, Hastings-on-Hudson, NY 10706.

No-Load Fund X (monthly), 235 Montgomery St., San Francisco, CA 94104.

Performance Guide Publications: Mutual Funds and Timing (monthly), Box 2604, Palos Verdes, CA 90274.

Spectrum 1: U.S. and European Investment Company Stock Holdings Surveys (quarterly), 11501 Georgia Ave., Silver Spring, MD 20902.

Spectrum 2: U.S. and European Investment Company Portfolios (quarterly), 11501 Georgia Ave., Silver Spring, MD 20902.

Strongest Funds (monthly), Box 6600, Rapid City, SD 57709.

**Very widely used

Trends in Mutual Fund Activities (monthly), 1600 M St. NW, Washington, DC 20036.

United Mutual Fund Selector (semimonthly), 210 Newbury St., Boston, MA 02116.

*Wiesenberger Investment Companies Service Current Performance and Dividend Report (monthly), 210 South St., Boston, MA 02111.

Options

Option Weekly (weekly), Box 124, Annandale, VA 22003.

Options Alert (weekly), published by Merrill Lynch, 1 Liberty Plaza, 165 Broadway, New York, NY 10006.

Options Handbooks (semiannually), published by Standard & Poor's, 25 Broadway, New York, NY 10004.

*Value Line Options and Convertible Survey (weekly), 711 Third Ave., New York, NY 10017.

Stocks

American Stock Exchange Stock Reports (weekly), Standard & Poor's, 25 Broadway, New York, NY 10004.

American Stock Exchange Weekly Bulletin (weekly), 86 Trinity Pl., New York, NY 10006.

Blue Chip Financial Forecasts (monthly), 1300 N. 17th St., Arlington, VA 22209.

Emerging and Special Situations (monthly), new issues, Standard & Poor's, 25 Broadway, New York, NY 10004.

Emerging Growth Stocks (fortnightly), 7412 Calumet Ave., Hammond, IN 46324.

Growth Stock Outlook (semimonthly), 4405 East West Highway, Box 9911, Bethesda, MD 20014.

Growth Stocks Handbook (semiannually), Standard & Poor's, 25 Broadway, New York, NY 10004.

Junior Growth Stocks (semimonthly), 4405 East West Highway, Box 9911, Bethesda, MD 20014.

Low-Priced Stock Survey (fortnightly), 7412 Calumet Ave., Hammond, IN 46324.

Market Chronicle (weekly), over-the-counter stocks, William B. Dana Co., Box 958, New York, NY 10277.

*Very widely used

Moody's Handbook of Common Stocks (quarterly), 99 Church St., New York, NY 10007.

Moody's Handbook of OTC Stocks (quarterly), 99 Church St., New York, NY 10007.

New York Stock Exchange Statistical Highlights (monthly), NYSE, 11 Wall St., New York, NY 10005.

New York Stock Exchange Stock Reports (weekly), Standard & Poor's, 25 Broadway, New York, NY 10004.

OTC and Regional Exchange Stock Reports (weekly), Standard & Poor's, 25 Broadway, New York, NY 10004.

OTC Chart Manual (monthly), Standard & Poor's, 25 Broadway, New York, NY 10004.

OTC Handbook (semiannually), Standard & Poor's, 25 Broadway, New York, NY 10004.

OTC Review (monthly), 110 Pennsylvania Ave., Oreland, PA 19075.

Penny Stock Performance Digest (semimonthly), 10076 Boca Entrada Blvd., Boca Raton, FL 33433.

Speculator (weekly), listed low-price stocks, 108 Columbus Dr., Jersey City, NJ 07302.

Standard & Poor's Dividend Record (daily or quarterly), 25 Broadway, New York, NY 10004.

Standard & Poor's Earnings Forecaster (weekly), 25 Broadway, New York, NY 10004.

**Standard & Poor's Stock Guide* (monthly), 25 Broadway, New York, NY 10004.

Unlisted Market Guide (weekly), 48 Glen Head Rd., Box 106, Glen Head, NY 11545.

Value Line OTC Special Situations Service (fortnightly), 711 Third Ave., New York, NY 10017.

Weekly Insider Report (weekly), Box 59, Brookside, NJ 07926.

U.S. Government Publications

Broker-Dealer Directory (quarterly), from Securities and Exchange Commission, Washington, DC 20549.

Federal Reserve Bulletin (monthly), from Federal Reserve Board of Governors, Washington, DC 20551.

Investment Adviser Directory (quarterly), from SEC (see above)

*Very widely used

Monthly Review of Federal Reserve banks, especially those of Cleveland, New York, and St. Louis

Publications Services
Division of Administrative Services
Board of Governors of the Federal
    Reserve System
Washington, DC 20551

Research Department
Federal Reserve Bank of Atlanta
Federal Reserve Station
Atlanta, GA 30303

Public Information & Education
Federal Reserve Bank of Boston
30 Pearl St.
Boston, MA 02106

Publications and Reports Section
Research Department
Federal Reserve Bank of Chicago
230 South LaSalle St.
Chicago, IL 60690

Publications Section
Federal Reserve Bank of New York
33 Liberty St.
New York, NY 10045

Research Librarian
Federal Reserve Bank of St. Louis
411 Locust St., Box 442
St. Louis, MO 63166

Bank and Public Relations
    Department
Federal Reserve Bank of
    Philadelphia
925 Chestnut St.
Philadelphia, PA 19101

Public Information Director
Federal Reserve Bank of Kansas
    City
925 Grand Ave.
Kansas City, MO 64106

Research Department
Federal Reserve Bank of Cleveland
1455 East 6th St.
Cleveland, OH 44101

Research Department
Federal Reserve Bank of Dallas
Station K
Dallas, TX 75222

Bank and Public Relations
    Department
Federal Reserve Bank of Richmond
100 North 9th St.
Richmond, VA 23213

Administrative Service Department
Federal Reserve Bank of San
    Francisco
200 Sansome St.
San Francisco, CA 94120

SEC News Digest (daily), order from Superintendent of Documents, GPO, Washington, DC 20402

Survey of Current Business (monthly), order from GPO, Washington, DC 20402.

Market Letter Ratings

Hulbert Financial Digest, The (monthly), 643 South Carolina Ave. SE, Washington, DC 20003.

Appendix C

IMPORTANT STOCK INDEXES/AVERAGES

Name	Made up of	Weighting*	Subindexes	Base year & level
American Stock Exchange Market Value Index (AMVI)	Common stocks, warrants, and ADRs traded on American Stock Exchange	Market-weighted	16 subindexes (8 industrial, 8 geographic)	1983 = 50.00
American Stock Exchange Major Market Index	20 blue-chip industrial stocks traded on New York Stock Exchange	Price-weighted	—	
Dow Jones Averages: Dow Jones Industrial Average	30 blue-chip stocks traded on New York Stock Exchange	Idiosyncratic weighting system		
Dow Jones Composite Average	65 stocks comprising the Dow Jones Industrial, Transportation, and Utility Averages		Dow Jones Transportation Average (20 transportation stocks); Dow Jones Utility Average (15 utilities)	
NASDAQ Composite Index	All domestic common stocks traded over-the-counter	Market-weighted	6 subindexes (industrial, bank, transportation, insurance, other finance, utility)	1971 = 100.0

Name	Made up of	Weighting*	Subindexes	Base year & level
New York Stock Exchange Composite Index	All common stocks listed on the New York Stock Exchange	Market-weighted	4 subindexes (industrial, transportation, utility, finance)	1965 = 50.00
Standard & Poor's Composite Index of 500 Stocks (S&P 500)	500 stocks, most traded on New York Stock Exchange but some on American Stock Exchange or over-the-counter, 400 industrials, 40 utilities, 40 financial, 20 transportation	Market-weighted	90 industry subindexes	1941–43 = 10
Standard & Poor's 100 Stock Index	100 stocks for which options are listed on Chicago Board Exchange	Market-weighted	—	1941–43 = 10
Value Line Composite Index	About 1,700 stocks, including some from New York and American stock exchanges and some over-the-counter stocks	Equally weighted, geometrically	—	1961 = 100.00

*Market-weighted means each stock is multiplied by the number of outstanding shares and influences the index in proportion to its market importance; price-weighted means each stock is multiplied by its price and influences the index in proportion to its price; equally weighted, geometrically means the index shows an average of the percentage increases or decreases in the price of the stocks, so that if it included only two stocks and one advanced 5 percent and the other 10 percent, the index would advance 7.5 percent.

By the year 2000, 2 out of 3 Americans could be illiterate.

It's true.

Today, 75 million adults...about one American in three, can't read adequately. And by the year 2000, U.S. News & World Report envisions an America with a literacy rate of only 30%.

Before that America comes to be, you can stop it...by joining the fight against illiteracy today.

Call the Coalition for Literacy at toll-free **1-800-228-8813** and volunteer.

Volunteer Against Illiteracy. The only degree you need is a degree of caring.